DATE DUE

AUG 1 6 1994	Oct 13 03
AUG 8 1994	11→3
AUG 2 4 1994	12-6
SEP 2 8 1994	JUN 1 3 2011
OCT 4 1994	
OCT 2 9 1994	
OCT 2 9 1994	
DEC 1 4 1994	
JAN 1 8 1995	
FEB 2 3 1995	
NOV 1 7 1996	
DEC 2 3 2000	
SEP 1 1 2001	
OCT 2 7 2002	
NOV 1 3 2002	

The
Fourth
Instinct

THE CALL OF THE SOUL

Arianna Huffington

SIMON & SCHUSTER
New York London Toronto Sydney Tokyo Singapore

SIMON & SCHUSTER
ROCKEFELLER CENTER
1230 AVENUE OF THE AMERICAS
NEW YORK, NEW YORK 10020

DESIGNED BY EVE METZ
MANUFACTURED IN THE UNITED STATES OF AMERICA

1   3   5   7   9   10   8   6   4   2
LIBRARY OF CONGRESS CATALOGING-IN-PUBLICATION DATA
HUFFINGTON, ARIANNA STASSINOPOULOS (DATE)
THE FOURTH INSTINCT : THE CALL OF THE SOUL / ARIANNA HUFFINGTON.
P.   CM.
1. SPIRITUAL LIFE.
2. HUFFINGTON, ARIANNA STASSINOPOULOS (DATE)   I. TITLE.
BL624.H845   1994
291.4—DC20   94-4411
CIP
ISBN: 0-671-69229-1

To Christina and Isabella

Contents

The Search for Meaning

We left for our long-awaited vacation in Greece, two days after I delivered the manuscript of this book to my publishers. On our first night on the island of Límnos, consuming several rounds of oil-soaked eggplant, octopus and aged ouzo at a taverna by the sea, we struck up a conversation with a friend of a friend, who mentioned in passing his remarkable experiences in the monasteries on Mount Athos. The evening swirled around us in Greek dance and laughter while silence settled on our table as our new acquaintance painted a picture of a different world: monks in long black robes and long white beards, gliding silently down centuries-old stairways; candle-lighting ceremonies signifying the light of eternal life; hours spent speaking nothing to no one but volumes to God. The man had barely disappeared into the night when Michael and I looked at each other, knowing, before we had even exchanged a word, that we were going to change our plans and leave for Khalkidikí, the peninsula jutting out of northeastern Greece, the fertile soil from which rises Mount Athos, its pyramid-shaped summit soaring some two thousand meters above the Aegean Sea.

There was only one hurdle to overcome: a permit to visit the mythic mountain. Mount Athos with its twenty monasteries is a virtual state within a state, under the jurisdiction not of the Greek government, but of the ecumenical patriarchate in Constantinople. We were told that Michael would have to go to the

American Embassy in Athens and, through the Embassy, apply to the Greek Foreign Ministry. As fate would have it, that night we met a charming Greek woman who just happened to be extremely adept at negotiating byzantine bureaucracies. Coincidences are indeed the small miracles that God performs anonymously. The next morning her office in Athens had the permit faxed to Michael at the hotel and it was slipped under our door before we awoke.

On the three-hour bus trip that took us from the airport in Thessaloníki to the small village of Ouranoupolis at the foot of Mount Athos, we began to wonder if we had made the right decision. Our children, refusing to sit still, were careening from one side of the bus to the other, which became less and less amusing as the mountain road grew more and more winding, and the turns sharper and sharper.

Women have never been allowed in the monasteries, although some have smuggled themselves in. Michael's womenfolk—which included our two daughters, Christina and Isabella, my mother, my sister and me—waved goodbye to him as he left for the boat that would ferry him to the monasteries. We stayed behind in little cottages at the foot of the mountain—all whitewashed walls, ascetic single beds, and blooming jasmine framing the front doors. Even our irrepressible Isabella seemed subdued by the mystery and majesty of the place. There we would spend the next few days together with my father. Over the last two years his eyesight had deteriorated until—and this, he said, was his greatest regret—he could no longer tell his two granddaughters apart. "The outer world has softened," he told me as we took a sunset walk on the beach. Mixed with a sadness in his voice, there was, surprisingly, a sense of relief, as if the man who had survived a German concentration camp, years of financial hardship, divorce, and myriad disappointments welcomed some softening of the world's harshest edges.

So here we were, as the red sun was setting, looking up toward the monastery of Simonopetra where Michael would spend this and the next few nights in silence, prayer and contemplation. Here we were—a man in his seventies using his approaching blindness to look within, almost prepared to accept that the world could no longer be as much with him, almost (although never quite) prepared to sacrifice, as so many

12

heroes have done in so many myths, outer sight for the sake of a greater vision; and I, his firstborn, more than ever convinced that we are all prodded and prompted to look inward, to follow an instinct that will lead us to spiritual fulfillment.

It is an instinct felt with different degrees of urgency. For a few it dominates every action, every decision, and every breathing moment. For the rest of us, it breaks into our everyday reality and demands attention or whispers in the still, small voice of the soul trying to be heard above the static of our busy lives. In the silence of this solitary shore, skirting the shadows of Mount Athos, the voice grew louder.

It was the voice of what I call the Fourth Instinct. And it speaks to us with the power of the forgotten truth on which every major religion, every successful recovery program, every ancient myth is based, the truth that has been embattled and belittled since the Enlightenment, and which, if it were anything other than indestructible and eternal, would have been dealt a deathblow by our modern culture of relativism, nihilism, and secularism.

While waiting for Michael to return, I had time to reflect further on this forgotten truth at the heart of the book I had just completed. During the process of writing it—indeed, living it—I had been on a journey of my own that had led me to the conviction that there is such a thing as human nature, transcending the imprint of our environment, and that embodied in our Fourth Instinct is a clear disposition toward goodness, compassion and human fellowship. It is the Fourth Instinct that urges us to become ourselves, to "exceed" ourselves, not in the Nietzschean sense of idealizing the will and the intellect but by awakening our intuitive selves, and striving to become all that we were intended to be. It takes us beyond self-centeredness and enables us to resist the combined forces of indifference and meaninglessness. It awakens us to a sense of responsibility for those most in need in our society as well as for the world that future generations will inherit. For some, that first awakening remains nothing more than a fleeting glimpse into another reality; for others—and for increasingly larger numbers—it is the first step on a journey to spiritual growth.

Our Fourth Instinct, like the legendary lost city of Atlantis, has long lain buried in our common culture and in ourselves.

13

Biologists, psychologists and social scientists have tried to define us exclusively through only three instincts. They have given them different names, but with varying emphasis have agreed that the three basic instincts are that of survival, the drive toward self-assertion and power, and the sexual urge. They are the instincts that tie us to our animal past.

Only when we awaken to our Fourth Instinct, the instinct that links us to our future, do we take the next step in our evolution, toward an understanding of life's true meaning. The Fourth Instinct serves as our "highest common denominator," enabling us to overcome alienation and achieve community. It leads us to inner peace and outer harmony, reconciling our first three instincts with our spiritual purpose. To follow the Fourth Instinct is to obey the law of human development. It is a universal law, but it expresses itself differently in each individual. Indeed, there are as many paths to wholeness as there are those who would walk them, threads through the labyrinth of life that we can follow to the center of ourselves and of all existence.

The charge of our Fourth Instinct is to move us from the tyranny of our fight-or-flight mechanism to the liberation of a practical spirituality that transforms our everyday life. And when we choose to evolve, when we choose to listen to the Fourth Instinct and live under its reign, we will have fulfilled the promise on the back of every dollar bill: *Novus Ordo Seclorum*—"a new order of the ages."

So it matters, it matters very much, what each of us chooses to do. The journey toward self-discovery and self-knowledge is not only life's highest adventure, but also the only way to transform society from one based on self-centeredness and compulsory compassion to one based on service and mutual responsibility.

This is the journey of exploration—the adventure—that I had written about in my book. And during our vacation in Greece I realized that, in a sense, I have always been on this journey. We all have, whether consciously or unconsciously. My conscious journey began when I was twenty-four and I had just completed a worldwide tour promoting my first book, *The Female Woman*. Until then, I had never been quite sure where the money would come from to pay my fees at Cambridge or my rent in London. Would my father be able to send me what

I needed this month? Would my mother's brothers be willing, once again, to help her give her daughters things they were not quite sure we really needed—like an education abroad? And now, suddenly, at the beginning of my career, a "best-seller" published around the world had brought me things that I thought would take a lifetime to achieve: financial independence; offers to lecture, to write books, to appear on talk shows. Courage, it has been said, is the knowledge of what is not to be feared. That knowledge has always sustained me, but in my early twenties my courage was based, almost exclusively, on naïveté. What you don't know, they say, won't hurt you. In my case, at the time, it might have even helped.

Yet, behind all my apparent confidence, there grew a cloud of uncertainty—a confusion between secular seductions and spiritual yearnings, between hopes for the ephemeral and glimpses of the eternal. I remember it as if it were yesterday. I was sitting in my room in some anonymous European hotel during a stop on my book tour. The room was a beautifully arranged still life. There were yellow roses on the desk, Swiss chocolates by my bed and French champagne on ice. The only noise was the crackling of the ice as it slowly melted into water. The voice in my head was much louder. "Is that all there is?" Like a broken record, Peggy Lee's question kept repeating itself inside my brain, robbing me of the joy I had expected to find in my success. "Is that *really* all there is?" I wanted to know, and I wanted to know now. If this is "living" then what is life? Can life's goal really be money and recognition, followed by the struggle for more money and fame? From a deep part of myself came a resounding "No!" that turned me gradually but firmly away from lucrative offers to speak and write, again and again, on the subject of "The Female Woman." It started me instead on the first step with which the journey of a thousand miles begins.

I was born into a household of many and sometimes conflicting Greek passions. My mother, whose family had fled Russia during the Revolution, had a passion for marathon midnight cooking—culinary binges that ranged from Russian piroshki to Greek stuffed grape leaves—and marathon reading sessions in psychology and the Greek classics. Entirely self-taught herself, she didn't care much if her daughters ever married, but cared deeply that we get university degrees. She took us to England, and by the time we arrived she did not own anything anyone would want to buy. From the heirloom carpet spirited out of the Caucasus to her last pair of gold earrings, she had sold everything along the way to pay for the schools and the private lessons that prepared me for the Cambridge entrance exams, and my sister for the Royal Academy of Dramatic Arts.

My father was a passionate dreamer. As a young man, he joined the resistance to the German occupation of Greece by editing *Paron* ("The Present"), an underground newspaper. He was caught. And what he experienced in a German concentration camp forever marked his life. From the time he met and married my mother (while they both were recovering, he from the war and she from tuberculosis), he oscillated between the world of business to make a living for his family and the world of ideas and publishing that made our living precarious. Most of what he made he would lose in launching another magazine or his latest newspaper. I remember many overheard conversations about how much money it would take to stop the paper from folding. And I would lie awake at night hoping and praying that I could be bigger or smarter so that I would know how to find the money he needed. I never thought my father was irresponsible. Whatever the hardships involved for our family, and however painful his separation from my mother when I was ten, I idealized both him and the world of writing and ideas he loved so much that sometimes, secretly, I felt a flash of burning jealousy over a pile of his manuscripts.

While I was at Cambridge, he launched another effort, this time a financial newspaper. And on the first page of its first issue, he published my interview (as the paper's ad hoc London correspondent) with Lord Drogheda, the chairman of the *Financial Times* (and, as it happened, chairman of Covent Garden as well). The paper folded after 194 issues. It was his last publishing effort. He had spent himself, literally, pursuing dreams—the dreams which had kept him alive during the nightmare of the camps.

Ever since I could read, books were both my delight and my refuge from life. In the quiet of an improvised study, often sitting by my mother's all-night oven, I was growing increasingly curious. I would discuss with her not only the answers

16

to life's emerging questions that I found in my books but also the greater questions left unanswered. At seven, I started wearing glasses, a little caricature of the earnest academic which I might have become were it not for my sister. Agapi was my thread to life lived in the present, not in the pages of books—to the world of laughter, of song, of imagination. Her favorite game was to peel me away from my books and dance me around the room—a tango, a two-step, a cha-cha.

Our favorite poem was "Ithaca" by the Greek poet Kaváfis, and we recited it long before we could properly pronounce all the words, let alone really understand its meaning.

> *When you set out on the voyage to Ithaca,*
> *pray that your journey may be long,*
> *full of adventures, full of knowledge.*
>
> *The Laestrygones and the Cyclopes*
> *and furious Poseidon you will never meet*
> *unless you drag them with you in your soul,*
> *unless your soul raises them up before you.*
>
> *But you must always keep Ithaca in mind.*
> *The arrival there is your predestination.*
> *Yet do not by any means hasten your voyage.*
> *Let it best endure for many years,*
> *until grown old at length you anchor at your island*
> *rich with all you have acquired on the way.*

My own journey to Ithaca—the one that started consciously years ago in a lonely hotel room—has included many adventures and many confrontations with one-eyed Cyclopes of my own making. It has led me to spend a small fortune on library "late fees," attend countless religious retreats and dream workshops, and amass an arsenal of metaphysical literature. It has spanned travels to Shantaniketan University in India, studies in comparative religion, the writing of six books, and my most profound spiritual teachers, marriage and motherhood.

Despite the obvious differences in the subject matter of my books, a common stream has run through them—the same stream that is running through my life. Socrates said that the unexamined life is not worth living. This urge to examine—the impulse to understand the forces that, hidden beneath the surface, control the life of an individual or a culture—has been the dominant theme of all of my books.

In *The Female Woman*, published in 1973, I explored the longings of women for intimacy, children and a family—longings threatened to be buried in the legitimate and overdue quest for equal opportunities and equal pay. These longings were denigrated and even denied in those days but, as more and more women discovered, they could not be extinguished.

In *After Reason*, I looked at Western culture since World War II, at its domination by politics, and at the failure of political solutions to deal with the proliferation of human casualties —from violent criminals and the mentally sick to drug addicts and the homeless. I wrote that in the major battle of our age, the battle of the individual for the meaning of his life, these abnormalities and aberrations were, in fact, tragic reflections of our century's neglect of the spirit in man. I quoted Peer Gynt: "The world behind my brow, *that* makes me what I am and no one else." And I looked at the truth our age seems to have lost, that our strength and our happiness lie not in our tortuous dealings with the outside world but preeminently in our dealings with the world behind our brow.

In my biography of Maria Callas, I showed that until we have mastered the "world behind our brow," our dealings with the outside world are bound to remain tortuous. Underlying the unresolvable conflicts and tempestuous relationships in Callas' life was the never-ending struggle between the legend and the woman, between the image and the reality.

In *The Gods of Greece* I revisited the myths of my childhood and found in the gods and goddesses guides to forgotten dimensions of ourselves. Personifying the contending forces in us as gods and goddesses acknowledges their emotional power over us and the need to give them conscious recognition— because if we do not, they will rise up and take their revenge.

Picasso did not. As a result, as I wrote in *Picasso: Creator and Destroyer*, he was a man who was an absolute master of his art, yet was tragically mastered in his own life by inner forces he never understood and never sought to understand. In his work he threw the glaring light of his genius into the darkness and the depths of evil in man. But in his life he was overpowered by that same darkness until the destroyer in him overcame the creator.

In all my previous books, as well as in my lectures around the country, there has been a central theme: my belief that a dimension is missing from ourselves and our culture which is reflected in our inability to reconcile the competing demands of our inner and outer lives. As a result, most of us make use of a very small portion of our possible consciousness and of our soul's resources.

In my new book I also explore this missing dimension in our lives. Yet I realize that this book represents a departure for me. It is the first time I have written about myself, bringing my own life and experiences—of pain and joy—into the narrative. But there was *no* other way to talk about the Fourth Instinct— the instinct that makes us all into one family—except in the intimacy of a personal voice that invites readers into my life.

This book is dedicated to my children, partly because in a very important sense I wrote it for them to read when they begin to ask themselves the questions it tries to answer. I know they are already asking some of these questions now: "Who is God, Mommy?" "Why do I have to share?" "Where did your friend go when he died?" For the moment, all they need to know is that these are good questions we must continue to ask throughout our lives. As long as we don't sweep them under the carpet and forget them there, absorbed as we are in life's distractions, the answers will be revealed. And we will be able to live our lives in accordance with the purpose for which we were created, a purpose enshrined in our Fourth Instinct.

There are doors in space you look for, Françoise Gilot once told me, and doors in time that you wait for. Her remark has a new resonance for me now, because it is a premise of this book that we are facing such a door in time—an opening for great possibilities of new being, for a breakthrough in our evolution. For the first time, something as vast and epic as the destiny of mankind depends on something as personal and intimate as the way each one of us chooses to live, think and behave. Everything—the loftiest intellectual concept, the most complex scientific equation—can be connected to the familiar experience of everyday life. And this is what I have attempted to do in *The Fourth Instinct*.

"The great revolution of our generation," William James wrote, "is the discovery that human beings, by changing the inner attitudes of their minds, can change the outer aspects of their lives." This conviction is at the heart of *The Fourth Instinct.* The first step toward changing the world is changing our vision of the world, and the first step toward changing ourselves is changing our understanding of ourselves. The modern equivalent of the pre-Copernican vision of the world as flat is our secular view of man as an exclusively material being. When Madonna sings the ecstasies of being "a material girl . . . in a material world," she is tapping into our age's metaphysical misunderstanding. The moment we recognize the spiritual dimension that animates the material, we will change our view of human nature, and since to see falsely is to live falsely, we will change our lives and the world.

Everything is connected to everything else; every *thing,* every molecule, every rock, every living form, is infused by the same force. To say this is to put the lie to a million false dualities, to all the forced separations between spirit and mind, soul and body, God and man. "God is in the sky and God is in the trees! God is in you and God is in me!" That is how my four-year-old expressed this cosmic theory.

To speak about this universal force that will lead us beyond the last horizon of our known self toward a wiser, more loving, more luminous state of being, we do not need to invent a new language. But we do need to learn to listen to the old, the ancient one, not with our jaded minds, but with our awakened souls. The food that feeds the hunger of our Fourth Instinct is known by many names. We recognize it in the touch of a child's tiny hand, in a violin performance that pierces our hearts, in the crispness of an autumn afternoon, in those still and solitary times when we have felt a presence nearby. Sometimes we call this presence Spirit, sometimes Being, sometimes Truth. I really do not believe that God cares what we call Him —but rather that we care to call at all.

Whenever we speak of God, of the soul, of the formless in the world of forms, we are bound to fall into metaphor. Translating these highest mysteries into our supremely rational world can at best be an approximation. Many who resonate to the Fourth Instinct and to the need to tend to our souls, are nevertheless uncomfortable with the word "God," a word that for some of them conjures up the white-bearded faraway gentleman of their childhood or, much worse, the atrocities perpetrated in His name. But to avoid using the word "God" is to amputate from our spiritual experience thousands of years of Judeo-Christian and Eastern wisdom that evokes God, not to mention some of the most profound poetry and greatest literature.

There is, however, a fundamental difference between today and other historic times of spiritual renewal. Ours does not revolve around any one concept of God or require that we believe in any one set of dogmas, any one doctrine, any one recipe for redemption. It is true that every age needs to find its own language to express eternal truth, but what our age needs more than another debate—this time on spiritual linguistics— is the experience of eternal meaning in the here and now. That is why I have written of the Fourth Instinct as the force within us all that urges us on beyond faith to understanding, knowledge and the actual experience of its power to transform ourselves and our world when it is translated into values, priorities and behavior.

It is a personal journey through the labyrinth of modern life that takes us sometimes down dead ends, sometimes face-to-face with one-eyed Cyclopes, sometimes to the still center around which all else revolves. And, if we follow the threads that guide us through the labyrinth to the end, we will end at life's beginning—and know it for the first time.

When Michael came back from Mount Athos we looked at each other, as we often do, as if for the first time. His stay at the monastery of Simonopetra had been an inner adventure of reflection, silence and prayer. As for me, I had basked in the love of my extended family—my children, my parents, my sister, my cousins, my nieces, my friends. We had both listened to the call of the soul, and now it was time to follow it home.

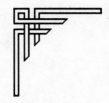

PART ONE

---

*The Anatomy
of the
Fourth Instinct*

1

Why Now?

The human heart can go to the lengths
of God.
Dark and cold we may be, but this
Is no winter now. The frozen misery
Of centuries breaks, cracks, begins to
move;
The thunder is the thunder of the floes,
The thaw, the flood, the upstart Spring.
Thank God our time is now when
wrong
Comes up to face us everywhere,
Never to leave us till we take
The longest stride of soul men ever took.
Affairs are now soul size.
The enterprise
Is exploration into God.
Where are you making for? It takes
So many thousand years to wake,
But will you wake for pity's sake?
—Christopher Fry, *A Sleep of Prisoners*

"To every thing there is a season and a time to every purpose
under the heaven." So it is written in Ecclesiastes, and given

this eternal truth, why now? What is it about this time in our history, a heartbeat removed from the millennium, that marks it as a turning point in our human evolution? Or do all generations assume they have been placed at a crossroads in the history of civilization?

In truth, every age is an age of transition, but it's hard to fully comprehend a turning point when you are living through it. We are simply too close to what is happening to gain the perspective that comes with distance. But the signs are everywhere around us that one age is dying and another is being born—a historic moment such as has not occurred since the Middle Ages gave way to the Renaissance.

The imagery of death and renewal is, of course, very old, and in myth, death always signals transformation. The sun advances across the sky, warming the earth even after it has actually begun to set at noon. Similarly, a civilization both advances and declines at the same time. The stream of literature on the decline of our civilization began in the eighteenth century, at the very moment when the Western world was experiencing unprecedented, exuberant vitality in the sciences and technology, in the control of our environment, and in standards of living, health and comfort. Yet, there were good reasons, despite these advances, for predicting the decline of the West. The spiritual strength of the age was being sapped by the more tempting and more tangible creation of a terrestrial paradise. Man's soul was being diverted. Pascal actually called the Western adventure a *divertissement* from man's true nature and highest destiny. And to the extent that progress within our civilization depended on this *divertissement*, the flowers of the West's success carried in them the seeds of its decline. The evidence of decline is undeniable, although the "decline of the West" has come about in a less theatrical fashion than many had predicted and a few had hoped. But just as undeniable is the fact that when sifting through the evidence of decline we uncover more and more proof of rebirth.

Many and varied routes of inquiry—scientific and religious —are converging at this hour to give us a perspective on human possibility that belonged strictly to the world of the imagination only a decade ago. From genetic engineering to spiritual healing, old assumptions about man's limitations are being altered or erased. Of even greater importance, many people are growing more spiritually sensitive, and they are translating their heightened sensitivity into attitudes and actions that are changing not only their own lives, but the lives of those around them. In mainstream publications and Main Street conversations, there is talk of a new beginning.

The expectancy surrounding the world's spectacular birthday, the day we enter the next millennium, is helping to prepare us psychologically for a breakthrough. We know this experience on personal grounds: One day we are thirty-nine, the next morning we are "in our forties." Enormous expectancy accompanies such a tiny chronological change. Approaching the year 2000 is having the same effect on the world. There are groups preparing for Armageddon, the Second Coming or some other earthly fulfillment of fin-de-millennium prophecy. Others are expressing deep-rooted fears of apocalypse or exultant hopes of revelation. Predictions and prophecies seem to rain around us. Regardless of whether we relegate them to the realm of possibility or party game we will soon know what is going to happen.

If a literalist wanted to count years, since our A.D. calendar has no year zero, the new millennium—the third thousand in this era—will begin not on January 1, 2000, but on January 1, 2001. That we are hardly likely to delay our celebration on grounds of technical accuracy merely confirms the fact that the approaching millennium is an event less of the calendar than of the imagination. What gives the year 2000 its power is what we bring to it: our dreams, our myths, our stories and our deepest inarticulate fears and hopes.

"Ye know neither the day nor the hour," Jesus told his followers. And those looking to spot the day and the hour get precious little encouragement from Saint Peter, who observed that "one day with the Lord is as a thousand years, and a thousand years as one day." No wonder pastors who herd their flocks to hillsides, there to await Christ's return, have been wrong every time. If we had to understand God's timetable, we wouldn't be able to catch a train, let alone an apocalypse.

Yet no qualifiers can detract from the symbolic power of anno Domini 2000. Even those who are not looking for "a new heaven and a new earth," a new messiah, or the Four Horsemen of the Apocalypse, recognize that what the millennium

27

requires from us above all else is a psychological shift, a spiritual breakthrough, a new readiness to rediscover what it is to be human and a thorough reformation in understanding ourselves. Social utopians may hope for the new millennium to usher in the triumph of justice and brotherhood. That would be nice, except that justice and brotherhood are unlikely to triumph unless we start demonstrating them in ordinary, everyday ways that cumulatively begin to transform the world. But for most utopians, the incremental approach is far too slow and unglamorous. It lacks cataclysmic drama. They want to save the world today and send out a great press release tomorrow morning. Feeding a hungry child tonight doesn't draw a crowd.

Many modern intellectuals are incapable of conceiving of social renewal that is the result of human action, but not of government design. Convinced that man must be the architect of mandated blueprints of renewal, they dismiss as frivolous and quaint the notion that we could act in accord with a higher will embodied not in some centralized agency but in the human spirit. One hint that a new age is being born is an increased trust in the ability of each one of us to move from the debris that surrounds us to a higher plane of consciousness, rich in compassion and creativity, from which to respond to the decline and reverse the disintegration. From Spengler and Toynbee to a multitude of modern scientists, we have had plenty of theoreticians of evolution. What we need now is *practitioners* of evolution. And we're beginning to find them all around us.

Something is definitely stirring within the spirit of the age, but darkness and suffering surround the germ of the coming era. The glue that has been holding together our present age has started to give way; consumption has been substituted for passion and ostentation for true culture; and many are fighting off a nasty case of existential dread. Like all turning points, this is a time of great tensions. Conventional answers no longer satisfy ancient questions now being asked with new urgency. There is grave danger in our discontent, but also great opportunity—if we use it to discover new ways of dealing with ourselves and with each other. If we see these tensions in an evolutionary framework, as the natural pain of leaving what we know to venture into the less familiar, we will uncover guidelines for our choices and we will not be left to face today's growing problems armed only with the bankrupt solutions of yesterday. And instead of avoiding the changes by clinging to the old, we will embrace them with anticipation.

Whether we are optimistic or apocalyptic about the future depends on our perspective. Do we focus on what is dying or on what is being born? On the miraculous power contained within man's spirit or on the universal presence of man's destructiveness? Both sides clamor for our attention. But optimism, a confident hopefulness, is neither a blindness to real tragedy nor a personal quirk, fueled by naïveté. It is the hallmark of spiritual thinkers throughout the ages who have been most awake to the truth of our Fourth Instinct. Through and beyond the cruelty, injustice and suffering of the world, they have seen perfection in the making; and although they speak in various languages and images, they have delivered a single message. All have seen, and all teach, that the key which will unlock the next stage in our evolution is already within ourselves. It has been implanted in us.

"Despite so many ordeals," cries out Oedipus, "my advanced age and the nobility of my soul make me conclude that all is well." "I consider the sufferings of the present to be as nothing," wrote Saint Paul to the Romans, "compared with the glory to be revealed in us." Ultimately, pessimism is a denial of the reality of God and the power man draws from being connected to it. It's fed by the signs of disintegration all around us and by our impatience with the sluggish pace at which we choose to move, to evolve beyond our fears and hatreds and our self-satisfied limitations.

In December 1988, *Life* magazine tackled the big question: *Why Are We Here?* When *Life*'s senior editor, David Friend, had first raised the idea of a feature focusing on life's meaning his colleagues brushed off his proposal and dismissed him as a "space cadet." Five years later the idea resurfaced, and this time a team of reporters was sent to the four corners of the earth, charged with finding answers to the "meaning of life." Questions of meaning, God and immortality, once the exclusive province of professional theologians and philosophers, had become topics for Everyman. One of the characteristics of the turning point we are living through is that spiritual development is no longer seen as the prerogative of a few luminous figures, with the mass of humanity destined to remain on the lower ranges of life, but as the destiny of all mankind. The marks of spiritual growth we have seen in recent years are merely the first blush of what will come—the first blossom in an orchard of renewal.

Many of those responding to the question posed by *Life* reflected their own, sometimes powerful recognition of this growing awareness. The author Tom Robbins said, "Our purpose is to consciously, deliberately evolve toward a wiser, more liberated and luminous state of being. . . . Deep down, all of us are probably aware that some kind of mystical evolution is our true task." The poet Maya Angelou said, "Each of us has a responsibility for being alive: one responsibility to creation, of which we are a part, another to the creator—a debt we repay by trying to extend our areas of comprehension." Elie Wiesel said that "our obligation is to give meaning to life and in doing so to overcome the passive, indifferent life." The Dalai Lama stressed that "what is important is to see how we can best lead a meaningful everyday life, how we can bring about peace and harmony in our minds." Stephen Jay Gould said, "We cannot read the meaning of life passively in the facts of nature. We must construct these answers ourselves—from our own wisdom and ethical sense. There is no other way." Islamic scholar Seyyed Hossein Nasr said that "man can be defined as a being born to transcend himself." Choreographer and dancer Twyla Tharp said that "there is an overall order to life, and art wants to be in sync with it." Rabbi Harold Kushner reflected on his own life experience: "I no longer ask the young man's question: How far will I go? My questions are now those of the mature person: When it is over, what will my life have been about?" And social psychologist Kenneth Ring said, "The meaning of life has something to do with realizing that our essence is perfect love, then going on to live our lives upon that truth, experiencing each day as a miracle and every act as sacred."

Philosophical and ethical reflections such as these are refreshingly at odds with the prevailing worldview that sees us as accidental specks in a universe indifferent to our fates, our lives meaningless, our evolution an aimless process of happenstance.

The keynote of our established civilization, the age we are about to leave, is disillusionment bordering on despair—disillusionment with politics and politicians, disillusionment with modern art and organized religion, disillusionment with marriage and with divorce, disillusionment with both the old values and the new freedoms. We wake up disillusioned, we vote disillusioned, we *are* disillusioned—especially with ourselves.

In 1993, Bill Bennett, former Secretary of Education and onetime drug czar, released a list of indicators he used to measure the rise and fall of American culture. Findings from his measurements painted a depressing picture. Since 1960 there had been "a 560 percent increase in violent crime; more than a 400 percent increase in illegitimate births; a quadrupling in divorce rates; a tripling of the percentage of children in single-parent homes; a tripling of the teen-age suicide rate; and a drop of almost 80 points in the SAT scores." During this same period, the gross domestic product had nearly tripled and social spending by all levels of government had risen from $144 billion to $787 billion. Spending on education alone had increased 225 percent. Whatever else we got for all our spending, we did not get cultural progress or solutions to our social problems.

The evidence of disintegration—statistical, anecdotal and personal (the evidence of our own eyes and hearts)—is overwhelming. Ask any teacher. In 1940, teachers identified the worst problems in public schools as talking out of turn, chewing gum, making noise, running in halls, cutting in line, dressing inappropriately and littering. When teachers were asked the same question in 1990, the problems they listed were drug abuse, alcohol abuse, pregnancy, suicide, rape, robbery and assault.

Montel Williams, the former football player and current talkshow host, who in 1988 mounted a one-man war to save a generation, has been traveling the country teaching teenagers what he calls the new "three R's: responsibility, restraint, respect." This is how he summed up his experience: "I talked to teenagers sniffing airplane glue in Tennessee, taking acid on Long Island, smoking heroin in Georgia and buying 'ice cream' in Mississippi. . . . Kids get high to take away the pain they are dealing with."

Confronted with the wasteland of modern life, many skip over the false escapes and take themselves straight down the final exit, which is why the suicide rate among teens has more than tripled in the past thirty years. Whatever one's age, depression is the most prevalent mental illness in America. Consider this staggering statistic facing me and my daughters: 25 percent of women in this country are expected to suffer from depression during their lifetime; for men, the risk factor is 12.5 percent. Depression has reached epidemic proportions, with nearly 10 million Americans suffering from a depressive disorder or seeking escape through drugs, alcohol or whatever might anesthetize them against the pain of living.

"I've been feeling really good lately," said a new friend in Washington. "Prozac has made all the difference." She was blissfully untroubled—not a question flickered in her mind—over the fact that she needed a mood-altering chemical to feel good. I'm constantly surprised—and I refuse to stop being surprised—at the number of friends leading successful, productive and in many ways enviable lives who cannot go to sleep without a sleeping tablet, who make no distinction between feeling good from Valium and feeling good from life, and who seem convinced that masking symptoms with drugs is the best way to continue leading their busy lives. Our souls want to get our attention, but we have no time to stop. We gulp down another pill and head for the next meeting. Millions of such victimless crimes are committed every day—victimless only because the victim is the invisible human spirit, its cries for help efficiently stifled with a succession of chemicals, some of them reliable old warhorses and others newly manufactured designer drugs.

Those who have not mastered the many socially refined ways of doing violence to themselves are busy augmenting the statistics of violence to others. And the fastest-growing segment of the criminal population is found among our nation's children—among the affluent as well as the poor, with all races well represented. In Blue Ridge, New Jersey, a group of teenagers raped with a baseball bat a mentally handicapped classmate. In New York City, seventeen-year-old Christian Abakpa was stabbed through the chest with his young brothers looking on; he stumbled home to die in his mother's arms. Popular films and books mirror the violence in the streets and glorify it. In *The Silence of the Lambs*, a serial killer skins his victims. In *American Psycho*, the sexual torture of a young woman is depicted with graphic gruesomeness: "The fingers I haven't nailed I try to bite off. . . . I occasionally stab at her breasts, accidentally (not really) slicing off one of her nipples. . . ." No wonder we are depressed.

In every medium, art that deals with rage, violence, disgust and brutality rises to the top. And the way we are dealing with the rising tide of brutality—in our neighborhoods, on our screens and in our bedrooms—is, as Daniel Patrick Moynihan observed, to redefine it, to raise the threshold of what we consider "normal." In the 1929 St. Valentine's Day Massacre, seven gangsters were killed. Headlines across the nation carried the news to a shocked America. Today, equivalent "massacres" that take place every day barely merit a murmur of shock. We are accommodating ourselves to the violence as we have been accommodating ourselves to depression.

Mothers in city parks put their toddlers on chain leashes. We invest in mace, rape whistles, bullet-proof fashions, and in the ultimate status symbol: bodyguards to shadow our every movement. Eight out of every ten of us, statistics predict, will fall victim to violent crime at least once in our lives. Our response? To quote a line from Pink Floyd, we "have become comfortably numb." Or as New York State Supreme Court Judge Edwin Torres put it, "the slaughter of the innocent marches unabated: subway riders, bodega owners, cab drivers, babies; in laundromats, at cash machines, on elevators, in hallways. . . . This numbness, this near narcoleptic state can diminish the human condition to the level of combat infantrymen, who, in protracted campaigns, can eat their battlefield rations seated on the bodies of the fallen, friend and foe alike. A society that loses its sense of outrage is doomed to extinction."

In the meantime—constantly bombarded by visual representations of gruesome statistics—we suffer acts of violence in our minds even before we experience them in life. "I . . . have known many troubles," Mark Twain once said, "but most of them never happened." Stunningly awful things are happening all around us, but what we fear may happen compounds them with a screaming, nightmarish reality inside our heads. To escape both realities we run to drugs, to alcohol, to a desperate, serial sexuality. Our addictions deliver momentary forgetfulness—although the law of diminishing returns sets in earlier and earlier. "Why ask why?" declares a Budweiser commercial, unaware of its own existential irony. We keep trying to escape veritas in vino or Valium or Vegas, to barricade ourselves against the demands of our Fourth Instinct with booze or barbiturates.

Alcohol and drugs have for centuries been used both to escape our Fourth Instinct and to release it. The dual properties of drink were personified in myth by the god Dionysus who could both inspire and destroy, just as they were in the Bible when Jesus turned the wedding water into wine. But many have mistaken the spirits for the Spirit, a drunken numbness for a state of ecstasy. "When, for whatever reason, men and women fail to transcend themselves by means of worship, good works and spiritual exercises," claimed Aldous Huxley, "they are apt to resort to religion's chemical surrogates." Today, the rush to chemical surrogates has turned into a stampede. And despite the destruction it has wrought in broken lives and failed dreams, rock and rap continue to glamorize the return of marijuana with "Marijuana's Greatest Hits Revisited," "Hemp," "Tasty Greens"—all reminiscent of the "angelheaded" junkies of *Howl* "burning for the ancient heavenly connection to the starry dynamo in the machinery of night." LSD use among teens is at its highest level in seven years. More kids have tried stimulants, more are using tranquilizers and cocaine. And those who can't get their hands on drugs are reaching for household inhalants such as glue or air freshener —anything for a fix, a hit, a trip into unreality.

We leave the hostile, incomprehensible world behind. We lose, for a chemically sodden moment, our feelings of fear and isolation. We are united with something vague but powerful, fleeting but comforting. Then the trip ends. The world returns and is all the more alien. The separateness and the meaninglessness which goaded us to drugs in the first place are all the more intense and painful. John Lucas, former guard for the Seattle Supersonics, described his journey into drugs in language that echoes the experience of millions: "You get into drugs, and that's what you can think. Nothing else matters. Not wife, not kids, not basketball, not parents, not team, not money, not anything. Only the coke." Lucas worshiped the white powder as if it had been sent from God. But what seemed at first to provide the meaning and measure of his life only ended up taking them away: "With drugs, it isn't that you lose your dreams. You lose your soul. You lose you."

An account executive for a San Fernando Valley manufacturing company described her drug-addicted state as "spiritually dead." And this is the tragic irony of trying to find through drugs the connections that can be found only through the spirit. Chemical shortcuts leave us deadened. And solutions to the drug problem that revolve around funding alone—more money for enforcement, more dollars for arrests—are bound to fail because they ignore the transcendent need at the heart of the addictions. Confronting the supply side of the problem undoubtedly helps, but only at the margin. The need that must be met is spiritual.

Even though America is gradually admitting that our social problems go much beyond economics and that solutions will not be found through social spending, many intellectuals are still finding it hard to think outside the framework of government. Michael Lerner coined the phrase "the politics of meaning" and became the Clintons' mentor in spotlighting our culture's spiritual crisis, but when it came to the diagnosis and the cure, he blamed the capitalist marketplace for the crisis and proposed a Department of Families to stave off the cultural disintegration. In the end, the "politics of meaning" has been reduced to a spiritual spin on a secular agenda—another defense, this time metaphysical, of an intrusive state.

Those addicted to political salvationism clearly cannot shake off the conviction that no endeavor—not even strengthening the American family or restoring meaning to our lives—can succeed unless it is sponsored by the State. But the rest of us are coming to the realization that deep cultural change cannot be imposed from distant quarters even by sincere politicians and earnest reformers. Lasting social change unfolds from inside out: from the inner to the outer being, from inner to outer realities. I can change nearly everything about myself. I can run from my children and trade in my spouse, move to another country and raise green rabbits for a living, but unless I care for my soul, I will not have changed who I am. We can doctor up a neighborhood, fix broken windows, clean littered parks, inoculate infants and sweep the drunks off the streets, but until we care for the soul of the community, we are merely tinkering at the edges.

This is a law of life as immutable as the law of gravity. We think twice about defying the law of gravity in the world outside. We know that breaking our necks, or worse, would be the inevitable result. But in the past we have, as a culture, been oblivious to the laws of the world within. And our communal lives are polluted with the consequences of our transgressions of these laws.

The most promising aspect of the turning point we are in is the growing recognition of these inner realities. We cannot go back to a world where duty, honor and self-discipline were inherited values, unquestioningly accepted. But neither can we go forward on the magic carpet of the sixties, seeking liberation from responsibility, crying for "authenticity," clamoring for the right to indulge our every impulse, regardless of the consequences for everyone else. John Lennon's "Imagine" became the anthem for an entire generation, played by pied pipers who would lead our culture off a cliff. This was the kind of spiritual vapidity engendered in a world of rights devoid of responsibilities. Soon the hippies of the Beat Generation were replaced by the yuppies of the Me Generation, and self-expression gave way to self-promotion. Either way self-centeredness reigned supreme.

In the spiral of our evolution, individuals have, since the Renaissance, been freed from preconceived definitions based on their membership in certain guilds, groups or traditions, or in the roles they have assumed in families or society. Man discovered that he matters independently of his social definitions, that his soul is not captive to duty and honor.

But on the journey that took us from the Middle Ages and deposited us at the Me Generation, we turned down a blind alley. We have come to a self-consciousness that is weary not only with all the conventions of the world, but with all the values and responsibilities of the world as well. If something challenges our narrowly defined self-interest, it is an unwelcome intruder. At this dead end, everything that enables human beings to create and sustain community has been put in jeopardy. And if we cannot transcend selfishness, we become prisoners to our own limitations—caged away from our fellow men and from our own souls.

Until a century ago in the industrial nations, and still today in developing countries, for the majority of the population—men, women and children—life was more a question of mouthfuls than soulfuls, of survival rather than evolution. It stands as a testament to the tenacity of the spirit that it lives on even in the midst of suffering and degradation, and without the luxury of contemplation during idle hours. In every age, in every culture, there have always been those in search of the spirit. Today, that search has reached new dimensions. In the whole of human history there have never been so many avenues to spiritual awareness being explored nor anything remotely approaching the proportion of people seeking such avenues for themselves.

"There are more people into this stuff than I ever thought," a bewildered friend told me recently. This "stuff" includes everything from explorations into the great religious traditions, to rolfing, rebirthing and past-life regressions. I have personally sampled a substantial variety of what is available—including fire-walking. (I emerged on the other side with a few blisters, evidence, I was told, that my faith in the power of mind over matter had faltered.)

Two-thirds of the Baby Boom generation dropped out of traditional religious involvement along the way to their midlife crises; now, 40 percent are returning. Wade Clark Roof, a professor in UCSB's Department of Religious Studies, describes an additional 10 percent as "intense seekers," whose lives center on a spiritual search, some of whom may join an uncounted but expanding group of "believers but not belongers." And someone should label the zealous questioners, men and women I have met who ache to be convinced, who challenge me—sometimes angrily, sometimes pleadingly—to provide them with proof that there is meaning and truth available through a life of spirit.

Baby Boomers notwithstanding, since 1960 there has been an increase in American church membership from 114 million to 156 million. Especially large increases have come in churches that emphasize an intense personal relationship with God and the believing community—Pentecostals, Assemblies of God, and a host of nondenominational "Bible" churches. These are high-expectation involvements, not low-energy investments. Meanwhile, churches with a more intellectual message and a low-demand approach to members have experienced striking declines—the Episcopal Church, for example, losing a third of its membership since 1960.

"It is not just the religious right, the New Age swamis or the

Twelve-Step enthusiasts who have discovered this secret of modern living," Norman Lear wrote recently. "Theoretical physicists, deep ecologists and many business leaders are coming to this realization as well." The fact that no one element in society can stake a claim to this sweeping spiritual quest is a distinguishing characteristic of the modern search.

When I started searching—my friends in England called it "groping"—in the middle seventies, the reigning presumption among fellow seekers was that the beneficiary of a spiritual search was the seeker. If asked the question "Whose life will your quest improve?" the quick response would have been, "Mine, of course." We were young, immature. Very few who kept to that quest are still involved only with their own search. Those who have matured spiritually, now put service to others at the center of their quest and of their lives.

Moving ourselves to the background and others to the foreground is evidence that the search is achieving its purpose. A friend whom I had considered a kindred spirit on the spiritual path, but had not seen in some years, recently spent a few days at our home. After ten minutes' discussion, I began wondering if my search had been as self-indulgent, as shamelessly narcissistic, as his sounded. The dominant message was: "Clean up your personal neuroses and that will heal the world." I don't think so. Analysis for everyone—even great analysis—will not by itself feed the hungry, or ease the burden of despair and meaninglessness in our communities. A search that begins and ends with one's self isn't going very far, and certainly won't lead us to the heart of spiritual fulfillment. "And behold you were within me," said Saint Augustine, "and I out of myself, and there I searched for you." But to really find God is to search for Him not only in ourselves, not only in our loved ones, not only in our neighbors, not only in the strangers we encounter, but, ultimately, in our enemies as well.

The modern landscape of our search may seem like a gigantic medieval fair where we wander between stalls and booths and hawkers selling promises: peace in the next world, success in tomorrow's business deal, happiness in tonight's love affair. There are priests and psychics, all-night pitchmen and spiritual counselors, faith healers and research scientists, offering promises of salvation in the here-and-now as well as the hereafter.

I remember visiting India's holy shrine of Benares when I

was sixteen. Bodies floated by on the Ganges while others were being burned nearby. Emaciated holy men knelt in prayer among goats and pigeons. Pilgrims, most in rags but one in a gold sari, listened to gurus and hawkers, making me wonder how they could tell who was proffering truth. Even at sixteen, I was more fascinated by those searching than those proffering. What was it, I wondered, that would so possess a pilgrim's soul that he would walk his feet bloody just to arrive at this place? As years have passed, the pilgrim's search has itself become the evidence of what I then suspected. In our seeking —from India's shrines to the Vatican, from the mountains of Peru to the deserts of Arizona—we prove the universality of the human drive to find meaning and purpose in our lives, to find God. It is the drive of the Fourth Instinct.

Spirituality can, of course, slide into superstition. "You mess up and leave the horoscope out of the paper for one edition," said the editor of the *Houston Chronicle*, "and there aren't enough telephone operators in town to handle the irate calls. We know. It's happened." No doubt. *The Washington Post* recently found that nearly "one out of three Americans believes that some fortune tellers can foresee events," and one out of five agreed that good-luck charms probably work. What, fundamentally, distinguishes these people's beliefs from those of the one third who believe in faith healing, or the other third who claimed "contact with someone who has died"?

Some cases seem clear-cut. After spending years in pain from an injured back, Danish telephone lineman Jorgen Korsholm suddenly "discovered" his power as a healer of "everything from cancer to psychic problems." And if this was not enough cause for amazement, he also changed his name to "Janada" and claimed he had arrived in "this solar system 18 million years ago."

Drawing attention to the nonsense that lines the road of our search is irresistible. Some hucksters are amusing, some dangerous. But even the rubbish of a society can be revealing. Bones and bottles in a garbage can suggest that somebody has been eating and drinking. Outlandish psychics who draw a crowd, no less than inspirational preachers who draw a congregation, are evidence that somebody's spirit is hungering for God.

Counterfeiters only exist because there is true gold. Some

analysts of the spiritual awakening in the West have concluded that it's all counterfeit. It was, after all, minted first in the late sixties by an obsession with "Me." If we jumble together evidence of the past few decades, group sex appears next to Gnosticism, and Zen retreats are staged next to Pentecostal revivals and "harmonic convergences." Given this caricature, it does look like a mishmash of egocentricity, the sort of thing that entertains weary readers of the Sunday supplements.

Such analyses may amuse, but they don't explain the Babel of tongues we hear all around us, raised in excited argument along the peripheries of the central question. Are we ready, individually and collectively, to unlock and set free the great promise of renewal within us? That is both the promise and the challenge of the new millennium. But how is that challenge to be met, that promise fulfilled? What thread, or combination of threads, will guide us through the labyrinth of our lives into the center of our souls—and out again to transform our world?

It is not for reasons of divine economy alone that the ancient Chinese ideogram for crisis is the same as that for opportunity: the moment of crisis and supreme danger, whether in the life of an individual or in the life of a community, is also the moment of the greatest opportunity for renewal.

My conviction that we will choose to act on the present opportunity is based on a trust in the power of the human spirit. It is the morning-of-creation feeling that I have seen shining through suffering and death. It is the belief that Gandhi gave expression to, and to which I keep returning whenever I feel disheartened at the evidence of disintegration all around me: "I have found that life persists in the midst of destruction. Therefore there must be a higher law than that of destruction. Only under that law would well-ordered society be intelligible and life worth living."

We sense that higher law often long before we are able to articulate it, or even believe in its existence. To live by it in our everyday lives, we need only reach out toward what Plato called the Beyond and millions call God—the God who, incidentally, is still reaching out for us.

2

"A Parliament of Instincts"

> What sort of God would it be who only
> pushed from without?
>
> —Goethe

What is it that leads the Buddhist monk to endure a lifetime of self-denying contemplation? Or Rembrandt to produce during his life more than a hundred self-portraits, each one in succession drawing away yet a little bit more of what shrouded his soul? Or the miserly old man to bequeath all his wealth to charity? Or the successful financier to devote hundreds of hours to practicing the cello? Each is driven by the most relentless, persistent instinct that man possesses: the instinct for meaning, transcendence, wholeness and truth. The Fourth Instinct.

There are around us people who have not forgotten this instinct, who live by it and allow it to guide them. The cultural elites have variously forgotten, ignored, derided or repressed it; churches, temples and mosques have sometimes succeeded and sometimes failed to satisfy its longing; and thousands of self-improvement manuals may have sensed the instinct but failed to identify its spiritual nature. The signals our mainstream culture sends us simply deny it. The pursuit of happiness is reduced to the pursuit of pleasure, with the quality of

41

life dependent on an ever-improving appearance, more and more toys and better and better sex. The film industry in the West and the stock market in the East have for years bracketed the nation with a single ethic, the ethic Mike Royko defined in *Boss* as the motto of Chicago: "Where's mine?" Whether it's gratuitous sex and violence on the screen or insider trading behind the scenes, it is the first three instincts—survival, power and sex—that are pursued and, until recently, glorified. The message echoing through is simple: "This is it. This is all there is." Life and its meaning reduced to scrapping over sex and power, ignoring the one instinct that makes us uniquely human.

Over the past several years, countless books have appeared in the West seeking to explain man's nature in terms of his kinship with animals. Man is only another animal, governed by age-old instincts, wrote Konrad Lorenz, Robert Ardrey, Desmond Morris and their innumerable rivals and successors. Understand animal instincts and they will unlock for you the mysteries of "human" nature. The astonishing popularity of books that make such claims has shown that they touch some chord corresponding to a deep hunger in our culture for answers to the most haunting riddles about who we are. Yet for all the fascinating and undeniable parallels between the behavior of men and animals which these books adduced, they left the ultimate riddle as puzzling and unresolved as ever. Because none of them explored the existence of the instinct which deeply divides man from other animals, and which is the cause of our greatest glories and our deepest discontents.

Give a gibbon a mate, a peaceful stretch of jungle and plenty of figs to munch on, and he will most likely live in contentment for the rest of his days. Give a man or woman an environment correspondingly idyllic—say, a Garden of Eden or, in today's terms, a successful career, a beloved spouse, adorable children and all the comforts civilization has to offer—and we feel dissatisfied, restless and vaguely aware that there is something very important missing from our lives. "Having it all" is clearly not having enough. We feel *incomplete*—and more often than not we rationalize that sense of incompleteness by ascribing it to some concrete cause: "If only I possessed this or had accomplished that, then I would be satisfied." We are surrounded by successful bankers wishing they were landscape architects, successful Hollywood film writers wishing they were serious novelists, serious novelists dreaming of one day writing a successful screenplay, and prominent academics nursing a secret hankering that they had used that childhood skill at baseball to play for the Dodgers. It is the irony of the old joke about the chicken that crosses the road just to get to "the other side." And these examples speak only of the very limited number of people who have managed to make it to the top, excluding all those millions of others who are still dreaming that one day when they have climbed those last few rungs up the ladder, they will indeed have "it" made.

The source of our discontent is lodged in the Fourth Instinct. The impulse for spiritual fulfillment is as deeply imprinted within us as the drive to live, to master our environment and fill it with our children. In the same way that physical systems embody information and purpose, our Fourth Instinct embodies our search for transcendence and communion. The barriers between the physical and the spiritual, built by the narrow rationalism of the Enlightenment, are now being dismantled by modern science and a growing chorus of personal experiences. And yet our conventional way of thinking about the world remains profoundly dualistic: the biological is pitted against the cultural and the physical against the spiritual. When Darwin shattered the literal interpretation of the creation myth, many gave expression to the forlorn feeling that mind and spirit would be dethroned from their old supremacy, and, at best, might find a place as mere appendages of the material creation. It was either/or all over again. Spirit *or* matter. Genesis *or* evolution. The Fourth Instinct confounds all this. It is a genetically based, physical instinct that has a metaphysical purpose. It is a natural hunger for supernatural food, the fulfillment of our spiritual destiny, inbuilt from the beginning as part of our human design. It is our bridge out of duality and into wholeness: "Let us make man in our image, after our likeness," says God in Genesis. And let man *evolve*, first unconsciously, then consciously, into his God-like nature, says evolution.

Genesis is unfolding in the evolutionary epic, and the Fourth Instinct is the driving force. It's more than a force, however.

It's a longing, an aching to complete ourselves, to unite with that which makes us whole. We are longing for God the way a soldier longs for his wife faraway. It's a relentless homesickness that, however desperately we try, will accept no substitutes. It has been this way from the beginning. Human history is the record of our search for the way back to Paradise—a state of being, more than a place, both behind and before us—this time regained in full consciousness. It was the choice to grab and taste "the knowledge of good and evil" that tripped us into history with a thundering fall, the necessary fall. "Man is become as one of us, to know good and evil." But this prize came with a price: Eviction. Exile. Alienation. Since the day we left Eden we have missed home. The hunger for meaning and thirst for purpose are nothing less than the human homing instinct—the Fourth Instinct—at work, turning us in the direction of God. But in the tangled maze of history, we have been sidetracked; in the long journey home, we forgot our destination. Indeed, we were told that it does not exist.

We forgot that we are born with a design and a purpose. We fell under the spell of those social scientists, biologists and psychologists who told us that the individual contributes only baby bawlings and mewlings and a capacity to be socialized—utterly malleable and utterly hollow. Goodbye, human consciousness. Human nature, goodbye. A human being is a computer with no software. Society, culture, the environment, the outside world supply the programs. And if there is no such thing as human nature, there is no such thing as a moral sense, and then no one way of being and behaving is better than any other—at least, not in any absolute sense.

Evolutionary psychology, with very little fanfare so far, is proving that this view of human nature is not only metaphysically untrue, but scientifically false as well. If a human being is a computer, then it is a computer pre-equipped with its own programs. But each individual has to choose at every turn which program to call up. We come with the Fourth Instinct installed in us. Yet our modern culture ignores or denies it, rarely sending requests or evoking in us the need to call up the forgotten instinct. Lack of use makes it harder for us to access it and, therefore, harder to see the end of the journey and know its purpose. "Use it or lose it" is a law of nature, but mercifully "not a soul will be lost" is a law of the spirit that

supersedes it. No matter how many times the Fourth Instinct may seem to have been erased, there are infinite backups of this particular program.

When Christ proclaimed that these things that I do, you too shall do and even greater, he was giving voice to a very important law of our evolution: Everything that anyone has ever done during the course of human history establishes the minimum boundary of the possible for those who follow. The maximum, we can only imagine. "The greatest discovery," said the electrical engineer Charles Steinmetz, "will be made along spiritual lines. The spiritual forces have as yet hardly been scratched. When this day comes, the world will see more advancement in one generation than it has seen in the past four."

For the moment, our proposals for social reform are based on an incomplete understanding of human design. We are built with an instinct which we ignore at our peril. So it is hardly surprising that there is such a chasm between intentions and results. Indeed, even identifying a universal human design out of all the buzzing expressions of human diversity is a task rejected as quixotic by modern psychological and social theories—which explains why expressions of a Fourth Instinct that we share with all humans, however diverse, remain blurred and out of focus. The goal that has dominated psychology the past half-century has been the development of a "technology of behavior" as envisioned by B. F. Skinner, according to which effects once assigned to states of mind are traced instead to states of culture and the environment.

But it is the instinct dominant at any one time that determines which aspect of our culture we interact with, what part of our environment we let in. We are shaped by the program in our human computer we choose to bring up, the instinct we choose to follow. We are constantly adapting to the world but we are just as constantly adapting the world to us—a paradox that runs counter to all our post-Enlightenment assumptions, according to which the human mind is a one-way receptor of information, designed only to interpret and respond in adaptive ways. Anyone who has ever seen healing beyond the power of medicine or walked on red-hot coals without being singed knows that reality is a continuum that extends from thinking to the denser world of physical form. "For as a man thinketh in his heart, so he is." The flow of adaptation between our mind and our world is definitely two-way.

The "Great Chain of Being"—from matter to body to mind to soul to spirit—requires man's active participation before it can unfold. Man, who has mastered so many secrets of his world, is now uniquely responsible for his future. Free will, the most glorious of our divine attributes, is also the one responsible for most of the suffering we have heaped on ourselves. Shall we advance, or shall we retreat? Shall we embrace our instinct to evolve in consciousness, or shall we position ourselves among the other animals?

"A human being," wrote Einstein, "is a part of the whole, called by us 'Universe'; a part limited in time and space. He experiences himself, his thoughts and feelings, as something separated from the rest—a kind of optical delusion of his consciousness. This delusion is a kind of prison for us, restricting us to our personal desires and to affection for a few persons nearest us. Our task must be to free ourselves from this prison."

What helped free me from this delusion of separateness was not so much my metaphysical studies as the expanding experience of marriage and then, uniquely, motherhood. A son lost before birth some years ago can still cry to me in the night. The beauty of two laughing daughters can pull from me as a mother what I, as a younger woman, did not yet imagine. In learning more to love, I have also learned more to listen and trust. In the process, I have been convinced that Einstein was right. Life and love are not essentially about "a few persons nearest us." They are found in the spiritual nature that unites us, even if everything else separates us. Apart from this unity, we are still lonesome and alienated—we are merely lonesome together, alienated together.

The struggle for survival, so far man's struggle against nature, has now extended to a struggle with our own nature. Inside each of us there is what Konrad Lorenz called "a parliament of instincts." To which of the four will we cede most influence? Freeing ourselves from the prison of our first three instincts is the mandatory next step in our evolution. It means stepping out of Plato's cave of shadows and finding the Light of Being. It is Christ's admonition to seek first the Kingdom of God. It is what Hindus and Buddhists mean by enlightenment, or liberation, or satori. It is the truth expressed in the Jewish folk saying: "We do not see things as they are. We see them as we are."

The Fourth Instinct is both the bridge to this next stage in man's evolution and the voice calling us to cross over—from competition to cooperation and community, from the exclusively material to the all-encompassing spiritual. In the fulfillment of man's being in nature, the ultimate scheme of nature itself is fulfilled. Beyond biology, it is an evolutionary spiral based on a different set of imperatives—for now the survival of the fittest will be the survival of the wisest.

As individuals, certainly survival is our first and most basic instinct. In the context of the Fourth Instinct, it is vital that we survive not only for survival's sake, but because the soul needs the human body to bring to it the experiences necessary for its unfolding. There were times at the beginning of my spiritual journey when I thought I had to deny one thing before I could affirm another, to deny the physical before I could affirm the spiritual. Humbled by the heightened reality of spirit, I tended to gravitate toward those religious thinkers who saw this world as an illusion—our life and body only means to help us escape from life and body.

Our survival instinct belies this. Armed with an automatic biological reflex to counter physical danger, it is here to ensure that we keep body and soul together. For millennia it has compelled us to seek food and shelter, to master our environment. Today, it is a tragedy of urban America that too many cities are being turned into war zones that threaten our survival. But more often, wherever we may live, it is *perceived* dangers that primarily trigger the survival instinct—the adrenal rush before we ask for a raise, or the clammy hands before we ask for a date. It may be a false alarm, but it trips a flood of anxiety no less real than if we were confronted with a mugger in a dark, deserted street. It is a reaction that runs counter to all the animating impulses of our Fourth Instinct: trust, acceptance and the peace that passes all understanding. Worry is a form of atheism. And so is most fear.

When in the prism of our perception we focus on the narrow band of survival, much of our behavior is dictated by fear—

fear that is rarely evoked by actual threats to physical survival. "Survival behavior" can be triggered by the fear of losing anything we perceive as being part of our identity: a relationship, a position, the approval of our parents, a pair of our favorite earrings or golf clubs. The survivalist mind does not differentiate between real and perceived danger. Once the fight-or-flight response of the survival instinct has been triggered, it exercises manual override and everything not connected to the perceived danger—no matter how connected it is to life—is filtered out, while the mind focuses on finding further evidence of what is wrong. The mind is now *looking* for danger, intent on spotting the roaring lion and ravenous tiger. The modern market analyst drags himself from bed to peer into his home computer screen as it delivers news on bullish trends and bearish slumps thousands of miles away. His face, illuminated eerily in the darkness by the pale-green, flickering screen, looks faintly like that of an ancient ancestor who stood at the cave's entrance, lit by a flickering fire. It is the same intensity, driven by fear of failure and death. Survival behavior, now rarely necessary as our first priority, has nevertheless become our second nature.

The Fourth Instinct connects us with an inner knowledge that can liberate us from the fears, anxieties and attachments of our survival behavior. It brings perspective to what we value and what we fear, restoring the first instinct to its original purpose of protecting us from actual threats to our survival, thereby preserving body and freeing soul.

I saw the survival instinct at work as I watched my newborns groping their way to my breast moments after they were born. And, in the months that followed, if Mommy's manna wasn't instantly available when the hunger pangs kicked in, my daughters' instinct prompted the wails that sent me running, my heart jumping and my blood racing, as if my babies were in mortal danger.

More recently I watched the second instinct begin to emerge as it urged both my daughters to assert and define themselves, propelling them to explore the world enticing them beyond the nursery door. The instinct to grow and expand into the world pushes the baby out of the orbit of the mother. The universe beckons and the baby, perched on the frontier of the mother's lap, plunges into its first brave foray—if only quickly to return.

There is excitement in exploring alone, stretching one's self, testing new boundaries. Reaching out is irresistible; however, many a wary and wistful backward glance makes sure that Mother is still there.

In its positive manifestations, the second instinct is an irrepressible current that sweeps the baby—despite all its fears— off the mother's lap on a journey of self-expression, curious and conquering. This is the second instinct, fulfilling its function, laying the groundwork for future journeys. It is only when the Fourth Instinct is forgotten or repressed that the second is drummed into service to fill the gap, turning explorers into exploiters and the quest for self-expression into the frantic pursuit of self-aggrandizement.

Already my younger daughter wants to *become*. It's not enough just to *be*. She wants to become more like her older sister, to probe and prevail. She wants her world (Mommy and Daddy and significant others) to watch, to clap, and adoringly to encourage an encore. Our presence is both reassuring and rewarding. "Watch, Mommy, watch," says Isabella, as she once again tries to demonstrate her dominion over gravity. Indeed, what's the point of conquest if there is no one to applaud? It is the Fourth Instinct that opens our ears to the inner ovations. When it fails to develop, the second instinct is forced to play understudy and the quest for celebrity becomes the adult equivalent of "Watch, Mommy, watch." Unchecked, the charming and adorable "Me, Me, Me" cries of the two-year-old become the self-centered manipulations of middle age.

"Without an attachment to a mother," wrote child psychologist Louise Kaplan, "a child cannot locate himself in the world. . . . Deprived of the beacon of a mother's presence, a child has no place to return to, no way to imagine how far or where to creep or walk. . . . Instead the child falls and bumps into the objects of the out-there world in a desperate attempt to locate the edges of his body and the boundaries of his world." It is also what happens later in life when as adults we bump into the objects of the "out-there" world, lacking an inner center.

Insofar as we can characterize qualities as feminine or masculine, intuitive or analytical, the second instinct clearly falls into the category of the masculine—as clearly as my husband who, when lost in unfamiliar territory, refuses to stop and ask for directions. This is not to say that instincts have a gender, but rather that they have qualities that we, with our limited understanding, describe metaphorically.

It is, of course, the old debate between the masculine and the feminine, the yin and the yang, the intuitive and the rational; between the right and the left brain, between the heart and the head. The second instinct is Nietzsche's will to power, the cornerstone on which Alfred Adler built his psychology. It is the instinct by which we choose our options in the world, make plans, execute them, and commit ourselves to a life of action. Here is self-assertion, the drive to exert ourselves as a force with which creation will need to reckon. Without the push of our second instinct, we might still be making mudpies in the sun. Under its stern guidance, we have conquered the world. We have shed the light of reason on it, but we have missed both the source of a greater light and what the dark corners have to teach. We have mastered nature, but in the process we have cut ourselves off from nature's master plan.

Even the feminist movement, which, in theory at least, should have been at the forefront of efforts to release the intuitive, feminine principle, in practice has with few exceptions idealized the masculine values of the second instinct. At the very time when masculine values are suffering an extreme case of virility-draining exhaustion, women have been trying to appropriate them for their own. A new series of dolls I was checking out for my daughters featured female role models: a doctor, a scientist, a senator, a policeman, a business executive, etc., etc. There was a childcare provider but there was no mother. The message was clear: Mothering is okay only if it's a nine-to-five job with a paycheck at the end—only if you do it "like a man."

The paradox is that while many women in the feminist movement have rejected the "feminine," it is their presumed association with it that has given the movement its power. The mainstream culture recognizes, however unconsciously, that it owes a debt to the feminine and that the debt must be paid. Call something "women's so-and-so" and the opposition will automatically be on the defensive. But this is hardly the true reconciling of opposites found through the Fourth Instinct.

Our second instinct is still clearly in command. And to fulfill it, we sundered ourselves from the substance of what it means to be fully human—mind and spirit, body and soul. Contrary to the contentions of those valiant social reformers who pit benign human nature against a corrupt and corrupting society, aggression is instinctive in human beings. Whether we call it, as Robert Audrey did, the territorial imperative or, as Konrad Lorenz did, a sine qua non of life, aggression is inherent in our genetic makeup. Social conditioning and social values alternately fuel and serve to check the darker impulses of man.

"To say that people have a moral sense," James Q. Wilson wrote in *The Moral Sense*, "is not the same thing as saying that they are innately good. A moral sense must compete with other senses that are natural to humans—the desire to survive, acquire possessions, indulge in sex, or accumulate power—in short, with self-interest narrowly defined. How that struggle is resolved will differ depending on our character, our circumstances, and the cultural and political tendencies of the day. But saying that a moral sense exists is the same thing as saying that humans, by their nature, are potentially good." We build up our moral muscle by exercising it. We become virtuous by the practice of virtue, responsible by the practice of responsibility, generous by the practice of generosity, and compassionate by the practice of compassion. Yet without the authority inherent in the Fourth Instinct, our moral sense becomes nothing more than a fear that there may be something or someone watching. A hundred values and a thousand laws disconnected from the absolutes inherent in the Fourth Instinct are powerless to prevent the demonic explosions of cruelty that have dominated our century and are still dominating our culture.

Ultimately, only the Fourth Instinct can redeem the aggression inherent in the will to power of the second. By connecting man to the true source of his power, the Fourth Instinct eliminates the experience of powerlessness—a key element in the drive, the "absolute necessity," for power, whether felt by Alexander the Great driven to conquer the world or a Wall Street executive driven to take over yet one more company. When the hoped-for resonance is not there, the conqueror's assumption is that it will simply take one more country or one more company to fill the vacuum and quench the thirst. Often the wish to conquer and the will to power remain lodged in the unconscious, as if a life plan dominated by our second instinct has been set on automatic pilot and, no matter how loudly the captain of the ship protests, the direction of the journey has been determined. The second instinct even spills over to the third—our sexual drive—with aggression posing as love. Marriage is reduced to the successful acquisition of trophy wives or trophy husbands, a means to the end of more power, more prestige and more recognition—one more way to compensate for the feelings of insufficiency and inferiority that Adler sees at the heart of the striving for power.

As the second instinct drives us toward what we can hold in the here-and-now, the Fourth summons us toward the infinite. In a healthy interaction between the two instincts, we are driven to accomplish not only for ourselves but also for the community, for the sake of the whole of which we are a part. And in the active embracing of our interconnectedness with others, we glimpse the infinite that eludes us when we remain barricaded in the prison of self-centeredness.

Plato wrote that most people want power, not virtue, and must be trained to prefer virtue. Once his Fourth Instinct is awakened, the pilgrim in Plato's *Republic* passes through different states of awareness—from the shadows cast on the wall of the cave in which he is chained to the final confrontation with the blazing Sun, a Form for the source of all Life, Truth and Goodness. The second instinct is to be superseded by the cultivation of higher desires. But in Plato's philosophy, the third instinct, the sexual drive, is a cosmic power which contains within it the transformation of this commonest human desire into a transcendent experience. Eros finds expression both in the unbridled appetites of the *Republic*'s tyrant and in the passionate longing for beauty—not only of the flesh, but also of the mind and spirit. In the *Divine Comedy*, as Dante pulls away from Virgil's human wisdom and gravitates toward Beatrice's divine wisdom, he feels the stirring growth of wings on his back. He knows then that Virgil was right: happiness and wisdom will both finally be his.

Falling in love and the awakening of the third instinct are for many people the most extraordinary and revelatory experiences of their lives. Our center of gravity is suddenly shifted, and we are, at least temporarily, off balance. The self-centered ego is shocked into awareness of a heightened reality. We are

—in the clichés of romance—"walking on air," "in heaven," "on cloud nine."

In our century, Freud, acknowledging his indebtedness to Plato, enthroned sexuality as the most powerful universal force, an ambiguous force that explains all and rules all, that sinks men into the depths of destruction or lifts them to the heights of cosmic union. Unlike other species of the animal kingdom that are sexually active only for a limited season, man is a sexual animal for all seasons—sexually available all year round. And affluence, both historically and today, has been accompanied by intense efforts—ranging from the imaginative and inventive to the perverse and even brutal—to heighten sexual pleasure. From rouged nipples showing through the transparent dresses of women in ancient Egypt to Nero's trying to turn the boy Sporus into a girl by castration, sexual indulgence has preoccupied humanity for centuries, often coupled with what is most barbaric in man.

The sexual instinct that men share with the beasts they also share with the gods. The earthly Aphrodite, known to the ancients as "the dark one," has her counterpart in the heavenly Aphrodite. Whether thwarted or fulfilled, this is a drive that can defy and overwhelm man's reason with glory or terror. In Andrew Lloyd Webber's musical "Aspects of Love," the lyrics of the central theme give contemporary expression to the vulnerability of our rational selves when confronted with our third instinct: "Love bursts in and, suddenly, all our wisdom disappears. . . . All the rules we make are broken. . . . Live or perish in its flame. Love will never let you be the same."

In our current atmosphere of omnipresent eroticism, it's hard at times to remember that procreation remains the primary function of our sexual instinct. This truth impinges upon our world like a strange and unwelcome visitor in an era in which billions of dollars are spent to glorify the pursuit (and perception) of sex, free of inconvenient details like conception, commitment and emotional consequences. The portrayal of sex on television is thirteen times to one sex outside marriage. It is no wonder that young people are sometimes amazed that, yes, married people do have sex.

The ancients recognized the ambivalent power of our sexual instinct—a tidal wave beneath which we drown or on which

53

we ride into a life lived more intensely, more truthfully, more consciously. Socrates called the "divine madness" of the lover a much higher form of being than the "man-made sanity" of mundane existence. Our century set out to liberate the sexual instinct from taboos and bounds of duty, in the process stripping it of its spiritual context. In our ultimate hubris, we put sex under the microscope and left it there. We speak about it coolly and clinically, in the pseudoscientific language of the Kinsey Report. The extraordinary mystery revered through the ages has given way to a numbers game and to a woman's "inalienable right" to multiple orgasms.

As a culture we have reduced sexuality to biology and given it, in this reduced form, to our children: candy-striped condoms in their Christmas stockings. We package it in videotapes and value-free classrooms. We venerate it in our fashions and revere it in our advertising. And when the Dionysian power, gussied up and clamped down, erupts in a rage of rape and abuse, we blame it on "society"—whoever that may be—and a lack of adequate social spending. Clearly, we need to stop pretending that we can understand the true nature of sex by merely viewing it through the biologist's lens, the advertiser's fantasy, or the feminist's scowl.

When we recognize the powerful, complex nature of the sexual instinct, we will know what to teach our children about sex: not how to put a condom on a banana in fourth grade, nor the approved, technical text on intercourse and abortion, but the truth contained in the annals of our cultural log—from ancient myths to modern plays. "It's to do with knowing and being known," wrote Tom Stoppard in *The Real Thing*. "I remember how it stopped seeming odd that in biblical Greek knowing was used for making love. Whosit knew so-and-so. Carnal knowledge. It's what lovers trust each other with, knowledge of each other, not of the flesh but through the flesh, knowledge of self, the real him, the real her, in extremis, the mask slipped from the face. Every other version of oneself is on offer to the public. We share our vivacity, grief, sulks, anger, joy . . . we hand it out to anybody who happens to be standing around. . . . Our lovers share us with the passing trade. But in pairs we insist that we give ourselves to each other. What selves? What's left? What else is there that hasn't been dealt out like playing cards? A sort of knowledge. Personal, final, uncompromised. Knowing, being known. I revere that."

Reverence as well as mystery seem largely out of date in our modern world. When we put sexuality under scientific observation, we thought we had placed it under our control. Only when we recognize again the power contained in our sexual instinct will we stop acting as if we can reduce it, without emotional cost, to fun and trivial satisfaction—and only then will we be able to teach this to our children. Meaningful sex education would devote a lot more time to literature than to plumbing. What a good novelist can teach us about the pain of sexuality cut adrift from connectedness can bring us face-to-face with the very isolation we are too often trying to overcome through sex.

In February 1991, the Presbyterian Church Special Committee on Human Sexuality produced—after three years of deliberation—a two-hundred-page report on sexual behavior that sums up every illusion about human sexuality. Camille Paglia ridiculed its "happy, bouncy vision of human life that would have made Doris Day and Debbie Reynolds—those 50s blond divas—proud." And what are teenagers to do with other emotions—some infinitely more glorious and others profoundly more disturbing? Suppress them, deny them, or drown them in drugs and alcohol? And now that we have eliminated evil from our sunlit moralities, how do we explain the horror of heavy metal and rap lyrics of "Gangster of Love," "Mind of a Lunatic" or "Bodily Dismemberment"?

> There's no need to worry bitch, Just lay there and relax
> And as you reach your climax, I'll be reaching for my ax
> Well you're fuckin' history bitch
> First I'll slice your tender leg off just above the thighs
> Then I remove your slender arms, my passion running high . . .
> A masterpiece of blood and flesh lies twitching on my bed.

We hear such things and quickly look around for someone to blame. This is not *our* view of sexuality, for goodness' sake; this is not *mine*. But as a culture, our fingerpointing is meaningless. The ugly rap lyric merely says graphically what we have been teaching for decades: sex, like surgery, is all about anatomy and physiology. The rap "artist" has simply chosen to do surgery with an ax. With all our dissections of human sexuality, freed from its mystery and its enormous power for both good and evil, we have taught a sexuality that is amputated from meaning. When we hear the rap lyric or see the jaded look on a teenager's face as he mouths the words, we have graphic and unhappy evidence that Wordsworth was right: "What we love, others will love, and we will teach them how." It is our culture which taught them to sing.

"This thing of darkness I acknowledge mine," says Prospero of Caliban in *The Tempest*. The transformation of darkness can take place only when we acknowledge it and integrate it into the light. In the *Eumenides*, Orestes, pursued by the dreaded Furies, finally owns the darkness of his own actions. Two hundred pages on the joys of emotionally unencumbered sex have less insight into our third instinct than two sentences from Aeschylus or Shakespeare. We can acknowledge the darker elements in the sexual instinct and not be overwhelmed by them only through accepting the higher reality to which our Fourth Instinct points—the light into which the darkness is absorbed.

The third instinct, more than any other, can be a bridge to the Fourth and to our future—by removing the dullness of habitual perceptions, by awakening the exaltation of love, by transcending both the self-centeredness of the second instinct and the self-preserving calculations of the first. Through the third instinct we stand naked, vulnerable to each other, and through each other, to God.

We hear it in the stanzas of popular love songs or in the sensual mysticism of Saint John of the Cross: the principle of union, of the binding that frees and the love that liberates. Perhaps this is why the third and Fourth instincts share so much common vocabulary. Motel, the tailor in *Fiddler on the Roof*, sings of his love as if it were a biblical event: "Wonder of wonders, miracle of miracles. I was afraid that God would frown, but like He did so long ago in Jericho, God just made a wall fall down." Our desire for wholeness, for at-one-ment, can drive us both into the arms of a lover and into the arms of God. "If I can say to somebody else, 'I love you,' " wrote Erich Fromm, "I must be able to say, 'I love in you everybody, I love through you the world, I love in you also myself.' " Love is the bond we share with each other and with God.

With the rise of secularism has come the blurring of this connection. We have so completely divorced sexuality from the transcendent that to speak of the third instinct in spiritual terms is jarring to our modern ears. But if we fail to see the connectedness here, we misunderstand both the nature of the instinct and the character of love.

No biblical writings are more sensual than Solomon's "Song of Songs." Eight chapters of erotic poetry nestle between Ecclesiastes and Isaiah. From the opening words ("Let him kiss me with the kisses of his mouth!") to the closing stanza ("Be swift, my lover, like a gazelle or a young stag on the mountains of spices!"), the "Song of Songs" is an ode to God in the language of an aroused lover. Even the vows of chastity taken by Catholic nuns are less a manifestation of prudish repression than a recognition that they are indeed "brides of Christ."

Whether through the vows of chastity or the whispered words of a mother's goodnight kiss, the Fourth Instinct finds expression in love's devotion and commitment. Procreation remains an evolutionary imperative: "Thou wast begot; to get it is thy duty." Yet it is the experience of bringing children into the world and bringing them up in it that is one of nature's most universal ways to activate the Fourth Instinct. For many, loving their children is the closest they ever come to the unconditional love of spirit, and nurturing their children the closest to caring for or giving to others. Although, sadly, there are some that even this elemental grace passes over; the average six-year-old will have spent more time watching TV than speaking to his father in his entire lifetime.

Perhaps I always knew a child was a gift of God. But the experience of parenthood has underscored another truth: a child is a gift of godliness, a creation to love and love through, a gateway to the path of empathy and understanding. At this point in our evolutionary history—when children need not be a primary economic unit in the work force, or a commodity to be treasured for what they can bring by way of material gain— the path of the parent, when chosen consciously, could become for the first time no less effective than the path of the ascetic in reaching the fulfillment of our Fourth Instinct.

In Classical Greek 101, we learned to distinguish that love which is *eros* (sexual love) from that which is *philia* (friendship) and from that which is *agape* (unconditional love). Most English

57

versions of the Bible translate all three words as "love." God is alternately our lover, our father, our friend, our fellow man. The Fourth Instinct pushes back the boundaries of our caring —from our solitary selves to our families and friends, to our communities, to the world. The story of the Good Samaritan answers the question "Who is my neighbor?" Spirit, not blood, makes us a family of men.

In a study on the roots of altruism, Dr. Ervin Staub analyzed men and women who had risked their lives during World War II to protect Jews hiding from the Nazis. What turned an ordinary bystander into an intrepid defender? "Goodness, like evil, often begins in small steps," Dr. Staub wrote. "Heroes evolve: they aren't born. Very often the rescuers made only a small commitment at the start—to hide someone for a day or two. But once they had taken that step they began to see themselves differently, as someone who helps. What starts as mere willingness becomes intense involvement." Indeed, heroes evolve, but they could not evolve if the seed for heroism, for goodness, for transcending our self-interest, had not been planted a *long* time ago. It is this capacity, this potential to love others more than ourselves, that is our common heritage, waiting, like a seed, to be watered by the first tender drops of compassion. The self so carefully nurtured by the first three instincts becomes less important to us than the promptings of our Fourth Instinct. Its fruits may range in bounty from death-defying rescues to daily acts of kindness. As for the secret season of each man's spring, this is the mystery of grace. The seed may bear forth year after year, or it may lie fallow, wedged in the corner of an arid soul. Yet like the seed that lay buried in a sealed urn of a Pharaoh's tomb, the potentiality— the eternal impatience to be born—is there. When the conditions necessary for germination were met some five thousand years later, the seed burst forth into life as if it had been planted with last year's crop.

"I am come that they might have life, and that they might have it more abundantly," the Bible tells us. And we are recognizing in growing numbers that "Gimme, gimme, gimme" is not where joy lies, or abundance, or strength. The plenitude experienced in giving, the health and the power—that's the miracle. When we decide to lend a hand, we discover what strong arms we have. And we never feel as much gratitude for our good fortune or the rewards of our hard work as in the moment we give of them.

When I was growing up in Greece, I got my first taste of American values by reading the complete works of Ayn Rand at age eleven. Imagine what an unexpected ally *The Virtue of Selfishness* could be to a growing girl. My childish essays and all my schoolwork became so thoroughly imbued with the "virtue" of selfishness that the headmistress summoned my mother to warn her that she had a socially degenerate daughter on her hands. I grew up and out of Ayn Rand's virtue of selfishness. Eventually, I adopted—or was adopted by—my new homeland, America. Looking back to my childhood and around me at the needs of our nation, I realize that if we are serious about maturing as a civilization, we must do no less. We must restore the second instinct to its proper purpose and proportion in our lives. When our Fourth Instinct is repressed, the second strains to take its place. Into the space reserved for compassion comes competition. The imagination intended for caring is instead invested in calculations. Instead of nurturing the spiritual underpinnings that would give us inner peace and true strength, we launch yet another game of us versus them.

Transcending ourselves—our problems, cares and fears, but also our pleasures, hopes and joys—is at the heart of the Fourth Instinct. "Charity begins at home" is the cliché too often used to justify doing nothing for others until one's own problems have been solved and all one's pleasures have been indulged. It betrays the promptings of our first three instincts. Our Fourth Instinct knows better. Its promptings were personified for me by Kathy Ousey, a woman who, with six children of her own, three with special needs, and a husband working his way through law school, took on a special project for foster children. "When I help lift someone else's burden," she said, "my own are easier to bear." It's a radically different attitude from the prickly "What's in it for me?" and "When will the government do something about it?" The woman's story, and her strength, resonate with the wisdom of an age-old African proverb: "When the right hand washes the left, the right gets cleansed too."

Healing ourselves—making ourselves whole by helping others—is not some half-baked homily. As psychiatrist Karl Menninger has observed it, "Love cures people. Both the ones who give it, and the ones who receive it." Anthony Godby Johnson was a young teenager who in his early years never received the love he learned to give. In his wrenching autobiography, *A Rock and a Hard Place*, he described how he survived as a young child in a house where his parents and their friends regularly beat, starved and raped him over a period of years. He discovered an inner tenacity when he realized that the only way to hang on was to reach out. He found a friend, a stray cat named PG—a quirky little creature with a taste for leftover lunch meat. The cat became one of Tony's last links to life. "Even if I didn't eat that day, she wouldn't go hungry, and so, in my own twisted way, I was securing my own survival," he wrote. "It made me feel alive and vital."

In every major religion, giving and service mark the path back to God—back to a world in which we are no longer strangers and alone, but members of a vast yet tightly knit family. The longing to overcome our feelings of alienation and estrangement is present in each of us, motivating acts of selfish desperation at one extreme and selfless heroism at the other. Our Fourth Instinct is not an impersonal, detached urge. There is a longing to it which is intensely personal, a pressing homesickness for that something or someone we have left behind and long to reach. We ache to transcend time, transcend our limitations, transcend our material existence and embrace the eternal.

Despite the wizardry of new technology and the advances of modern science, the answers to life's larger questions still elude us. Able to expound at mind-numbing lengths about the minuscule moons of the planet Mars, we are struck dumb when a colleague suffers a sudden heart attack and we visit his wife, newly widowed. Powerful telescopes probe deep into outer space while microscopes map the molecular structure of a strand of DNA; psychologists diagnose our pathologies and sociologists analyze the dismal causes of mob violence. Then our three-year-old asks where she came from, or where Grandpa went when he died, and we are left speechless. "The basic problem," André Malraux wrote, "is that our civilization, which is a civilization of machines, can teach man everything except how to be a man."

We have measured every element of our structure, the intensity of our feelings and the exact nature of our behaviors. Still, we have not taken the measure of man. Our analyses have focused on one or the other of the first three instincts—man the survivor, man the aggressor, man the sexual animal. Ironically, most of these efforts have ignored the Fourth Instinct while demonstrating it in our longing to understand and connect, to find the ultimate unifying principle that makes sense of it all. The first three instincts may explain what has happened or what is happening, but they fall short of an explanation of what may yet happen when we tap into the truth of our being.

Like the mythic cosmic tree, rooted in this world and growing up toward heaven, man reaches out for God, for communion and at-one-ment. And God reaches back, unfolding his love in man and through man in the world. It is our rationalist hubris that uproots our everyday selves from this nurturing soil. And it is the din of our everyday "busyness" that drums out our soul's whispered pleas for attention.

"I felt it better to speak to God than about him," said Saint Thérèse of Lisieux. Speaking to God demands solitude. We can commune with God through our communion with others. But we also long to commune with God directly, to seek the truth about the world by withdrawing from it. Poets and mystics have to travel this path of withdrawal. It was through that "inward eye" that Wordsworth celebrated the bliss of solitude:

> *When from our better selves we have too long*
> *Been parted by the hurrying world, and droop,*
> *Sick of its business, of its pleasure tired,*
> *How gracious, how benign, is Solitude.*

Saint John of the Cross wrote about the dark night of the soul, the darkness we need to traverse in solitude: "Let that quiet darkness be your whole mind and like a mirror to you. For I want your thought of self to be as naked and as simple as your thought of God, so that you may be spiritually united to Him without any fragmentation and scattering of your mind."

My own search for this path across the darkness was at first a purely cerebral undertaking. It was the time when, shortly after I returned from my worldwide tour for *The Female Woman,*

I retreated into my small apartment in London, drew shut the heavy drapes, locked the door and read through the night, often falling asleep with my head on a page of Saint John of the Cross, Jung or Shakespeare. East, West and, of course, the Greeks were ransacked for their wisdom. I piled books around my bed, stashed them under my sink, stacked them on my kitchen counter. I began by diving into erudition and ended by nearly drowning in it. After a season of this isolation and intellectual indulgence, I discovered that I could not quench my thirst by merely studying the scientific properties of water. I learned what Plotinus realized some seventeen hundred years ago: "Knowledge has three degrees: opinion, science, illumination. The means or instrument of the first is sense; of the second, dialectic; of the third, intuition. To the last I subordinate reason. It is absolute knowledge founded on the identity of the mind knowing with the object known."

With the phone turned off and the curtains drawn, it was hard to know when dawn broke or the sun set—especially when I decided to embark on a long "water fast," partly because I was tired of living on cheddar cheese and crackers, but mostly because I so wanted to touch the spirit, to be filled by it, that anything that was not spirit or about spirit was an encumbrance. So, starving my body seemed like a good shortcut. Fortunately I realized, sooner rather than later, that treating physical reality as a dispensable illusion was no less misleading than dismissing spiritual reality as a hallucination. Even while this realization was taking hold of me, my first instinct ensured that I came out of my fast before I had weakened myself too much, although not before I could, blindfolded, tell the difference between sips of the various brands of bottled water I had in my flat.

When I decided to go beyond my books and my intellect, and try to gain access to my intuition and inner wisdom, I began to set aside some time every day not to read about God, not to talk about God, not even to talk *to* God, but to listen. The Quakers call it "quiet time." The Jesuits call it "spiritual exercises." Thomas Merton called it "contemplation." And, of course, Christians have for centuries called it prayer. In its latest incarnation it is known to many as meditation, and the mainstream culture dismisses it as the latest invention of Marin County, California.

Quietly waiting for God is not a novel idea, any more than eating is an innovative response to hunger. But quiet and solitude are rare commodities. The silence in our lives is under assault on all fronts: roaring jets and blasting Walkmans, numbing elevator music and blaring headline news. It's hard to genuflect to the beat of MTV. We are wired, plugged in, constantly catered to and cajoled. After a while we become terrified of the silence, unaware of what it has to offer. We drown out the simple questions of God with the simplistic sound-bites of man.

In the *Apology*, Socrates defined his life's mission as awakening the Athenians to the supreme importance of attending to their souls. This is the call of the Fourth Instinct. Christ expressed it in terms of the Kingdom within: "Seek ye first the Kingdom of God . . . and all these things shall be added unto you." We nod approvingly at this "poetic truth" and proceed to follow our second instinct—going after things of the world, securing our own little kingdoms, keeping tabs and settling scores. I remember, shortly before I left London for New York, speaking to an English lady who was even more emphatic. "I think," she said, "that looking into one's self is quite, quite disgusting, not a thing nice people do."

In recent years I have witnessed more and more people, on both sides of the Atlantic, choosing to sneak a look at their own lives and, eventually, themselves. Some have learned to listen once more to the silence. At the same time that mainstream culture is drowning out our still, small voice, postmodern pilgrims are following the path of the Fourth Instinct into silent retreats, monasteries, temples and the "cathedral of the outdoors"—wherever the body and the mind can find quiet and make room for the soul to awaken.

I remember walking in a rugged part of Cornwall to visit friends who lived in one of those grand old houses overlooking the sea. The basement, as I recall, was a fantastic place, antiquated plumbing mixed with even older antiques. The public rooms were eccentrically elegant, filled with odd curios and curious oddities. And then, through a hatch, there was another level yet above. It was the widow's walk, a part of the house and yet above it and outside it as well. It was a place to be alone, to sit and be still, to see things one could not see from below. It felt like what it was: the place from which to catch the first glimpse of the one you are waiting for, the one with whom you will be whole.

Looking for God, receptive, open, wrapped in the mystery of things, is the state prompted by our Fourth Instinct. In the noise and press of our lives, this seems a state alien to modern man. Exiled and dispossessed, we sit by the sidewalk of life waiting for Godot, knowing full well that he will not arrive. An anxiety hangs over us that we cannot ascribe to any particular cause or event. "Free-floating anxiety" is the term used by modern psychology, and by naming what we cannot explain, we delude ourselves with the notion that by classifying the symptoms we have somehow mastered the cause. A successful, fashionable playwright wrote a column a few years ago in an equally successful and fashionable magazine. He recounted a day in his life that would be the envy of many, full of drama and people and color. He ended his piece where he had ended his day: "I go to bed feeling that I have forgotten something." The nagging sensation of having forgotten something important is the Fourth Instinct breaking through our veils of comfort, sensation and routine—a warning that all is not well and the assurance that we have known better. If only we could remember . . .

That remembering can be the beginning of life's greatest journey. What begins as an inkling—as revelation, intuition or the sudden leap of faith—slowly starts to transform our lives and ourselves. When we deny revelation, shut down imagination, ignore the voice of intuition or faith, the moment passes. Like the smile on the face of a child seen for an instant outside the window of our train rushing by a playground, it is gone by the time it has registered. The flickering insight of the moment has disappeared, sometimes leaving us even more certain of our loneliness than we were before.

Whether through nagging anxiety or existential dread, we are goaded to find some explanation that makes sense of the chaos of life. This is the Fourth Instinct's quest for meaning. Despite all attempts by the existential philosophers and the culture they spawned to make modern man more comfortable with the meaninglessness of life, we are designed to keep looking for meaning because we are designed to embody it.

The trap of our proudly rational age has been to try—in vain, of course—to capture meaning and pin down God through intellect alone. Nietzsche tried it, but his brilliant aphorisms about God's nonexistence could not deny the reality of God in the depths of his soul. As the doors of his mental prison closed behind him, his idealization of man's proud ego led him to proclaim that there is room in the world only for hermits—or, at most, hermits in pairs. The denial of God is the denial both of meaning and of the brotherhood that only man's spiritual unity with others can engender. Human life is trivialized and each of us is reduced to "a feverish selfish little clod of ailments and grievances" dressed up in expectations, waiting for some new entitlement.

Of course, spiritual reality, like gravity, does not disappear just because we deny it. But as Plato noticed, the divine element in the world is persuasive, not coercive, which is why religious coercion is the most pernicious form of spiritual abuse. In the divine plan of man's evolution, man is indeed God's co-worker, but each of us has to consciously choose this intended role. The more inescapably obvious it becomes that the preoccupations of our daily life cannot satisfy our deepest needs, nor fulfill our native hunger for meaning, the more imperative the yearnings of our Fourth Instinct become.

The French philosopher Joseph Renan once said that you should never believe a German when he tells you he is an atheist. No man—German, American or Peruvian—is an atheist in those hidden depths of his soul which modern science has uncomprehendingly called his unconscious, and which modern man has all too often rejected as nonexistent.

When we visit these depths we discover a vast cauldron of realities holding both forces of destruction and seeds of creation. The Fourth Instinct encourages us to substitute the guidance of spirit for the guidance of our inadequate ego with its futile willing and striving. God is encountered not as a wishful, remote and unapproachable reality somewhere out in the blue of the heavens, but present and concrete, alive and well, with us and within us. Creation is not an arrested reality that can be captured, dissected and handed down in frozen creeds; it is, instead, a living process that can only be completed by our own full participation. We are at a giving end, not only at a supplicant, receiving end, living in our lives the answer to the problem of creation that theologians have sought to provide by using their razor-sharp logical minds to slash the air. Meister

Eckehart scornfully proclaimed in the fourteenth century that if God were good, He could be better. And he was right. Not, of course, in the sense that God lacks perfection, but in the sense that for this perfection to become manifest, we must choose to follow our Fourth Instinct through the unfolding of our spiritual nature.

Only then will we be whole and God's plan realized. The circle throughout history has been a symbol of wholeness, and squaring the circle has signified completion. Four points naturally and symmetrically divide the circle. The motif of "three plus one"—three parts animal and one part human—has appeared in Western literature from the writings of Plato to the theories of Jung. In Ezekiel's biblical vision of the four cherubim, each one had four faces. Our four instincts correspond to this ancient quaternity in the human soul. When the Fourth— the quintessentially human instinct—has been given its honored place in our lives, then the circle will have been squared and we will at last have arrived at our center.

3

Dead Ends

> The guests thought that they were happy, thought that they were witty, thought that they were profound, and, as they thought this, other people thought it still more strongly; and so it got about that nothing was more delightful than one of Lady R.'s assemblies; everyone envied those who were admitted; those who were admitted envied themselves because other people envied them; and so there seemed no end to it—except that which we have now to relate.
>
> —Virginia Woolf, *Orlando*

I moved too young, I suppose, from project to project, and place to place. Our mother was determined that, despite our modest means in Greece, she would find a way for her children to pursue fine educations. So, at age seventeen, I was off to England where, a year later, I was enrolled at Cambridge.

Many of the best things in my life were not planned. Certainly not my writing career. A British publisher, who had published Germaine Greer's *The Female Eunuch*, happened to see me on television debating my views on the importance of women not throwing, so to speak, the baby out with the bathwater, and sent me a letter asking if I would be interested in writing a book on my views. I was in my last year at Cambridge and was planning to leave the next year for the Kennedy School of Government at Harvard, and a postgraduate degree. I sent him a letter saying, Thank you, but I can't write. He wrote back: "Can you have lunch?" Thinking of all my friends wandering around looking for a home for their manuscripts, I decided it was definitely worth a train ride to London. By the end of lunch, Reg Davis-Poynter had offered me a contract and a modest advance. "If you really can't write," he said, "then I won't publish it, and you can go to Harvard a year late."

Call it coincidence, or fate, or synchronicity, or serendipity, or destiny—by whatever name it should be known, the publisher's letter sealed with a publisher's contract marked a new beginning in my life.

I was twenty-two when I finished *The Female Woman,* and both the publisher and I hoped for a few readers and perhaps one kindly review. What I got was a flood of media calls and a round-the-world book tour, followed by the beginning of my soul-searching, and six years as a journalist in London doing columns for the *Daily Mail,* book reviews for the *Spectator,* attempts at humor for *Punch,* and profiles and speeches for anyone who would pay. During this time I also wrote *After Reason* and *Maria Callas.*

In 1980, for no particular reason except a very strong intuitive pull to do so, I decided to move to New York. I was thirty and ready to begin a new chapter. Maybe I had had enough of pulling shut the drapes in my London apartment and in my life.

The "New York Chapter" of my life lasted four years. It was a very different time for me—a time when I stepped outside the cramped confines of erudition and joined the social whirlwind. Also a time when I broadened the scope of my writing and did a lot of speaking around the country. When I had money, I loved giving dinner parties; when I was poor, I called my lecture agent and took speaking engagements in places I'd never heard of. Sometimes when today I read media coverage of me, I wince and blame the years in New York for the sobriquet of socialite that I earned there. And I definitely *earned* it! Lunches at Le Cirque, dances at the Metropolitan Museum, weekends in the Hamptons and intimate, black-tie dinners for thirty-six.

I would come home from the dinners, sometimes drained, sometimes elated. Nothing was more claustrophobic than sitting for an hour and a half next to someone who refused to move beyond small talk or a discussion of that day's *New York Times* editorial, and few things more recharging than a conversation with someone—an old friend or a new acquaintance—who was prepared to move beyond the surface.

I wrote about these dinners in my journal before I went to bed, and looking back, a single refrain seemed to run through them all. Night after night, I would sit next to someone very wealthy or famous or both, who was either visibly unhappy and in deadly denial of the fact, or eager to discuss the paradox of having so much and feeling so empty. So it came about that a lot of the research for *The Fourth Instinct* was conducted in the dining rooms of New York.

Among the people I met in New York were women and men with whom I formed relationships that have deepened over the years and become more and more valued. And there were others I remember as one remembers characters in a play, searching for their lives in all the wrong places: driven to be invited to the right dinner, to be on the arm of the right partner, to throw the perfect party featuring perfect table settings, perfect flower arrangements and, above all, the perfect mix of glamorous guests. It was not enough that they were well educated and attractive, well married and successful. They wanted —they needed, they were desperate for—the momentary security they drew from appearing at the right place with the right people at the right time. To see and be seen was their obsession, to be successful enough or at least close enough to success to be dusted by its glory. What they most dreaded was that they might not be invited to *the* event which defined, by its invitation list, the "Who's Who" of the hour. They were haunted by the possibility that they might be declared an FV ("Fashion Victim") by *W*, snubbed by Suzy or—horror of horrors—that the social train would pull away from the station without them. If even once they were not on board, they might never again travel in such fine company.

There is, of course, no social train—only a merry-go-round, a sometimes amusing, sometimes soporific way to pass time in the presence of others passing time. But for those hungry souls desperate to see their photographs in *W* or *Town & Country*—thus assuring them of new invitations in the morning—this was no innocent pastime. It was an addiction that hounded them, occasionally to their graves.

Among them were men and women who had invested so much energy honing their social skills that they were perfect at the game. There was the perfect courtier whose specialty was his concern for your children—provided your net worth was over $100 million. He knew how to get them into the school of your first choice, where to find the perfect present, who was the best—and most discreet—therapist when they got hooked on drugs or alcohol. There was the woman so ferociously chic that no flourish or ruffle was ever allowed to disturb the severe elegance of her silhouette; while fashion victims struggled in their overwrought Lacroix, she would steal the show in her monochromatic cashmere by Valentino. There was the master of the artful tease and the master of studied complicity, drawing you into corners to whisper "secrets" in your ear.

And then there was the master of indiscriminate seduction, whose high social spirits never faltered. I remember a dinner soon after he had come back from a cruise on the Nile visiting the Egyptian temples. (It was the season's "in" vacation—"There is nothing happening in Monte Carlo this year," he had said before he left.) "Ramses," he told me incredulously, "spent *all* his life preparing for death." Looking around the room, I thought that this was certainly a wiser choice than ours: spending our lives desperately pretending death would never come. "A life lived without taking death into account," I told him, "seems to me to be missing the point in a big way." "Death bores me," he replied, drawing an appreciative crowd around him. "In Central Europe they have coffeehouses for that stuff—*kaffee mit shlag, torten* and soul-baring about death and the hereafter. There is something very undignified about confessions. I don't want to know more about myself." There was laughter and relief all around and, on cue, our perfect hostess changed the subject.

But it was getting harder and harder to change the subject, harder and harder to believe in the splendor of the naked Emperor's clothes. "Is this," cried Orlando, "is this what people call life?" And Virginia Woolf went on to elaborate: "How, in so short a time, she had passed from intoxication to disgust we will only seek to explain by supposing that this mysterious composition which we call society, is nothing absolutely good or bad in itself, but has a spirit in it, volatile but potent, which either makes you drunk when you think it, as Orlando thought it, delightful, or gives you a headache when you think it, as Orlando thought it, repulsive."

I left New York for Los Angeles at the end of 1984, not because I found the social merry-go-round repulsive but because, listening to the same inner voice that had taken me from London to New York, I knew that the New York stage of my life was complete, although I had no idea what the new stage might hold in store. At farewell dinners given by my friends, the same note of wonderment was struck in the toasts: How could anyone *voluntarily* exchange New York for California?

We don't, of course, have to move to a different city every time a stage in our journey comes to an end. From New York to New Delhi, from London to Los Angeles, we are pushed and pulled by our own soul's hunger for something more substantial than finger food and light conversation. Whether we are conscious of it or not, wherever we may be, we all want to find our way to meaning in life. We are drawn into the search simply on account of being human. And more often than not, we rush headlong into one blind alley after another. The number of dead ends being explored daily in our modern culture is limitless, and as quickly as we discover that a particular road leads nowhere, a tempting new path emerges from the mist. We sense that life is incomplete—our Fourth Instinct makes sure we do—and we respond to that sensation by hunting for some magic potion which will relieve the symptom, some quick fix which will offer instant meaning, some paperback answer to life's most challenging questions: "Why are we here?" and "Is that all there is?" We become pilgrims to the modern meccas of meaning: shopping malls and sports arenas, cocktail parties where we slurp down calories and health clubs where we work them off. We are looking for the new idol, new lover, new clothes or new body—something that will either satisfy our desire to feel better about ourselves, or silence our

71

dissatisfaction. But by looking outside ourselves, we are guaranteed to be charging down a dead end. We cannot find the answer there because—as Gertrude Stein once said of Oakland —"There is no there there."

My father brought back a story from the concentration camp— a story another prisoner had told him one day while they were waiting for they did not know what. Somewhere in the bowels of Dachau or Auschwitz—so the story went—sat a perfectly ordinary German man, drafted into Hitler's army from a nearby village, honored to serve the fatherland in some small way. It was his task to count, precisely and daily, the number of people being fed to the ovens. His goal was to make the grim work as efficient as possible, to see if trends emerged or patterns appeared which would show means by which productivity could be increased. And so, with an eye for detail and a commitment to accuracy, day after day he made careful entries in a book. When the numbers not only added up but also assured him that on average the daily score was growing larger, he went home satisfied that his work had paid off. Life for him was about the detail, the task immediately at hand. It never occurred to this otherwise kind husband and gentle father that he was calmly counting history's greatest carnage. He was committed to simple accuracy, not great truths; to legible entries, not moral conclusions.

And for millions, in infinitely less dramatic settings, life has been reduced to the task immediately at hand, with the larger questions that gnaw at us sometimes in the morning's early hours left unexamined. Once we've made ends meet, is our primary calling merely to measure our progress toward the supreme goals of wealth, position, reputation and celebrity? Is it merely to count the days, or to live each day to the fullest? Is it to satisfy the hungers of our first three instincts while starving those of the Fourth? Or is it to integrate both body and spirit on a journey through life that will have purpose and meaning? What does it mean that we, unique among all living creatures, have the power to choose to evolve and the longing to understand and to know?

Why are we here? "I fall into a depression just thinking about the question," a lawyer friend told me recently. "I've never found any satisfying answers before and I expect none now." Pessimistic about ever finding any answers but unable to stop asking the questions, he identified, he said, with the character played by Bill Murray in *Groundhog Day*. Murray wakes up each morning to the day he had finished the night before, trapped for eternity in the same old routine. Between disappointments and the daily grind of life, it's easy to feel trapped on an endless treadmill. The Fourth Instinct calls us to meaning, but not having trained our soul's ears, we hear only a muffled voice urging us to move. And so we shuffle along, likely as not down another dead end.

"Glory is fleeting," wrote Napoleon, "but obscurity is forever." And we definitely don't want forever. However fickle a lover it may be, we want celebrity. Fame. Headlines. Cheering crowds and thundering ovations. If only our names could be in lights along the Great White Way, and spelled correctly, then we would be satisfied. Celebrity will fulfill our cavernous longing. Or so we have been led to believe.

In a secular culture, fame is advertised as both a substitute for immortality and the means by which to attain it. In an age of doubt and uncertainty, celebrity bestows existence. "You think I am, therefore I am." "Fame is a narcotic," fashion designer Bill Blass once said. "Once you are hooked on it, you are hooked for life." Like other narcotics, this one induces its own stream of illusions. When supply meets demand, the need to be worshiped meets the longing to worship and celebrities are both created and create themselves. They are the high priests of film and fashion, books and baseball, camp and capitalism. There they sit, demigods in the cradle of a modern Mount Olympus.

Many of the rich, having discovered that lives littered with things do not make them happy, spend more of their millions in pursuit of fame, hoping that *that* will bring them happiness. Leona Helmsley, once beaming from the pages of every glossy magazine (before she was sent to jail for tax evasion) epitomized the hunger for self-promotion in the course of product promotion. And memoir after memoir tells us that when the rich and famous go home, they head for the medicine chest or the liquor cabinet to make it through the night. If there is a lesson to be learned, it is that having other people know their names is no guarantee that celebrities know who they are.

The meteoric rise to fame which comes to music and movie stars has left many who took the ride staring at a dead end. Janis Joplin and Jimi Hendrix fell out of one generation; Judy Garland's rise and fall spanned several. "How come I'm not happy all the time?" asked Eddie Murphy when fame had sent him to new heights. "There's a couple of times I really thought I was going to go under," Bette Midler recalled—not of her days singing in bathhouses, but of the problems of dealing with success. Robert Mitchum, who achieved fame through countless movie roles, looked it straight in the eye and said, "I don't feel successful." Anthony Perkins, afflicted with AIDS, said the only time in his life he had experienced true support was within the anonymous AIDS community made up of others who, like him, were dying. Sir Laurence Olivier, revered worldwide for his genius as an actor, said despairingly: "I just don't like me . . . I don't like my own company very much." If the goal of one's journey is a sense of peace that comes with self-knowledge and a sense of purpose that comes with knowing God, then the path of celebrity is—according to the testimony of those traveling it—a dead end.

Fame is a fickle mistress. One week the champion athlete hears a stadium rocking with cheers for his exploits; the next week, he drops a ball or misses a shot and the crowd rains down a chorus of abuse. Things change. If we expect fame to bring us constancy and security, it can't. And even at its height, it is never enough; it reinforces our masks, and leaves our souls undernourished.

The life of a celebrity consists in wondering and worrying about the audience. If a spiritual journey requires a direct response to the question "Who am I?", the quest for celebrity revolves around the question "Who do others want me to be?" We must play to the adoring audience, or it will turn its back on us and go next door for a better show. The more actress Kim Novak—"the next Marilyn Monroe" three decades ago—succeeded in her film career, the more miserable she became. What had gone wrong? "I was sinking," she remembered in an interview. "All I wanted was for them to tell me that I was doing something right and let me find some way I could be good. . . . I was lost. . . . I felt an incompleteness, like an unfinished song."

For all these examples and thousands more, our urban playgrounds are teeming with young men who believe that the ticket to life's satisfaction is a shattering slam-dunk, or twelve-year-olds with a guitar, too young to remember Joplin's agonizing performances or Hendrix's onstage collapses, who imagine that hard-rock fame must be the greatest experience in the world. The road to celebrity dazzles those who turn toward it. It gives no hint that it's a dead end.

Indeed, advertising—the magic mirror reflecting Western culture in thirty-second spots and full-page ads—proudly lures pilgrims to this path. The Gap, a popular clothing chain catering to and defining the tastes of teenagers, is unabashed about this phenomenon. "Gap people," wrote Henry Allen in *The Washington Post*, "are people who trade in image and performance, people who make you want to be with them, be famous, be in a Gap ad, people who offer transcendence, evangelists of a sort." Their copy is cribbed from the realm of the sacred: "Our religious art is advertising. Our sainthood is fame."

Fame is not only a dead end, but potentially a dangerous one, for those we would crucify, we first worship. The real-life price of fame is gossip, rumor and venom. Fans at rock concerts are whipped into a fever which can be matched only by religious fervor; and stars on stage must guard against being ripped into relics as their faithful grab for the sacramental scrap of clothing or hank of hair. If fans grab out of frantic adoration, critics fix their sights on the famous calmly, for a living. As enthralled as we are at the prospect of being mobbed by adoring fans, the next-best thing to becoming a celebrity is toppling one.

Because we are born human, we have an instinct that continually reminds us that to be *somebody* is not the ultimate satisfaction. It is our Fourth Instinct that impels us on a journey to *become* who we really are—to reach both within and beyond ourselves to find what will fulfill our true purpose in life. When we head down the road to celebrity for its ephemeral and often self-destructive rewards, we are being taken for a ride to disappointment.

Consumption. Acquisition. Possessions. Harvesting goods and displaying what we have gathered. Investing our life-blood in an effort to ensure that we have at least our rightful share of things, knowing that "our rightful share" will always be just a bit more than we have now. The path of consumption leads to the dead end of discontent.

Maybe what makes this path especially alluring in America is that, lacking a line of royalty, we have elevated to princely realms the champions of success. Since one gains the American throne not by fortune of birth but by success, we dream of the day we might be crowned. Or perhaps it's merely the constant expectation, drummed into us from kindergarten onward, that no matter how humble our origins we too can achieve the American Dream, defined as the acquisition of things: houses, cars and a variety of toys.

No matter how loudly we protest that we have seen the hollowness of materialism, our behavior indicates otherwise. In the early 1990s, commentators and citizens joined ranks in judgment against the spirit of consumption that had marked the preceding years they christened "the Decade of Greed." From Wall Street's insider traders who broke the law to a host of financiers who used their profits to parade lavish lifestyles, headlines were dominated by masters of acquisition and display. The promise of the eighties was the dream of consumption come true. If someone had referred to "The Donald" in the 1970s, Americans would have thought of the duck; by 1990, every head turned toward Donald Trump, the man 81 percent of *USA Today*'s readers once agreed "symbolizes what makes the USA a great country."

Then we came to our senses and said that, on reflection, all this was misguided and even frightening. We rejected consumption as a value and began to recognize the need to replace it with compassion. During the 1992 presidential campaign, there were new calls to sacrifice and service. The age of consumption, it was broadly agreed, had been eclipsed. We agreed on everything, and—as nearly as can be determined from the evidence—changed nothing.

The shopping mall is no less the American temple in the 1990s than it was in the 1980s. Credit cards are proliferating at the same pace at which they are sinking users into debt. The devotion with which we attend sales and the veneration we hold for our playthings, our fascination with the latest gadgets and our obsession with the latest fashion trends—in every respect our behaviors show that the only real change is in our words, not our actions. We explain to each other why the gods of materialism are false and dangerous. We pick up books on the inner journey, and we read them with interest between midnight binges of ordering from glossy catalogues and morning-after sessions of figuring out how to whittle down the mounting pile of overdue bills. Agreeing that consumption will not fill our empty lives or bring us joy is a step in the right direction—but only a step. What's needed is some demonstration that we believe what we are saying enough to act on it.

In the great spiritual literature we have inherited, the admission price for salvation has always been detachment from material possessions. "It is easier for a camel to go through the eye of a needle, than for a rich man to enter into the kingdom of God," the Bible tells us. According to the Buddhist tradition, only when we overcome our selfish cravings will our sorrows fall away from us "like drops of water from a lotus flower." "Give me neither poverty nor riches," the Book of Proverbs tell us. It is not that wealth or material things are evil. It is rather that when they are moved from the background to the foreground of our lives, a fateful imbalance occurs and we are possessed by our possessions.

The pursuit of wealth is, in its most common form, a response to our second instinct. It's our desire to assert ourselves and take control. Alan Durning, an environmental researcher, recently assembled an interesting study showing that "psychological data from several nations confirm that the satisfaction derived from money does not come from simply having it. It comes from having more of it than others do, and from having more this year than last." Money becomes the standard by which we measure not merely our productivity but our progress. As one Wall Street banker put it bluntly in the *The New York Times*, "Net worth equals self worth."

But when the drive to accumulate takes on mythical proportions—beyond the bounds of a second-instinct drive for comfort and security—it may be a misbegotten response to an otherwise legitimate prompting from the Fourth Instinct. As

Viktor Frankl pointed out, "Sometimes the frustrated will to meaning is vicariously compensated for by a will to power, including the most primitive form of the will to power, the will to money." Wanting to have some sense of our own meaning and purpose, we look about to see how others have met this need. We look for role models. And what we see is a nation of shoppers. Shopping, reportedly the favorite activity for 93 percent of American teenage girls, appears to be the chosen path. Between 1986 and 1989, total retail space in shopping malls grew by almost 80 million square yards. Since 1987, America has had more shopping malls than high schools. What do we *really* value, as opposed to what we say we value?

The retailing analyst Victor Lebow once delivered himself of a memorable homily in praise of consumption as redemption. The American economy, he contended, "demands that we make consumption our way of life, that we convert the buying and use of goods into rituals, that we seek our spiritual satisfaction . . . in consumption." It turned out to be modern history's best-heeded sermon. Advertisers have used Fourth Instinct litanies to reinforce it: Soaking in Calgon will "take you away," while commercials for chocolate-covered candy bars urge us: "When it all looks dark, look within."

Advertisers are no doubt the most effective of all television evangelists, unscathed by scandal and undeterred in their objective. "What might once have been called an information industry," wrote Eric Clark, author of *The World of Advertising*, "has become an all-out persuasion industry." According to one study, the typical American endures between 50 and 100 advertisements each morning before nine o'clock. Within their twenty-two-hour weekly diet of television, American teenagers consume nearly four hours of TV ads each week, exposing them to approximately 100,000 advertisements from television alone before high school graduation. "That happiness is to be attained through limitless material acquisition is denied by every religion and philosophy known to humankind," sociologist Robert Bellah wrote, "but it is preached incessantly by every American television set."

In Max Apple's novel, *Free Agents*, the story is told of a father who takes his two young children to the ultimate amusement arcade for dinner. He finds himself instantly abandoned in favor of the machines. Turning to another deserted parent, he laments, "I want my children to eat with me, talk with me." The other parent looks about and concludes with resignation: "There hasn't been this kind of hard investment in idolatry since the days of the Pharaohs."

Capitalist societies, of course, have no monopoly on this idolatry. When the Iron Curtain was finally rent in the late 1980s, the manifestations of greed which poured out were a striking testament to the pent-up demand, after years of repression, to have, to get, to consume. There have been many more opportunities for materialist excesses in the West, and they have been much more widely publicized, but it isn't clear that a pair of Levi's is craved any more deeply by a teenager in Moscow, Idaho, than his counterpart in Moscow, Russia.

On May 15, 1993, on Sunset Boulevard, 125 glittering Rolls-Royces paraded past the homeless and into *The Guinness Book of Records* as the longest unbroken procession of Rolls-Royces ever assembled. Anyone finely tuned to the Fourth Instinct, watching the cavalcade roll by, might have recalled the ancient text: "What shall it profit a man, if he shall gain the whole world, and lose his own soul?"

Perfection. The ideal. Workout videos before a bran breakfast and dinner with all the right friends. Husband strong and sensitive, wife beautiful and busy. If the house is exquisitely decorated and our bodies are honed to perfection, if we're up for Boss of the Year and make the Best-Dressed List, we are well on our way. And as soon as we are perfect, we will be happy.

It's true that the Fourth Instinct calls us toward perfection. We hear the echo of a voice we recognize. In the middle of tension and anxiety, we are suddenly enveloped by a sense of peace. In circumstances of intense hatred, we are given glimpses of the power of love. All is evidence of the perfection to which the Fourth Instinct points. But it is a perfection we can achieve only through our soul. When we look for it elsewhere, we are worshiping idols.

"In the last twenty years," observed psychologist Melvyn Kinder, "we have developed this treadmill mentality. We think that by always reaching higher, accomplishing more—more money, a better body, the perfect mate—that we will automatically be happy. That's an illusion. All this reaching is just making us crazy. We need to rest." Rest takes a beating in America's thousands of health clubs. Here, the perfect body is god, exercise is the order of worship, and the personal trainer today's high priest. "I believe in physical perfection," Linda Evans professes. And Jamie Lee Curtis, star of *Perfect*, assures the sweating congregation that "there's an unlimited beyond" of bodily improvement.

Diets and other disciplines of deprivation, joined by muscle-pumping hard work, promise the perfect body and the salvation that accompanies it. When our physiques are finely molded to the proportions of a Michelangelo figure, then we will be happy. Lovers will find us irresistible. Strangers will throw us admiring glances. Shopping will be an incomparable adventure when everything we try on fits as if we were runway models. Not only will others worship us, we will finally have beauty enough even to love ourselves. Inner joy and outer status will be the earthly rewards of our sacramental workouts. And cellulite will be no more.

What exercise and diet cannot achieve, the surgeon's scalpel can provide. Three million Americans each year commit their quest for physical perfection to the ministrations of plastic surgeons. In a futile fight against heredity, gravity and age, we launch another attack against ourselves. Earlier cultures saw old age—given a life expectancy generally around the age of forty—as a great gift, rarely bestowed, with wisdom as its crowning glory. As Betty Friedan wrote in her book *The Fountain of Age:* "The blackout of images of women or men visibly over sixty-five, engaged in any vital or productive adult activity, and their replacement by the 'problem' of age, is our society's very definition of age. Age is perceived only as decline or deterioration from youth." The denial of aging is a reflection of the frustration we feel when the stomach muscles are not as flawless at fifty as they were at twenty, when the wrinkles reappear after the third face-lift and when no amount of cells from an unborn baby lamb can restore the bloom of eternal youth.

"No one in our time finds it surprising," Solzhenitsyn wrote, "if a man gives careful daily attention to his body, but people would be outraged if he gave the same attention to his soul." Exercise buffs who spend hours each day polishing muscle tone are viewed with admiration; someone confessing that she spends an equal amount of time each day in prayer and meditation is a certifiable fanatic, most likely dangerous to the community's children. During my New York social period, I decided once again to go on a ten-day water fast. I knew that if I called it a liquid diet for reducing purposes, it would be perfectly acceptable, but if I confessed my spiritual motivations, I would be thought weird. I decided to say nothing. After all, at fashionable dinner parties, rearranging food on priceless china was what the "social X rays" called eating.

Teenager Robyn Notrica's family paid ten thousand dollars to have a doctor suck the fat off her legs. "Liposuction," she said after surgery, "made me happy." The question is how that happiness will hold up in a few years—or rather months. Elaine Young, a Beverly Hills real estate agent, went through six marriages and "dozens" of plastic surgeries on her way to discovering that she "had a false sense of thinking that if you look better, it's going to make you better. It's inside, and it took me all these years to realize that it's an inside job."

The Fourth Instinct urges us to know what it is that makes us human—uniquely and distinctly human. And it is not physical perfection. It helps us explore the meaning of our mortality, rather than run from it. It's when we lose sight of the spiritual realities within and around us that, in increasingly desperate behaviors, we hang on wildly to our material existence—our bodies and our possessions. Death and its attendants, sickness and pain, have us cornered, trapped, hopeless—until we listen closely to what it is that the Fourth Instinct is actually saying about our mortality. It welcomes it as a challenge we can meet. Saint Paul calls death our "last enemy"—but an enemy that has already been defeated.

To pursue good health and balance in our lives is an admirable goal, but there is a quiet desperation in searching the world for a perfection that is not of this world. If we have become obsessed with perfecting our bodies, we seem no less concerned with protecting them. Every year a growing number of Americans are participating in an intriguing variety of self-defense classes. In one recent year, Americans spent $29 billion for various calibers of armed and armored protection: bodyguards, burglar alarms, saturation floodlights, electronic surveillance, cans of mace and bullet-proof cars. There is a mechanic in Miami who charges fifty thousand dollars to equip a new Cadillac with gunports, floor armor and the capacity to release tear gas. He had so many back-orders the day of his interview that he had stopped promising delivery in less than six months—telling testimony to the indomitable belief, despite evidence to the contrary, that somewhere, somehow, an unbreachable line of security can be established. And then we will be safe. Secure. Happy.

Columnist Ellen Goodman recently recalled that our "ancestors talked about risks to the soul, and we talk about risks to our bodies." But our concern, she observed, "is religious in its intensity. . . . We are less likely to count our sins and more likely to calculate our risk factors. What's at stake is not the hereafter but the here-and-now. . . . It turns out that we share something with these ancestors: a thoroughly ancient and thoroughly modern desire to cheat fate."

The desire to cheat fate by protecting and perfecting our physical well-being is a desire bound to be thwarted. Sooner or later, we will get caught cheating. The perfect mate will prove to be as we all are: imperfect. Perfect children will grow to be as their parents already are: imperfect. We may search for perfection, and even claim its discovery, but then gravity and slowing circulation, or simple wear-and-tear on a machine, however lovingly tended, will make their demands. Sooner or later, our bodies will yield, and our search for perfection will end with death. John Donne's warning that death should not be proud is a confident statement of faith; death will not have the final victory. But, along the way, it will prove the futility of our search for the perfect body and the perfect lifestyle. Dead ends.

America has been dedicated from its founding to "Life, Liberty, and the pursuit of Happiness." But true happiness eludes us in the frantic pursuit of power, perfection and possessions. It is the Fourth Instinct which warns that what will lead to happiness is not an excessive concern with our security, our status or the fulfillment of our sexual desires. When we recognize and begin to fulfill our spiritual needs, when we reach beyond ourselves and wipe away another's tear, then we will be happy. "Happy hours" will leave us stumbling through the carnival of life. "Happy Meals" can barely nourish the body, let alone the soul.

One may wonder why, as George Will asked in *Statecraft as Soulcraft*, the Founding Fathers declared themselves for "life, liberty and the pursuit of happiness" instead of life, liberty and the pursuit of virtue. They were not guilty of rhetorical oversight. The confusion over words and meaning is not theirs. It's ours. When I'm reading historical documents, I try to put myself in the place of the authors. What were the things they took for granted? What the signers of the American Declaration of Independence assumed is that some truths did not have to be proven; they were "self-evident." One such truth is that man should be free to pursue doing good—knowing, because it is self-evident, that doing good yields joy to him who does it. "Happiness" was not imagined as a giggle; it was the happiness of the Book of Proverbs: "Happy is the man that finds wisdom" and "Happy is he that has mercy on the poor." It was the happiness, as Lincoln said, that a slave owner lying about the plantation while others sweated for his bread could never know.

Nor was this a "secular" happiness. The legislators who launched Americans on their famous "pursuit of happiness" also approved the following clause in the Northwest Ordinance of 1787: "Religion, morality, and knowledge, being necessary to good government and the happiness of mankind, schools and the means of learning, shall forever be encouraged." Inherent in that one clause was their belief—their assumption—that schools would, in fact, teach religion and morality as well as knowledge.

Washington did not quibble about the meaning of happiness. He assumed it. Which is why, in 1783, he offered this prayer for his nation's happiness: "That God would . . . incline the hearts of the Citizens . . . to entertain a brotherly affection and love for one another . . . and finally, that he would most graciously be pleased to dispose us all, to do Justice, to love mercy, and to demean ourselves with that Charity, humility and pacific temper of mind, which were the Characteristicks of the Divine Author of our blessed Religion, and without an humble imitation of whose example in these things, we can never hope to be a happy Nation."

We have come a ways since George Washington's prayer. What is considered "happiness" in today's lexicon is the near-exclusive domain of the first three instincts. Happiness has been reduced to instant gratification. It should be mine by right, mine without investment, mine because I am alive. Peggy Noonan, President Reagan's speech writer and now an author, identified a time in our recent past, somewhere in the sixties or seventies, when "we started expecting to be happy and changed our lives—left town, left families, switched jobs— if we were not. And society strained and cracked in the storm." It is not that people had not known dissatisfaction before. What was new was that we began expecting to find in changed material conditions the satisfaction that was eluding us. Marriages have been strained since Adam and Eve's first day exiled from Eden. But at some point husbands and wives began acting on their dissatisfaction in unprecedented proportions, convinced that the perfect mate was waiting over the next hill. Noonan attributed this phenomenon to a sense of loss: "We have lost, somehow, a sense of mystery about us, our purpose, our meaning, our role." We have, in other words, lost touch with our Fourth Instinct.

Our Founding Fathers believed that man should be free to pursue happiness—by pursuing justice and mercy, by living within the framework of God's law and being open to God's grace. A quiet voice within us keeps whispering that in getting things and getting status and getting weary we are not going to become happy. But the voice is drowned in the cacophony of our culture, commanding, ordering us to be happy. When we make happiness itself our goal, we are traveling down another dead end. Happiness will always stay ahead of us—out of reach. We are like the child who wants to camp out on the horizon, but the more he hikes toward it, the more it recedes. Eventually, he lies down and weeps in frustration—surrounded by mountain glories he never notices. Although we think of happiness as something to pursue, the original perception of that pursuit saw happiness as something that ensues— not as the goal, but as the consequence of having achieved the goals of compassion and understanding, of reaching out to help others and finding peace within ourselves. Given these things, happiness will follow.

Consumption, celebrity and the quest for perfection in this world are all subject to the law of diminishing returns: each successive acquisition and achievement will mean less than the one before. Diminishing returns are finally leading to diminished expectations about the promise of finding happiness without caring for our souls. Perhaps we are now ready to reject the hucksters of materialism that have lured us down so many dead ends, and start again on the road that will lead us back to God. The Fourth Instinct beckons us there.

PART TWO

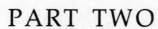

*Threads Through
the Labyrinth*

4

The Imperative Journey

> The real voyage of discovery consists
> not in seeking new landscapes but in
> having new eyes.
>
> —Marcel Proust

It was like the re-creation of a Greek myth of my childhood when, in my early twenties, I visited Chartres. Spanning the width of the nave was a maze of paving stones, shaped in spirals, 320 yards of twists and turns through which pilgrims had to find their way to gain access to the altar.

I entered the maze, and what had begun as amused interest turned, when the path became even more convoluted, into an anxious desire to find my way. I was walking in a circle, uncertain whether I was nearer to or farther away from the end. My steps quickened as I thought I was approaching the center. But I was wrong; there was yet another turn until, finally, I spun around and found myself at the end of the path. At the same time I realized that I had to find my way back out before this symbolic journey was complete; again I followed the tortuous path of the paving stones until I was out of the maze. It was the labyrinth of Greek myth, a maze built as a metaphor for the journey to God, walked by worshipers at Chartres for centuries.

THE FOURTH INSTINCT

Every New Year's Eve, I like to look back on the paths I have walked that year and the years before that have brought me to that moment. What I see is a journey through a labyrinth, turns taken or rejected, choices made, meanderings down dead ends and travels along main roads. The metaphor of the maze still grips me, a fascination sparked early on by a childhood game. My father believed in stretching minds. Before I could speak, he asked me questions. Before I could read, he bought me books. Before I could count, he taught me number games. When I was four or five, I grew especially fond of solving mazes. Cartoon mice stood at the entrance, waiting for me to draw a line so they could follow my pencil's path through the maze to their cheese. But when the mazes were too complicated for my childish mind, when the effort to find my way from beginning to end, avoiding blind alleys and dead ends along the way, was too taxing, I would improvise. If I couldn't bring the mice to the cheese, I would bring the cheese to the mice! I would go to the center of the maze and work outward, moving smoothly back to the entrance where the mice were waiting. I was unable simply to push aside the maze, even when I was too frustrated to complete it. One way or another, the center *demanded* to be touched.

Even in play, the Fourth Instinct calls us toward the center. The specific character of the call varies from person to person and, sometimes, even from day to day. There is no single blueprint to be followed, no scroll of instructions to be unfurled. There is only the inner voice that asks to be trusted, even if others do not hear it.

"If you build it, he will come. . . ." This was the voice a rock-solid Iowa farmer heard in the movie *Field of Dreams*. He heeded it and built an improbable baseball diamond in a field that should have been a cash crop of corn. It's a Hollywood metaphor for life lived in response to the Fourth Instinct—not according to some prescribed formula, but dynamically, with a willingness to listen to an inner call.

The Greek myth of the Labyrinth and the Minotaur was my favorite story when I was growing up—not only because I was named after its heroine, Ariadne. In the myth, Theseus, son of the king of Athens, is sent to Crete as part of the Athenian tribute of seven men and seven women who have to be sacrificed every nine years to placate the Minotaur. The terrible monster, half bull and half man, lived in the center of an impenetrable labyrinth. Theseus could only be saved and be free to return to Athens if he entered the labyrinth and slew the Minotaur. All who had gone before him had perished. But Ariadne, daughter of the king of Crete, fell in love with Theseus. Guided by the thread Ariadne gave him, Theseus was able to enter the labyrinth, slay the Minotaur and find his way back out, alive and victorious.

Greeks were not alone in seeing the labyrinth as a powerful metaphor for the path we must take to find the center of our lives and ourselves. Since before Christ, the labyrinth has represented the human journey as, at once, a road, a search and a conundrum. With evocative images of twisting passageways demanding that its traveler make life-and-death decisions, the labyrinth and its companion symbol, the spiral, appear in myths and ceremonies throughout the world. From the operas of Monteverdi and Richard Strauss to Victor Hugo's Paris with its labyrinthine streets and sewers, haunted by Jean Valjean, we are surrounded in art no less than in life by images of the labyrinth. Ariadne's thread, by which Theseus traces his way, finds a parallel in the "silver cord" that in the Hindu tradition leads to the divine. And in Polynesia, dancers wind their way through spiral gyrations clinging to a rope, while the labyrinth itself is seen as the vaginal entryway to Mother Earth.

In the twentieth century the image of the labyrinth has intrigued the great students of man's subconscious. Joseph Henderson, author of *Thresholds of Initiation*, concluded that in all cultures the labyrinth has a unique place in man's spiritual search, and "can be traversed only by those who are ready for a special initiation into the mysterious world of the collective unconscious." Edward Whitmont, the Jungian analyst who pioneered studies into the meaning of dream symbols, saw the labyrinth as "the way to the unknown center, the mystery of death and rebirth, the risk of the search, the danger of losing the way, the quest, the finding and the ability to return." Joseph Campbell found in the labyrinth a reassuring metaphor for the spiritual adventure: "For the heroes of all time have gone before us; the labyrinth is thoroughly known; we have only to follow the thread of the hero-path. And where we had thought to find an abomination, we shall find a god; where we had thought to slay another, we shall slay ourselves; where we had thought to travel outward, we shall come to the center of our own existence; where we had thought to be alone, we shall be with all the world."

For Bunyan's Pilgrim and for medieval Christianity, the road to God was the dominant metaphor for the spiritual journey. For Africans sold into slavery in eighteenth-century America, it was the river Jordan; for Plato it was the cave; and for Melville a whaling ship. But in the twentieth century, the labyrinth, a place of light and dark, of mystery, of the juncture between the known and unknown, has captured the imagination of many modern seekers. It has even dominated their dreams.

In my own dream journal, it appears with great regularity, and unlike the labyrinth of myths and childhood games it is always three-dimensional. Like the hero in a cosmic Pac-Man game, we enter at the lowest level and wind our way past danger toward the center. When we wind our way back out again, we travel away from the center at a level higher than where we entered. When next we return to the center, we again leave at a higher level. We never emerge quite the same from the center of the labyrinth—and never in quite the same place. Some Eastern faiths describe this process as the spiral of purification through which we move upward toward God. In Christianity, it's the process of sanctification by which our time with God enables us to live life not yet perfectly, but more lovingly, more generously, more joyfully. On our way home, we may follow for a while paths that take us away from ourselves, but the center we have experienced becomes a lodestar drawing us back—to confront the Minotaurs of our fears, to overcome our doubts and to prevail over all real or imagined threats that lurk in the labyrinth's shadows.

The Fourth Instinct is a human instinct. The massive Saint Bernard, keeping watch over a tiny baby's crib, is a noble creature, loyal and admirable. There is a lot we share with the faithful Saint Bernard. Yet we are unique—unique in what we are and even more unique in what we may *become*.

Human language is one aspect of our uniqueness. Computers have languages built of symbols, and animals communicate both with sounds and signals. But human language is unique in our capacity to talk about worlds we have not seen with our eyes and messages no audiotape can record—to use images and similes and metaphors, descriptions of things known, to evoke things only felt or imagined.

The most communicative parrot and the fastest computer have yet to match the capacity of my two-year-old daughter to pray. If the parrot could recite the Oxford English Dictionary by rote, it would be impressive; but could it comprehend, let alone compose, one of Yeats's sonnets? If a computer could solve problems of logic at the speed of light, and move pieces about a chess board at two million times the speed of master champions, it would be astounding; but could the computer weep when a child dies, and then rise from its weeping to comfort the child's mother?

The human will is another aspect of our uniqueness. For some, free will—our capacity to choose good or evil—is a frightening truth. They are those who find security in rules that don't bend and instruction manuals that leave no detail to the imagination. They prefer life's journey to come with a map from which they would never deviate, sparing themselves the blind alleys and the dead ends that come with free will. True, they have no freedom. But because they never make a decision, they never make a mistake. Instead of choosing their own route through life's labyrinth, they prefer to march in scripted time from one end of the maze to the other.

Whole societies have embraced this lockstepped life as their ideal. In their concern for "the good of the people," they have done everything in their power to stamp out whatever calls man to freedom and choice. True religion is usually the first and most widely noted victim, but it isn't the only casualty. Totalitarian societies often fear art as deeply as worship and suppress science as much as prayer.

The labyrinth, like life itself, is about choices. Nations that crush the human will, that eradicate choice on the grounds of eradicating error, inevitably lose their strength in a hopeless battle against man's spirit. And those who would merely follow in someone else's footsteps are missing the uniqueness of the human journey. We must choose to undertake that journey for ourselves. And we must choose for ourselves which threads, or combination of threads, to follow.

The Second World War, and the Civil War that followed it, were still fresh wounds in the Greece of my childhood, not yet healed into history. My mother would hurry me past young men who looked old, standing in quiet clusters smoking cigarettes or, sometimes, standing alone, staring at nothing but the distant horizon. "They've seen too much," she would say. "Now they do not look."

My daughters were born in a very different time and place. Their childhoods are being shaped not by a cruel war but by a generous peace. Yet, for them too, there will come a time when they will have to make the choices that are uniquely human. The week before Isabella was born I read an article which argued that a chimpanzee has 95 percent of our genetic makeup. Since I was already anticipating labor, and one's imagination can run wild in such moments, the article stirred zany images in my head. I was relieved to see that my child did not resemble a little chimp. Yet I remain amazed that so small a genetic variation was all that was necessary for God one day to create a chimp and, the next, a human being made in His own image, "a little lower than the angels." Because of the minuscule shift of five percent in their makeup, my daughters are heirs not just to all of human history, but to all of mankind's divine potential.

As surely as the color of our eyes is determined by a gene, so the drive to reach out for meaning and purpose is fixed within us. The Fourth Instinct draws us into the labyrinth as surely as the aroma of fresh bread draws a hungry man to the table. It's not an easy journey, but when the path becomes dark and uncertain, there are threads to guide us and messages from the travelers who have gone before us. Isaiah heard the voice of God, and now his message lights our way: "I will lead them in paths that they have not known: I will make darkness light before them, and crooked things straight. These things will I do for them, and not forsake them."

There are many threads that can guide us through the labyrinth, to wisdom and to the center of ourselves. Sacred texts and traditions are wound into the thread of religion. The values and myths that form societies and bind them together are woven into the thread of community. By following the threads of art and science, by picking up the thread of relationships, in the healing process, and even in pain, we can find purpose and meaning.

We come to many moments in our lives when we cannot stifle the Fourth Instinct. It demands we pay attention. We see the surgeon coming from our child's hospital room and we know, by the slowness of his walk, the news he does not want to give us. We watch our marriages weaken, then begin to crumble, and finally explode in an avalanche of pent-up anger and old hurts. We live with parents who age beyond wisdom and strength, and we grieve as we watch them die ever so slowly. These are the moments that pin us to the ground with sharp questions. We look at the course of our lives and at those we love, we see crushing pain and loss and we are slammed into the wall with doubt about the meaning of life. Ironically, it is in these moments that the journey toward our own soul is the venture that can no longer be postponed.

We plunge into the journey, and we pick up one, or two, or all of the threads that will lead us through the labyrinth. For a time we may follow false clues and counterfeit threads that lead us to dead ends. The greatest danger is not that the thread will be counterfeit, but that we will forget our destination and fail to recognize and follow the ones that are genuine. They are the threads that will take us to God, not to the veneration of false idols. They are a means of grace.

5

Seizing a Thread of Grace: Healing

MACBETH: Canst thou not minister to a mind diseased,
Pluck from the memory a rooted sorrow,
Raze out the written troubles of the brain,
And with some sweet oblivious antidote
Cleanse the stuffed bosom of that perilous stuff
Which weighs upon the heart?

DOCTOR: Therein the patient
Must minister to himself.

—Shakespeare, *Macbeth*

My friend Gail and I are only a few years apart. But while my girls were still in diapers, her daughter Dawn was already out of college and living in Los Angeles, at the beginning of an acting career. Gail is more than a friend; she's a gift in my life. We have spoken often and intimately about our children and ourselves, our hopes and our dreams. It was during one of my late-night conversations with Gail, when Michael and I were expecting Isabella, that she quoted Yeats's poem, "A Prayer for My Daughter," and gave me just what I wanted for Isabella's birth announcement. Her enthusiasm for life permeates her sense of motherhood. It seemed so right that she would have named her daughter Dawn, the beginning of a new day.

It was April 1990. Michael and I were in Houston when the phone rang in the middle of the night. It was a friend telling me that Gail was on her way to Los Angeles. Half asleep, I could not understand why someone would wake me to tell me about Gail's trip—until I heard the two words that told me everything: "Dawn's dead." Full of life and energy, Dawn had died in her sleep when her heartbeat grew wildly irregular—"fluttering like a butterfly," the doctor told Gail.

When I saw Gail at her home in Houston the next day, there were no words spoken for a long time. We just held each other and cried. And then Gail looked at me, and with a voice that seemed to come from a long way away, she said simply, "I'm broken."

We have, all of us, sometimes felt broken. Blows rain down on us too hard; we weaken and then we break. A little boy is told by his mother that she wishes he had never been born and something inside him breaks. A bright-eyed girl is visited in the night by her mother's boyfriend. . . . Weary from too many long days at the office, we make a catastrophic decision and are fired. . . . Driving home, wording the apology we owe our husband, we never see the child dart in front of the car. . . . We wait, night after night, to hear someone we love whisper in the dark, just once, "I love you." . . . We are broken people in a broken world.

The day before she died, Dawn had called her mother. At the moment of the call, Gail was already late for an appointment. "I can't talk now, honey," she said. "I'll call you tonight." And as she always did, before she hung up, she added, "I love you." It was the last time they would speak. When Gail called that evening, she heard Dawn's taped voice on her answering machine. In the grim early hours of her grief, the security of twenty-four years of love had faded into the agony of a single unfinished telephone conversation. Broken by the grief of Dawn's death, Gail was also haunted by the guilt of that one unfinished conversation.

For months after Dawn's death, Gail would pray—even beg —for one more moment with her daughter, a chance to say goodbye. Her prayer was finally answered in a dream. "I didn't even really know that you were sick," she cried out as soon as Dawn appeared. "How could you die?" "Mom, is that what happened?" Dawn replied. "Did I die?" And she walked away.

"The next evening," Gail told me, "I was reading Richard Bach: 'What the caterpillar calls the end of life, the master calls a butterfly.' " Still broken and groping through those dark moments to find some reason for Dawn's death, Gail picked up the thread of healing. In the process of trying to answer the question "Why did Dawn die?" she began to look for the answer to another question: "Why do I live?"

At first, what she wanted more than anything was another child. Her husband went through a vasectomy-reversal operation and even a couple of artificial-insemination procedures with patience and a sense of humor that made all of us marvel at his love for Gail and his understanding of her healing process. Finally, accepting that she would not get pregnant again, she came to understand that what she needed to give birth to was not another child but a deeper part of herself. It was the turning point in Gail's healing journey. She could not have another child, and she could not reach back and hold Dawn. At that moment of expanded understanding and surrender, she came to see her loss not as a gaping hole in her life but as a door through which she could pass into a greater spiritual awareness.

"I don't want to die," Gail had told me when she came to stay with us in California shortly after Dawn's death, "but it hurts too much to live." She had gradually begun to discover the difference between surrendering and giving up. And during meditation and prayer, she had one spiritual experience after another. Four times on four different occasions she heard the same words in answer to her prayers: "Seek Him only." Now, she felt God loving her through the pain, holding her up through it.

Gail embarked on a healing pilgrimage. At one point, her thread of healing took her to the Santa Fe office of Dr. Stephen Levine, who has written extensively on death and grieving. He listened to her recount an extraordinary dream in which she saw her daughter's face smiling, bathed in moonlight and water. Her arms were beckoning her, and when they embraced, the love between them was something that Gail will never forget. "It was not just a feeling," she later told me. "It was a thing, a tangible sensation. I understand now that when we say 'God is love,' we really mean not the emotion of love but the concrete experience." Dr. Levine listened to the dream, and told Gail that she was not alone, that other mothers and fathers who had lost children had also found them again under a moonlit sky.

Gail taught me so much about the healing process—the looking in and the reaching out. At the same time that she followed her grief wherever it took her, she never barricaded herself from life. When we planned a shower for Isabella's birth, a birthday party for Christina or a fundraiser for the Partnership for Children, we could always count on Gail being among the most enthusiastic guests.

On one of her trips to California, I introduced Gail to another close friend whose life could be measured in the before-and-after terms of losing a child—and who had also used her grief to open up rather than to close down. Jodie's daughter was taken from her just days before her second birthday. The ocean had suddenly turned rough and Jodie had to struggle to hold on to Lala. Then a wave broke and ripped them apart. Seconds later she caught the child again. But it was not to be. There was another wave—and Lala was gone.

In the years following Lala's death, Jodie gave birth to another child, a second son who is my precious godson. On the tenth anniversary of Lala's death, we talked on the phone: "I do feel healed. But not enough—never enough—to forget." And then, as always full of stories from her travels around the world, she told me of an Indian healer who cured a man of leprosy and took away all his scars, except one. When someone asked the healer why she hadn't taken away that last scar, she replied, "So he will always remember."

"When fall comes," Jodie continued, "and the anniversary is around the corner, or when I'm hugging Christina and Isabella, I see the huge waves in the sea and the pain grabs me and takes me back. What I do is to take that pain and channel it into helping others." Out of her pain Jodie created the Grief Recovery Center, which has spread hope to so many grieving parents. "In my prayers," she told me, "I thank God for the pain and for the joy, recognizing that they are the flip sides of each other."

Seeing Gail and Jodie together at my kitchen table brought

to life for me the truth that "only a wounded physician can heal." Bonded by the greatest challenge to our healing powers —the loss of a child—they reached out to each other, healing in the process of being healed. Both have now gone beyond being victims, beyond even being survivors of their own private tragedies. They have transformed their experience into healing, wholeness and a glimpse of holiness for themselves, for those whose lives they have touched, for their world.

"Why don't you commit suicide?" Viktor Frankl often asked his most severely depressed patients. Frankl did not take life lightly; he himself had barely survived Auschwitz. And yet his question was exactly to the point: What helps you hang on? What keeps you here despite your despair? His patients' answers varied. For some it was their love for their children; others harbored vague religious reservations; still others held dim hopes of an unfulfilled dream. In each answer, the doctor discovered a thread with which to lead his patient back from the abyss—a remnant of meaning from which to weave a new life.

Our understanding of sickness and health has changed radically over the past few decades. In one generation we have moved from Band-Aids to biofeedback. A "holistic" approach to health has begun to reconnect the soul with the body, the state of our mind with the state of our health, our lifestyles with our life expectancy. In the process we are healing—making whole again—not just ourselves, but the way we look at the world.

Healing is no longer seen as a passive experience, no longer pursued as a clinical undertaking, but increasingly embraced as a spiritual endeavor. We are again recognizing that we cannot separate what ails the body from what troubles the spirit. "Among all my patients in the second half of life, that is to say, over thirty-five," Jung wrote, "there has not been one whose problem was not that of finding a religious outlook on life. It is safe to say that every one of them fell ill because he had lost that which the living religions of every age have given to their followers, and none of them has been really healed who did not regain his religious outlook." It was not conversions that Jung sought. It was a reconnection with our spiritual dimension, without which there can be no peace, no harmony and no wholeness.

When our world is "shattered," "in pieces," "falling apart," healing—of mind, body and soul—does not only help us put the pieces together. In this largest sense, healing is about more than reconnecting the hip bone to the thigh bone to the knee bone; it is about reconnecting ourselves to God.

It is becoming increasingly irrelevant to speak simply of "curing" depression, "treating" an illness, or even "mending" broken bones—as if each part of the human experience were some isolated event. The modern trend of medical specialization has fragmented the healing process. But the mounting spiritual awareness converging from many fields is pulling in the opposite direction, with medicine shifting from a "need to know" to a need to grow. Doctors and patients alike are looking up from the minutiae to which man has been reduced and are taking an aerial view. Their holistic approach to health, far from dismissing what each discipline has to offer, seeks to unify the different parts of man.

Dr. Deepak Chopra taught at the ivied medical schools of New England before the radical ideas expressed in his best-selling books *Quantum Healing* and *Ageless Body, Timeless Mind* began to take root in the American medical community. "Every aspect of reality is one piece of a mystery . . . the totality of what is," he said, describing the wholeness of life and healing. "Atoms, molecules, rocks, stars, and the human body are material expressions of what is. Pain and pleasure are psychological expressions of what is. Compassion and love are spiritual expressions of what is. When the material, psychological, and spiritual dimensions are brought into balance, life becomes whole. . . ." If we are to be healed, Chopra said, each of us must "rise above the world of duality."

Whether our daughter has died at twenty-three or our son before birth, whether we welcome the messengers of our spiritual dimension or deny them, whether we cling to our favorite dualisms or hide behind the label of skepticism, the thread of healing carries a blaring message of its own: It isn't this or that, but this *and* that. There is one continuum of reality. Deny this, and we deny ourselves access to our very core.

As we move toward the next millennium, we need to embrace healing which treats our whole being. The National Institutes of Health have created an Office of Alternative Medicine. Medical schools have reintroduced courses in bed-

101

side manner, with 117 out of 126 accredited schools requiring some study of physician-patient relationships, which are seen as critical to the healing process. And recently, Mutual of Omaha—not known for its softheaded New Ageism—decided to reimburse patients for the preemptive, preventive program designed by Dr. Dean Ornish, which includes meditation, yoga, and a vegetarian diet.

Holistic medicine was one baby thrown out with the bathwater of the Middle Ages. The Enlightenment—in all its rationalist glory—was less concerned with "making connections" than with drawing distinctions. And now healing as a holistic endeavor battles not just the bureaucracy of an overwrought health care system, not just the preconceptions of the medical establishment, but the accumulated intellectual habits of several hundred years as well.

For all the Fourth Instinct's desire to bring things together, to make connections and find unity, our second instinct and our almighty intellect insist on setting things apart. It is the pervasive division of inner and outer reality, "thinking in opposites," the material against the spiritual, the secular against the sacred, the natural against the supernatural. Dualism— deeply rooted, historically defended, philosophically elevated, culturally pervasive—has led us to become specialists who have lost sight of the whole; while we learned how to build, we forgot what we were building for. Dualism has acted as an antibiotic, protecting us against chaos but also against mystery. As with all antibiotics, in the process of killing the bad cells it severely weakened some of the good—especially our sense of connectedness and our openness to the miraculous.

The modern age further fractured human experience into a complex set of cogs and wheels, pulleys and levers. No one better personified this mechanistic approach to human nature than B. F. Skinner. He was unconcerned about anything within man; indeed, he doubted that anything existed within man. What matters isn't what we feel or what we think, let alone what we *are*, but what we do. A person, a self, "is a repertoire of behavior appropriate to a given set of contingencies," he wrote near the closing chapter of his life. No room here for spirit or soul, no interest in any dimensions beyond our first five senses. In fact, Skinner bade feeling and soul and spirit "good riddance," and left us with the ultimate broken man: a man divided from himself. Like just another piece of equipment in a machine-filled world, we react according to what button is pushed. If we break, healing becomes a matter of mechanical repairs.

But healing is much more than a purely rational endeavor. "Imagination is more important than knowledge," Einstein wrote. Imagination acknowledges something in us before we know, sees before we see, and sends its vision to the surface in the form of faith. Inexplicable, perhaps. But illusory, no. Imagination and its components of visualization, prayer and meditation, are essential elements in healing. And imagination is hardly passive, because it leads toward experience, precipitates confirmation and evokes the cure.

When asked which patients he had found the most difficult to heal, Jung replied instantly: "Habitual liars and intellectuals." Both categories suffer the same delusion: neither can any longer distinguish reality, the liar because he has so frequently distorted it and the intellectual because he has defined most of it out of existence. The liar doesn't believe truth exists, and the intellectual is convinced that there is no truth beyond what can be scientifically observed.

The hardest thing for any therapist to do with a patient is to take him beyond what he believes is possible, physically, emotionally, spiritually—beyond his perceived limits of reality. The man who believes his legs are paralyzed will not flee a burning building, even if they are not. The woman convinced there is nothing in life but behavior will be incapable of feeling repentance or grace. We have taken the psyche—the soul— out of psychology and we wonder why we can dissect and analyze, but cannot heal and make whole. When we are convinced that we are bound to remain broken people in a broken world, the promise of wholeness is a cruel taunt.

Perhaps because I was brought up in a culture that still believed the world was full of gods, I have always enjoyed that delicious Greek stew of allegory, divinity and earthy humanity. Plato ladled the mix out into three parts. Man may be one being, he argued, but within that being there are different, distinct realities, mirroring the different classes of the city-state. At bottom was "the belly," the basic, instinctual side of man's nature. Governed by forces beyond its control, the belly was represented as the slaves and plebeian masses of Greek society. Next in our nature came "the chest," the assertive, passionate part of man. The warrior class—the guardians—embodied this aspect of human nature. And then, there above the din, reigned "the mind," like the philosopher king it represented, at once rational and spiritual.

Freud also painted man's portrait in triptych: the id, the ego and the superego, all essential elements of our personality. The id is our basic, instinctual self lodged in our unconscious. The ego is the part of our conscious mind that mediates between the needs of the id and the demands of our superego. And the superego is the part of the mind that censors and censures the relationship between the ego and the id, our conscience.

Freud's great contribution was to burst open the dam holding back the flow of the unconscious. He exposed the irrational forces that can drag us down into the mud, but offered nothing on which we could stand to lift ourselves out of it. He was blind enough to believe that it is possible for "enlightened" patients to achieve a totally rational approach to life. Yet all experience has shown that it is not that simple, and that unless we discover a spiritual center we will never be able to climb up out of the mud of the irrational, or move beyond the commonplace conventions or repressions of our lives.

Whatever names we choose to give to the different parts of ourselves, the evidence shows an "adult self" emerging by mid-childhood with all the marks of our individual personalities. It is the "self" we know and others meet. Before this adult self begins to develop at around age seven or eight, it is the "child self" which is dominant. This aspect of us, which never leaves, is rooted in emotion rather than intellect. As we grow older it says things our adult self was determined not to say; it eats things our adult self was determined not to eat. Biologically, the child self carries the influences of millions of years of evolution; culturally, it is still the four- or five-year-old we carry with us into adulthood, capable of tantrums and rages and the enormous self-pity of a child shouting "You don't love me!" Where the adult self seeks power and conquests, status and achievements, the child self is focused on survival and pleasure.

Behind the restless power of our adult self—the power that acts, works and experiments—and the compulsive power of our child self, there is another power that knows, supports and inspires. This is the energy of our "spiritual self." It puts us through loops of learning and observes as we endure grief and celebrate joy, guiding us to understanding, and helping us reap wisdom from it all. This is the center of the consciousness toward which we are evolving, free from both the compulsions of our child selves and the limitations of our adult selves.

It is the Fourth Instinct which propels us toward the alignment of these three selves that will open the combination lock to an understanding of ourselves and our purpose in life. The aim is alignment, not dominance or suppression of any one "self." In the balance we strike among these three aspects of our self, in the harmony we achieve among them, lies the power of health and healing.

When I was a young graduate of Cambridge, newly a published author, freshly minted and fully degreed, I knew that something in my life was out of balance but I did not know what. Then, by coincidence, I was given the opportunity to write a biography of Maria Callas. I discovered that, consumed by her career, she had pushed aside the passionate woman in her. When she finally gave expression to that part of her nature, she surrendered to it entirely and, in the end, became its victim.

While looking into Callas's life, I looked also into my own and saw an imbalance. I realized that I had so heavily stressed the cognitive, the intellectual, the professional—those aspects of myself that had secured first my education and then my career—that other elements were going undernourished. I was starving the woman within me who was longing to be a wife and mother.

Whether we acknowledge it or not, each "self" is real. We are not *merely* soul, or *merely* body, or *merely* mind. We are not one-dimensional, but neither are soul, body and mind divisible. When our feelings change, our bodies change. Anger produces strong breathing, fear creates shallow breathing, and sorrow expresses itself with broken breathing: sobs. We have known for years that psychological stress can cause severe and even fatal physical illness. Experiments rigorous enough to convince the most adamant rationalist have shown that 30 percent of patients experiencing severe pain receive exactly as much relief from a placebo as from a prescription painkiller. In other experiments with placebos, gastric secretions in ulcer patients have stopped, blood pressure has been lowered and tumors have shrunk. The boundaries between our bodies, our minds and our feelings are extremely permeable.

A stunning illustration of how completely connected our bodies are to our minds and our feelings came during research into the electrical charge produced by strong emotion such as that felt when reliving a past trauma. It was shown that even when we remove cells from the body, the cells themselves will respond to stimuli when the person does. A polygraph expert at the Backster Research Foundation in San Diego scraped cells from the mouth of an ex-Navy pilot, placed those cells in a distant laboratory and then asked the veteran to watch battle films. When the man saw a fighter plane being shot down, his polygraph showed a strong emotional response. At exactly the same moment, the polygraph of his cells—which had been moved seven miles away—also responded. When the pilot relived his fear, every cell of his body relived it with him.

We understand our emotions and thoughts as being part of our psychological nature. But researchers such as the neuroscientist Professor Candace Pert are uncovering the material manifestations of our emotions—the flesh and blood of our hopes and fears. Pert has discovered opiate and other peptide receptors throughout the brain and body, leading to an understanding of how information travels throughout our system. Emotions, according to Pert, are the "link between mind and body. . . . Intelligence is in every cell of your body." Attitudes and feelings physically affect our tissues and organs. In a demonstration completed under the auspices of the Menninger Foundation, a man consciously raised his heartbeat from 70 beats per minute to nearly 300. His heartbeat became a flutter. He could have died. Instead, he went on as if nothing much had happened.

When we are willing first to accept and then to explore the truth about ourselves, we will find enormous storehouses of energy there—not to defy nature's laws for the sake of producing parlor tricks and party games, but to challenge sickness and suffering and heal our wounded selves. Today, miraculous cures, dramatic and undisputed drops in blood pressure in programs that excluded drugs and relied on meditation, Norman Cousins's work, Bill Moyers's *Healing and the Mind*, and Bernie Siegel's *Love, Medicine, & Miracles* have established, much beyond the anecdotal, the effect of mental states on biology and health.

I was to experience the healing effects of the holistic approach firsthand during the delivery of Isabella. I followed a regular regimen of yoga in preparation for childbirth. It is a discipline I inherited from my mother as a kind of family tradition. In the concentration and relaxation, the inner discipline and outer postures, we feel aligned, a balance that stays with us long after the yoga mats are rolled away.

Yoga seemed a powerful corrective to the treatment of pregnancy as a disease and of delivery as a surgical procedure, with the incidence of Caesarian sections reaching 40 percent in some hospitals. I was blessed to have an obstetrician who was both one of the preeminent doctors in his field and supportive of a holistic approach to pregnancy and childbirth. Confining women to a hospital bed, tying them to an IV and wiring them to electronic fetal monitors is the denial of childbirth as a natural process, a collaborative effort of body, mind and spirit. My preparations for giving birth included visualizations to deal with the fear of delivery, meditation, breathing and yoga exercises right up to the day of Isabella's birth. I was unprepared for only one thing—when Isabella was born, she came so quickly, as I was walking around the room, that had we not caught her, she would have landed on the floor.

As a relentless researcher in the field, I have tried so many forms of alternative healing, so many seminars and retreats, that it seems amazing that I have never tried the analyst's couch. Perhaps I have neglected traditional therapy out of the fear, as one psychiatrist friend once kidded me, that I would be a "backseat healer." I may not have entered this particular classroom, but I have spent much of my time with my face pressed to its window. When I arrived in New York in 1980, it seemed that there were almost as many therapies as there were patients—from primal scream and rebirthing to past-life regressions and transactional analysis.

In a recent *U.S. News & World Report* poll, 81 percent of respondents agreed that going to a therapist would be helpful "sometimes" or "all of the time." Our culture increasingly celebrates therapy as an all-purpose panacea—from the public confessionals of daytime talk shows, through presidential re-treats featuring group encounters and hug-fests, to the diffusion of "therapy-speak," as in "getting in touch with one's feelings" and "needing one's space." Personal salvation is no longer expected to be found exclusively in a pew or on one's knees. The therapist's office is the new sacred place.

"A few decades ago, nobody believed in the confession of sins except the Church," wrote the author and theologian Fulton J. Sheen. "Today everyone believes in confession, with this difference: some believe in confessing their own sins; others believe in confessing other people's sins." But the new culture of confession runs the risk of being less about exoneration and more about exhibitionism. We fall prey to a similar danger when we use the thread of therapy not to grow through our problems but to rearrange them. What could have been a spiritual unfolding ends in a psychological refolding—therapy less as a bridge than a treadmill, less as self-awareness than self-absorption.

Still, millions of us take our hope for healing behind the closed-door sanctuaries of counselors and therapists. We bring with us the conviction that they are the healers of our age, the men and women who can shoulder our griefs and help us bear our sorrows. What we soon learn is the truth of a very old joke: "How many therapists does it take to change a lightbulb? Just one, but it must really want to change." Therapists cannot remake us; they can only point us to the healing power within ourselves and offer suggestions for tapping into that power.

I value what therapist friends have taught me and, like everyone else, I have had my bouts with denial and despair. I know that millions of families have been strengthened and millions of lives enriched by the professional contributions of therapists. But I am also painfully aware that for many therapists, helping a patient has come to mean merely making him adapt to the suffocation of a limited life and regard such adaptation as a sign of healthy maturity. The most disturbing aspect of this trend is the creeping transformation of therapists into pharmacists, quick to prescribe feel-good sedatives at the drop of a complaint. Sales of mood- and mind-altering drugs, baptized with utopian-sounding names like Xanax and Halcion, have skyrocketed during the past three decades.

Instead of listening to the messengers of our discontent, we

silence them with drugs. But it is the job of the Fourth Instinct to refuse to settle for the perfection of arrested development, to ensure in every way that we remain restless and discontented until we have achieved the wholeness that is the principle of our being. I remember years ago, in London, seeing Peter Shaffer's play *Equus*. It still remains for me the ultimate summing-up of the limitations of psychotherapy. "Let me tell you exactly what I'm going to do to him!" the psychiatrist explains. "I'll heal the rash on his body. I'll erase the welts cut into his mind. . . . When that's done, I'll set him on a nice mini-scooter and send him puttering off into the Normal world. . . . Passion, you see, can be destroyed by a doctor. It cannot be created. . . ." Soul can neither be destroyed nor created; it can only be evoked or driven even deeper into hiding. The best a therapist can do is hear the Fourth Instinct himself and perhaps teach someone to listen for it and follow it.

Over the past half-century group therapies have mushroomed alongside more conventional one-on-one approaches. Here, the thread of healing is reinforced with the rich weave of community, relationships, and even religion. These are groups whose aim is, in the Germanic accents of therapy, *Gemeinschaftsgefühl*—the sharing of social concern and common humanity.

Nowhere is the power of group therapy more evident than in the area of addictive disorders. It is here that therapy takes on the depth of a spiritual endeavor, in which initiates interact along themes of "surrender" and a "higher power." The recognition that addiction is more than physical is the cornerstone of Alcoholics Anonymous, the organization which has helped more alcoholics toward recovery than any other. How this cornerstone was put in place is in itself a revealing story.

Shortly before his death, Bill Wilson, who co-founded Alcoholics Anonymous, sent a letter to Carl Jung in Switzerland. "I doubt if you are aware," he wrote, "that a certain conversation you once had with one of your patients . . . did play a critical role in the founding of our Fellowship." Apparently, in 1931 Jung had been unsuccessfully treating an alcoholic man. "You frankly told him of his hopelessness, so far as any further medical or psychiatric treatment might be concerned," wrote Wilson, and then pointed him in the direction of "a spiritual or religious experience." Jung's counsel had led to a profound change in his patient who eventually met Wilson, giving him the benefit of his experience.

"Because of your conviction that man is something more than intellect, emotion, and two dollars' worth of chemicals, you have especially endeared yourself to us," wrote Wilson. It was a remarkable testimony not only to Jung's spiritual perspective but also to an understanding that since life is more than physical, healing must be more than physical too.

As a result of that chain of contacts, we can see Jung's fingerprints in the formulation of Alcoholics Anonymous's first two founding steps: "First, we admitted we were powerless over alcohol—that our lives had become unmanageable. Second, we came to believe that a Power greater than ourselves could restore us to sanity."

The positive power of group therapy is undeniable. I have seen glimpses of this power in retreat settings where honesty, empathy and exploration have come together in previously unexamined lives. I have also seen the danger in such groups when we are encouraged to hand over the wheel of our lives to the group leader, or find our identity not in our health but in our illness. We create communities of pathology and seek identity in the badges of our brokenness. We are brought together as drug abusers, battered wives or rape victims, alcoholics and workaholics, exhibitionists and cross-dressers. Our symptoms become our admission tickets: "Hello, my name is Caryl, and I'm a sex addict."

As the twentieth century bumps to a close and the next millennium opens before us, there's a new awareness of the power of groups to aid in our healing process. My hope is that as the Fourth Instinct becomes a more dominant voice in our lives and in our culture, we will see fewer communities of pathology and, everywhere, more healing communities—acknowledging our wounds but also our intrinsic wholeness.

The Fourth Instinct can point us to balance, to harmony, and hence to healing, at any time and any place—from the morning, as we slowly rise from our dreams, throughout the whole day as we not only learn to trust our intuition to speak to us, but train ourselves to listen, and to bring the timeless into the everyday.

. . .

At Gail's house, immediately after Dawn's funeral, a close friend took Gail aside: "I swear to you on my honor that I saw —not through a flash of light, not through a vision, not through loss of concentration or meditation—I saw Dawn sitting on her casket. And she was radiating love toward you."

He had been reluctant to tell Gail. After all, there isn't much tolerance in our mainstream culture for men of intelligence and sophistication seeing visions of the dead. But visions are only another reminder, as all the reports of near-death experiences have confirmed, that there are many bridges between the temporal and the eternal, between earth and the realm of spirit, between life and death. They may appear as opposites, but they are, in fact, expressions of the same reality, fired by the same breath.

Standing by Dawn's grave, I told my fellow mourners: "Last night Gail and I made a promise to Dawn, a promise that we would bring into our lives more of the purity and kindness and sweetness of soul that was Dawn, a promise that we will bring into our lives more of the forgiveness and grace that was Dawn, a promise that we will bring into our lives more of the unconditional loving and giving that was Dawn, a promise that we will keep the flame of love that was Dawn alive in our hearts."

It was a promise not only to Dawn, but to ourselves: to listen to the voice of the Fourth Instinct, to accept unconditionally the reality of spirit, and to reach toward the healing we can find when, beyond the aching void, life once again becomes whole.

Of all the threads in life's labyrinth, here is the one for which we grab when we cannot see through our tears, when our eyes are squeezed shut by pain. It may lead us to the thread of religion where our souls are most open to the Divine and our spirits long to go home. It may take us into a new sense of community where we learn to be one with others despite the divisions which once seemed important. We may find art breaking through the grief with messages of redemption beyond suffering, and of love beyond fear. We may discover in science the truth of life's harmony and order, getting a glimpse into God's workshop where all that is broken was once whole. Or we may discover that the incredible pain of loss is merely the shadow of the immeasurable joy of love—and so, in the hour of grief, we learn not to cling too tightly, lest love be reduced to nothing but possession.

Through the thread of healing, we may pick up any one of the threads through the labyrinth, or we may take them up all at once, for in the end they all lead to wholeness. It's a goal worthy of a promise, not only to Dawn but to ourselves.

6

"I Don't Make Strangers": Relationships

> There's no one more openly irreverent
> than a lover. He or she jumps up on the
> scale opposite eternity and claims to
> balance it. And no one more secretly
> reverent.
>
> —Jalaluddin Rumi

I knew my writing deadlines—knew them well—when the children and I left California to join Michael in our new house in Washington. Before the paint had dried, I was setting up files, installing computers and programming the fax machine. Furnishing and decorating the house could wait. My book deadline and being together as a family could not.

It was Michael who first remembered that I also had a birthday. A birthday, he decided, deserves a celebration. Despite a half-furnished house and my halfhearted enthusiasm, he was convinced that "one night off" would be a good idea. I nodded, giving it no more thought, except to look at the list of friends he had invited and, when other friends called, to invite them, too. Two days before my birthday, driving to Georgetown Hospital for a routine physical exam, I made my first

113

count of the guests. It was a sobering moment and I began to wonder how I would break the news to Michael that all of "his" guests at "my" dinner wouldn't fit at the dining room table—even when it was fully extended. I knew he would remember that for my fortieth birthday I had somehow transformed his "intimate dinner with close friends" into a tented event in the yard behind our house.

It's well known that opposites attract; I have personal knowledge that they also collide. When I first met Michael, only his five closest friends had his home phone number; when his mother, by mistake, gave it to a sixth, he changed it. And then we married. Now, as he says, when he walks into his home "on a good day," he knows only half the people talking together or snacking at the kitchen table.

When I arrived at the hospital I began to move mindlessly through my physical exam, trying to figure out where to seat our dinner guests. Someone measured my blood pressure while I made a quick list of things to get done. Nurses did their jobs and I did mine. The doctor was in, then out, then in again. At some point it occurred to me that she was speaking with unusual seriousness. I think she caught my attention with the word "lump." It needed to "come out as soon as possible," she said.

One of the problems with my philosophy of assuming the best until told the worst is that, in this situation, when I had noticed the lump I assumed it was another harmless cyst. It had happened before. No problem. But now the doctor was using words like "biopsy" and "surgery," and telling me the lump would not "aspirate," that she could get no fluid from it and wanted to get it out right away. I felt myself beginning to black out and I asked if I could lie on the examination table while she explained what this meant. As if through a thick fog I heard her talking about how long it takes to "get lab results after surgery" and that she always likes her patients to come to her office to review the results and discuss alternatives. Deadlines were disappearing and priorities were being replaced.

I called Michael from her office, forgetting that Congress was in session that morning. "He's on the floor," I was told. My mind was telling me to leave a message when I heard my voice pleading, "Can you *please* get him for me?" In the seven months Michael had been in the House, I had never asked for this. They knew it was important. All I knew was that I wanted to tell him, to know that he knew. Then I could walk out of the hospital with the strength to handle my life until Friday morning and the scheduled lumpectomy.

Michael and I had a long and quiet discussion that night, talking about everything except my Thursday-night birthday dinner. Suddenly, I remembered the guest count. I told him. "Don't worry about it, darling," he said. "We can use the table in my conference room. I'll sit there with all the guests who won't fit in the dining room." "Everything will be okay," he kept repeating like an incantation—more about life and Friday morning's surgery than about birthdays and Thursday night's dinner.

The events of that week brought home one great truth about relationships: the big crises in life wipe out the small ones. All the petty clashes and trivial disagreements are consumed when the recognition of what *really* matters suddenly flares up. Moments of high intensity, of life and sickness and thoughts of death, are accompanied by a higher Fourth Instinct clarity—moments when God taps us on the shoulder and reminds us of the impermanence of much that we assume is forever and the value of all we take for granted in our everyday relationships.

When I look back on what threads have pulled me through many of the tight squeezes, sharp drops and hard choices in my own life's labyrinth, I realize that the "what" was often a "who"—my sister, my mother, my husband, a colleague, a teacher, a friend, or even my baby daughter, who, with an insightful sentence or an unexpected smile, put everything in perspective.

The party went off without a hitch. The next morning, as Michael and I were waiting for me to be taken into surgery, he was making so many jokes to mask his anxiety that the nurse turned to me and teased: "Is *that* the responsible adult you brought with you?" A week later, we got the result. The lump was benign. It had been a long week, full of "what ifs," in which I leaned not only on my faith, but on the strength of my family and friends.

Prayer, meditation, and reading the Bible have always been important to me. But there were times when I needed to hold on to a living thread, a soul-to-soul connection with someone I loved. I needed not only to hold, but to be held. My sister

Agapi has always been a thread for me, and I have nestled in her unconditional love many a time. "School's in session!" was the rallying cry for midnight chats, pow-wows in the powder room during a double date, and late-night long-distance calls after my marriage. Secrets were shared with absolute trust and tears were shed in total vulnerability. She was the intuitive one; I, the cerebral. And when I wanted to catch up with her in matters spiritual, she was always my guide, sending books and people my way, nudging my spiritual explorations, calling to wake me up at a hotel in Kalamazoo, Michigan, at five in the morning so I could have time to meditate before another grueling book-tour day began.

We have always protected each other, Agapi and I, but never from the truth. This is a prerequisite for relationships to serve as a thread through the labyrinth. In most relationships we don't trust our love for each other enough to say what may be hurtful or, worse, what may momentarily turn someone against us. How many times, following a divorce, hasn't a friend asked, "Why didn't you tell me you knew my marriage would never work?" Fourth Instinct relationships are about paradox. At one and the same time I can say to someone I love: "Marrying so-and-so would be a mistake," and "If you choose to marry I will love and support you." To say the first without the second would be an infliction of a personal opinion; to say the second without the first would be not to trust or cherish the relationship enough.

There are many casual relationships with neighbors or co-workers that either never flower into intimacy or even become thorns in our side, many marriages that are ripped apart in a miserable divorce, many parent-child relationships that turn sour and never recover. Such relationships become threads through the labyrinth only when we consciously choose to learn from the pain they bring us or the distance we seem unable to span.

But many of our relationships are, or have the potential to become, direct threads toward our life's meaning. An admired teacher praises a gift we have and, in that moment, turns us toward a career. A parent's patient confidence encourages us to try again and again, until at last we succeed. Colleagues at work who, despite the pressures of their own jobs, take time to support or even rescue us; neighbors who find out we have

116

been laid off and bring a pound of coffee, a chocolate cake, and a hopeful enthusiasm that lifts our spirits—all are threads just waiting to be picked up and followed, even if only to the next level of understanding.

The highest function of relationships that are threads is to remind us of where we are going, of our spiritual purpose. We make hundreds of decisions every day—from what to wear to what house to buy—which may have no bearing on our spiritual growth. But we also come to forks in the road where one way leads down a dead end and the other closer to the center of our labyrinth. If psychotherapy is, as psychologist Hans Strupp described it, "the systematic use of a human relationship for therapeutic purposes," a human relationship that's based on love and acceptance can be the most meaningful form of therapy. There can be no judgments in therapy, and forgiveness lies at the heart of relationships which are a thread leading to God. This acceptance comes not because we have lost a sense of right and wrong, good and evil, but because a good friend, like a good therapist, understands that "missing the mark" (which is what sin means in classical Greek) is a daily event on the journey through the labyrinth. And missing the mark of our spiritual purpose is man's "original sin."

"Never get angry, never make a threat, reason with people," was the philosophy of Don Corleone in *The Godfather*. This, he believed, was the best way to get results. Getting results, especially the kind the Godfather had in mind, is not the highest function of life, but the same advice might help lead us closer to the center in the labyrinth. Of course, we will sometimes miss the mark, become angry and get hurt; but as long as we follow our Fourth Instinct, even experiences that bedevil our relationships can become ministering angels pointing out the false attachments, fears and unresolved emotions that may stand between ourselves and God.

Myths and fairy tales often show relationships as threads and guides—the helpful animals, wise old men and fairy godmothers who, in time of trial, make sure we don't lose our way. But the way in which relationships bring out our flaws and weaknesses is another aspect of their importance as a thread through the labyrinth.

Whether in Greek tragedy or in Shakespeare, it's the fatal flaw in the hero's character—the flaw unrecognized by the hero himself—that brings him down. Relationships are a uniquely direct way to gain a greater understanding of ourselves, including the traits that put at risk both others and ourselves. When a trusted friend is brave enough not only to point out our flaws and blind spots but also to encourage and support our growth, we have a relationship that is clearly a thread guiding us past potential minefields of our own making.

We can take or leave, pick up or put down, most threads in the labyrinth. But relationships, with all the pain and joy they bring, are an inherent part of life, as unavoidable as breathing. After all, we are born in relationship. We are conceived in the relationship of a man and a woman. Nine months later we emerge, not from an egg left to hatch on its own, but from the womb, wet and bawling, tied to our mother. We are programmed from the beginning, from the moment that first tie is severed, to feel that a relationship is what we must work on—relationships are what we must master. They are central to our lives, our learning, our work, our discovery of ourselves. Aristotle said that the man who lives alone, apart from his brothers, must be either beast or god. Perhaps. But few beasts live alone. And God Himself is deeply vested in relationships—spinning all reality out, as He does, and back upon Himself. Even His first words about us were spoken in the plural: "Let us make man in Our image, after Our likeness."

Relationships and the emotions they engender are not new. Love is as old as creation and anger is only a little younger. What is modern is the way we dissect our relationships, how we "deal" with them, "handle" them, "grow" through them and listen to what they are trying to "tell" us and what they reveal about ourselves. The self-help section of our local bookstore contains countless volumes on how to master relationships, how to start them, stop them, recover from them and get more out of them. But when we see relationships as a thread to our spiritual center, we don't see them just as ends in themselves, but as opportunities—often through ordeals and pain—to bring light into our lives, illuminating our blind spots.

It's through the weakness we don't see in ourselves, or don't fully recognize, that evil can work—and even take us over. "There are many events in the womb of time, which will be delivered," says Iago. And the only opening through which

118

death and destruction could be delivered was Othello's blindness, his ignorance of himself. The soul's compulsion is for light and consciousness. And unless we take refuge in our blindness, relationships are a vehicle through which we bring more light to our lives and ourselves.

In the myth of the union of Psyche to Aphrodite's son, Eros, the condition for their love is that they can unite only in darkness. When Psyche succumbs to her need to know, she violates that condition by lighting a candle and, in its light, seeing her lover in all his glory. "Love cannot live with suspicion," Eros cries and flies away, leaving her alone again. What is suspicion or even idle curiosity from one perspective is, from another, the soul's unwillingness to be in a relationship shrouded in darkness.

Psyche had to *know* Eros and *be known* by him, whatever the cost. It's the challenge of all relationships, but especially deeply intimate ones. And there are costs and a price to pay. In the myth, Psyche is punished by Aphrodite with a series of impossible tasks. Her final test is to enter the Underworld and there put into the box that Aphrodite has given her a drop of Persephone's beauty, the beauty of the soul. When she fulfills this ultimate task, she is at last able to be reunited with her lover—this time without conditions and not in darkness.

To reach the depths of the beauty of our souls in our close relationships, we must be prepared to walk into the dark side of intimacy and out the other side into the light. Our most meaningful relationships are based on what we are capable of becoming, rather than on what we have been or what we are, on our longing for expansion rather than our preoccupation with comfort and security. To live exuberantly—to fully know and be fully known—we must be prepared to risk lighting a candle to illuminate the darkness of even our most intimate relationships, revealing ourselves and seeing clearly all that is revealed. To grow in our relationships and to expand as individuals within them, we must exchange the glorious unreality of the honeymoon for something even better.

Michael and I had a dreamlike honeymoon—Anguilla, the Orient Express, Venice, Paris. We held on to it for six weeks. I had no desire to return to reality. The first morning we were back in Michael's home in Houston—now *our* home—we sat at the breakfast table, a pile of mail in front of each of us.

Within fifteen minutes, Michael had a neat stack of letters, opened with a letter opener, next to his cereal bowl, and I had strewn envelopes, torn open with my own hands, all over the kitchen floor, leaving the table littered with the letters themselves. We looked at each other, silently wondering what sort of person we had vowed to love, honor and cherish until death do us part. We said nothing. That we loved each other there was no doubt. But were we prepared to *know* each other—from the most trivial ways of letter-opening to the deepest ways two people can know each other?

That Sunday we went to worship together at the Houston Cathedral. The Cathedral Dean, Pittman McGehee, gave a memorable sermon on "becoming married." He talked about the illusion that we emerge from the ceremony of marriage truly married. He urged us to see marriage as a process and, especially, to be open to the negative side of intimacy, the hurt, the pain, the criticisms, the losses that bring depth to the relationship and, in that depth, bring us closer to God. He cautioned us to be wary of a relationship that has no room for anger or pain, that is lived on the surface of niceness behind smiling masks that block us from experiencing our own and each other's reality. He pleaded with us to be vulnerable in the face of each other and of God, to realize that the self-protective devices behind which we barricade ourselves are actually self-destructive.

As we lined up to greet the Dean at the close of the service, we heard others in front of us saying what was also in our hearts: "You were talking to us"—one of Pittman McGehee's great gifts.

Michael and I decided to put the sermon into practice. We committed ourselves to "becoming" married and to looking straight in the face whatever came up. It is the only way to grow within marriage, to make of this life partnership something larger than ourselves, satisfying more than our own needs and emotions. But without knowledge of our spiritual nature, it is hard to take too much reality. Intimate relationships like marriage are often seen exclusively as a safe harbor during life's storms, a haven, a retreat. And to maintain this image, we cherish our illusions; we cling to them. One of the most subtly destructive twists in relationships occurs when they become not a thread to truth, but a quilt we stitch to wrap around ourselves to protect us from the winds of reality which blow where they will.

The salvation of man is through love, but lovers are not saviors. "We may give our human loves the unconditional allegiance which we owe only to God," C. S. Lewis warned, "then they become demons. . . . For natural loves that are allowed to become gods do not remain loves. They are still called so, but can become in fact complicated forms of hatred." We become, in pairs, not partners in life's great adventure but accomplices, rationalizing our arrested development, self-satisfied in our limitations, squashing the intrinsic longing of the soul to fly. So great becomes the fear of losing what we have that many of us, even after having glimpsed another reality, instead of following the thread of revelation wherever it might lead, rush back to hide under the quilt. Given adequate time and sufficient fear, we may hide under self-made quilts so long that we hardly notice when we are suffocating.

"There is a passion in me," wrote the mystical poet Rumi in the thirteenth century, "that doesn't long for anything from another human being." Here is soul not running from human intimacy but recognizing there is something beyond it. It is the passion of our Fourth Instinct. Tragically, I've seen women and men whose partners, sensing this passion stir, do everything they can to stop it, to deny it, to kill the newborn longing before it can mature. Threatened by a passion they may not be ready to understand, fearing they will never share in it, imagining that its light will make everything else appear stark and bare, they panic at the thought of being left behind, abandoned. This is the danger of relationships that are all anchor and no sail. "Ships in the harbor are safe," someone said, "but this is not what ships are made for." God sets us free, and limiting, possessive relationships return us to our cells.

Relationships can become a doorway into a new life—surrendering, growing, giving, creating—or a revolving door which gives us movement without progress and deposits us back into ourselves, not as we could become but as we are. "There is no surer formula for discontent," wrote Fulton J. Sheen, "than to try to satisfy our cravings for the ocean of Infinite Love from the teacup of finite satisfactions." The Fourth Instinct will keep tugging at us until we start on the journey for the ocean. When we stop expecting some perfect human union and some endless human love to satisfy our soul's cravings, we will stop putting impossible demands on our most intimate relationships. Talking to a newly wed friend, I could hear the disappointment in her voice: "We don't have enough time alone . . . I don't feel his love as much . . . There isn't as much romance . . ." I could not help but think that the honeymoon was over, but their marriage had yet to begin.

In my experience, the key to loving relationships is in gaining access to the love inside ourselves. "I tried to die near the end of the war," Arthur Miller wrote in *After the Fall*. "The same dream returned each night until I dared not go to sleep and grew quite ill. I dreamed I had a child, and even in the dream I saw it was my life and it was an idiot and I ran away. But it always crept onto my lap again, clutched at my clothes. Until I thought, if I could kiss it, whatever in it was my own, perhaps I could sleep. And I bent to its broken face, and it was horrible. . . . But I kissed it. I think one must finally take one's life into one's arms."

We cannot truly love another until we have learned to love and accept ourselves beyond all shortcomings. God's spirit lives within us in a loving, intimate relationship. When we accept this reality, we can fill ourselves with it and bring it fully to our marriage and to all our relationships. The only sure way I know to gain access to this love is by tapping the spirit within us, drawing on the unconditional love God has for all His children—the love we replicate as parents ourselves. What we want more of—more loving, more romance, more tenderness— we must bring to our intimate relationships. As surely as we must bring food if we want a picnic, not hope to find it when we arrive, so surely must we bring love to our relationships rather than expect to draw it from them. As long as the expectation continues that relationships will fill our emptiness and insulate us from anxiety and loneliness, we will keep trying to find in them the lost oneness of our childhood—and we will keep finding disappointment instead.

A baby at the breast knows oneness with the mother, but it is not a conscious knowing. Babies nurse on instinct. But that was then and this is now. As adults we are, all of us, at a different point. And, for a very good reason, we cannot enter the same river twice. We left the Garden of Eden with its state of unconscious harmony and bliss to make the journey that, if

122

we persevere, will end in a state of *conscious* harmony and bliss. Loving relationships can help us get there by bringing out of ourselves the love that is already dormant in us. Guided by that love, relationships help guide us home.

My mother has lived with us for years. She loves to cook, but most important, she loves helping us raise her granddaughters. Having my mother at home is, for Michael and me, very little giving and a great deal of receiving.

I know it's different in other homes. Population graphs have always been shaped like a pyramid, broad at the base for the early years of life and narrowing to an apex for those few people over one hundred. But with better health increasing our longevity, the pyramid is gradually changing shape. The fact is that, today, the fastest-growing segment of the elderly population is people over eighty-five. This trend, however, conflicts with another. Traditionally, if aging parents needed care, they received it from their adult daughters. Thirty years ago, 38 percent of American women worked outside the home. Now, the figure is nearly 60 percent. Women are joining men in the full-time work force, leaving homes without either husband or wife available for most daytime hours. So while more parents and grandparents grow older, our ability to provide family care for them has diminished.

It isn't the sociology or the statistics that move me; it's the relationships themselves, threads which could lead us through the labyrinth, but instead, in many cases, lead to frustration, guilt and recrimination. Parents do not want to become "a burden" on their adult children, and children who love their parents and would value their wisdom have no time. We work to buy houses and cars, our children's education and our own insurance. When we are done working, we are drained. And the relationship which began decades ago at *our* mother's breast grows strained and unhappy. We do not want to put our father into an impersonal institution, there to languish and die. We do not want to think of our mother alone, hoping the telephone will ring, wondering why she had to outlive what she considers her "usefulness." I have watched friends become parents to their aging parents, and I have seen what a tear-stained process it can be.

I know and love dearly a couple whose hearts have been nearly broken by a daughter bent on indifference and even cruelty; if these parents someday need care, their daughter will not provide it. I have spent hours listening to children who, despite the best counseling, cannot shake the thought that they are somehow responsible for their parents' break-up; for the children of divorce, the parent-child relationship is, at best, a bittersweet reality.

All these elements of parent-child relationships can produce great pain. But if we do not run from the hurt, if we stay with the agony and confront it, listening to the messages our Fourth Instinct will deliver, they are still relationships in which even pain and stress can become the threads leading us through the labyrinth.

Of all the roles that can be a thread to meaning and purpose in our lives, none is stronger than the role of parent. Michael and I have followed this thread for the past five years. Like other parents, we have learned that children do not simply merge seamlessly and magically into the relationship Mom and Dad have already established. The adjustments required can by themselves become a spiritual thread to acceptance, giving, and an absolute commitment to something, or someone, outside ourselves. One thing on which all parents agree is that, whether you are eighteen or thirty-eight, you are never really prepared for having children. I was thirty-eight. And, yes, I picked up quickly on the diaper-changing and baby-burping routines. But what about the total surrender of my being—my sleep, my body, my interests, my friendships, my goals—to the well-being of another? Nothing could have prepared me for that.

I remember the conversations I had with a friend nine months after she had given birth to twins. The euphoria of early motherhood and the romance of the babies' sweet-smelling skin were giving way to the drudgery of diapers, tears and flying food. Having quit her high-powered job to stay home with her children, she was enduring unimagined depths of exhaustion. By evening, she just wanted to relax—to put the babies down and be taken care of. Her husband, a lawyer, had taken on extra cases to make up for their loss of family income and prepare for the expenses ahead. His usual day was an endless series of meetings, conflicts, and deadlines. By the time he inched his way home through the inevitable traffic jam, he just wanted to loosen his tie, put down his burdens and be taken care of. And, of course, the babies themselves wanted the same thing babies always want: to be fed and loved and coddled and cuddled—to be babies, and be taken care of!

My friend was left with four anxious "Me's" in a house without a lot of room left for "Us." She was afraid she and her husband were about to start on a downward spiral of guilt and recrimination, passing around the blame for failed expectations. She had seen the drama played out many times in many different ways, starting with strained sarcastic humor and ending in the divorce courts. Fortunately for my friend, she had a spiritual capacity to go beyond what seemed on the surface to be merely a matter of logistics and emotions. She and her husband kept the demons at bay, not just by calling a babysitter or Auntie Jane, or simply by declaring "Mommy Nights" and "Daddy Nights," but by resolving that they would do more than survive: they would evolve, together, through the hard times. They would nurture each other not just physically and emotionally, but spiritually.

"We are discussing whether to take the plunge and have a child," another friend in her late thirties announced on a morning hike through the hills of Santa Barbara. "What do you think?" I looked at her, slim, successful, dressed as though she had just stepped out of a *Vogue* shoot on rugged chic—her life, I knew, planned to the last second. I thought about how I should balance tact and truth. Finally, I said, "Yes . . . yes . . . yes—have a child. Do not think about it. Just pray that you get pregnant." Prayer, it seemed to me, was the right starting point. Many friends my age think they can plan getting pregnant with the same control and accuracy that they schedule a business meeting. The first lesson in surrendering to a higher will is accepting a timing that's not our own.

Then I debated with myself how much more to tell my friend beyond "Yes, have a child." Should I tell her that she would never again be able to answer the question "How are you?" in reference to herself alone? Should I tell her that, all her sophistication notwithstanding, she would be reduced to the primitive level of an animal protecting her young? Should I tell this woman, famous for her quick decision-making powers, that she would be reduced to a bundle of second-guessing insecurities over every tiny decision affecting her child? Should I tell her that she would never again look at a statistic of child abuse without feeling her blood boil, or a picture of a homeless child without hearing her heart cry out? It's not that every mother's circle of compassion automatically expands once her child is born. If this were the case, the world would by now be a very different place. But I knew this woman and why I loved her. And I knew that all this would happen to her.

What I finally told her is that all the sacrifices, all the loss of control and independence in her life, would be trivial compared to the gains. What's more, they would be necessary losses, welcome sheddings on her way from self-absorption to self-knowing, from the confining *I* to the liberating *we*. What Kahlil Gibran wrote about allowing love into our lives applies to parents as much as to lovers—perhaps even more:

> For even as love crowns you so shall he crucify you. Even as he is for your growth so is he for your pruning.
> Even as he ascends to your height and caresses your tenderest branches that quiver in the sun,
> So shall he descend to your roots and shake them in their clinging to the earth.

We pick up the thread of parenting when we let ourselves be truly vulnerable and open to all the transformations entailed in introducing—in most cases, for the first time—unconditional love into our lives. In the middle of all the PTA meetings, dental bills and endless loads of laundry, we somehow need to remember that our children are indeed the greatest miracle on earth—a witness to the creation of matter out of the energy of love. We should not have to wait to come to this realization when something happens to them or to the children of friends we love.

Yet parenting can become a twisted thread when it pushes aside all other needs and commitments. I worry when couples begin referring to each other only as "Mommy" and "Daddy." Men have made the shift from lover to husband to doting dad, but that doesn't mean that they no longer love the way lovers do, that they no longer need their wives intimately, passionately and physically. Unless we care for ourselves and for our spouses, we will be no good for our children. Flight attendants give voice to an important truth when they warn passengers that in case of an emergency they should put on their own oxygen masks before assisting their children with theirs. This is not callous corporate disregard for half-fare half-pints; it's a realistic reminder of the fact that we cannot care for our children without caring for ourselves. If we always put our children first, they may end up as the quietest spectators in a divorce court.

I recently told a young friend, who worried that having a child would take the romance out of her marriage, that she would fall in love with her husband in entirely new ways the first time she saw him changing their baby's diaper. I will never forget the love that welled up inside me one morning last spring. I had gotten up unusually early. Then about seven, I returned to our bedroom to find that Christina had crawled into our bed and was caressing her daddy's face, looking at him adoringly while he, eyes half shut, was soaking in all that four-year-old love. I don't know a deeper romance than that.

The love we receive from our children is, in itself, a thread we can follow to the source of all love. Because our young children are still so closely connected to it, their love has that morning-of-creation feeling about it—and the fingerprints of our Creator all over it. To return this love to them *unconditionally*—not to withdraw it from them because of behavior we want changed—is the greatest gift we can give our children. The child who grows up on unconditional love will blossom into the adult who gives it naturally in return.

Children learn early enough that the world "out there" does not love them unconditionally. Most of us make this discovery the first day we are sent out into it, lunchbox in our hands and terror in our hearts. We have embarked on a whole new universe, one where relationships are constrained by countless "rules," passing tests, making varsity teams and, soon enough, finding jobs. Regrettably, it is a world in which even our relationships are graded, as many an anxious parent learns when reading that fateful report card entry, "Does not work and play well with others"—and as many an adult learns when missing that promotion on the basis of something as amorphous as "attitude."

If relationships can be a thread to self-knowledge and understanding, the pressure to "make friends and influence people" can very effectively lead us away from both. We have all said and done things to gain approval; we want our friends to like us, we want strangers to become our friends. But there is nothing sadder than the sight of someone spinning like a weathervane to the whims and wants of others. A friend of mine who remembers resolving in kindergarten to do anything it took to win the acceptance of her peers woke up in her thirties to the bleak futility of her contortions. A lifetime of bending over backward had left her paralyzed. "I didn't really know who I was anymore. I thought I knew who, or what, *others* wanted me to be. But I had no idea who *I* was." She was blessed, in her darkest hour, to find a relationship that became a thread gently leading her back to herself.

Our Fourth Instinct knows that who we truly are is the original gift—a gift worth exploring at any cost, including the disapproval of friends, strangers and even family. "I came not to send peace, but a sword. For I am come to set a man at variance against his father, and the daughter against her mother," was Christ's stern message about the primacy of our relationship with God.

Someone said somewhere—probably on a farm where they still notice such things—that "you get a chicken by hatching the egg, not by smashing it." Patience is the key both in our relationship with ourselves and in our relationships with others—including God. God and man, Simone Weil observed, are like two lovers who through some terrible mix-up have missed each other at the appointed place and hour. Life stretches on ahead of us, and we start pacing, glancing ever more frantically at our watch. Where *could* He be? Impostors, sensing our frustration, approach us—each with some substitute, some alternative plan. Sometimes, losing heart, we go along. Patience built on trust is the great bulwark against discouragement, which in many spiritual traditions is the devil's favorite way of turning us away from God. Practicing patience is nothing less than practicing cooperation with God's will.

Of course, like all spiritual truths, this too can be abused. Patience is no excuse for putting up with destructive relationships. I remember the woman at a battered women's shelter who had been admitted with her two children a week earlier after her husband had beaten her nearly unconscious. "Whenever it would start," she said, "I would try to rise above it and concentrate on God." I interrupted. Submitting to evil, if we can flee from it, I said, is in itself a spiritual crime. Cooperating with our tormentors, when we can run away from them, simply adds to the sum total of evil in the world. Actually, what I believe goes even further than that. We need to protect ourselves not only from physical abuse, but from someone intent on destroying our spirit with hatred, spite and hostility. We must learn to make a distinction between the necessary sandpapering of our souls that can occur in relationships at times of hardship and turmoil, and the dangerous bludgeoning that takes place in relationships that are simply destructive. If someone is hurling sharp emotional spears our way, let us by all means try to maintain our spiritual center. But, first, let us duck.

The greatest spiritual challenge is to keep our hearts open while deflecting darkness and negativity. Until we can achieve this state of being, we must at least not allow painful experiences to close down our hearts permanently. At a conference on healing, Dr. Rachel Remen, medical director of the Commonwealth Cancer Help Program, told the story of a survivor of Auschwitz, a brilliant chemist with a heavy Polish accent, who was taking part in a spiritual retreat at which she was the medical director. Fighting cancer, he wanted to experiment with mental forms of healing, but he was uncomfortable with all the talk about loving and the hugging of strangers that went on. Even more, he was frightened by a vision he had during meditation in which he saw himself inside a big pink rose that grew out of his chest. He told the group that this huge energy field of love generated by his heart left him feeling very vulnerable; since he had been taken to Auschwitz as a twelve-year-old boy, he had closed his heart to all but a small circle of intimates. Now, here was this field of love extending from his heart to everyone around him.

On the last day of the retreat, Dr. Remen asked him how he was doing with his big rose. "Better," he said. "What happened that helped?" she wanted to know. "I took a valk and talked to God. It's better." "What did God say?" Dr. Remen asked. "Ah, I say to God, 'God, vot is this, is it OK to luff the strangers?' And God said, 'Harry, vot is this "strangers?" You make strangers, I don't make strangers.' "

Ultimately, the way we respond to the nameless, the homeless—the "strangers"—is the true test of our spiritual mettle, the true test of relationships as a thread through the labyrinth of our own lives. "Don't talk to strangers!" we are taught from the moment we are able to talk. But if we do not talk to strangers, if we do not expand the circle of our affections and our caring, then we simply are not choosing to evolve. I do not, of course, send my four-year-old to Central Park alone to talk to strangers. And yet, while I will teach her about caution and judgment, I will encourage her to trust, to learn to share with strangers, as she is learning to share with her sister. I would rather that she be duped a few times than that she go through life mistrustful and barricaded, never taken in because she was never vulnerable.

"First of all we want to make them feel that they are wanted," Mother Teresa explained about her work with those dying in the streets of Calcutta. "We want them to know that there are people who really love them, who really want them, at least for the few hours they have to live, to know human and divine love. That they too may know that they are the children of God, and that they are not forgotten. . . ."

So long as we are on a search for pain-free human relationships, or shifting responsibility for all our hurt and all our fears of abandonment, or seeking ourselves in others, we have not yet found the thread that will lead us toward God, or ourselves. When we learn to accept ourselves—not just our public achievements and private successes, not just the divine being we are evolving into, but also our failures, inadequacies, cowardices and fears—then we will be able to embrace the strangers among us, because we will, finally, have embraced the stranger inside ourselves.

7

Reconnecting to God: Religion

> How wonderful it is, this marrying of the ribaldry of gargoyles with the sublimity of steeples, this seeing of a saint in every clown and a clown in every saint, and the Fall of Man as being, at once, the measure and fatality of all our afflictions and the old banana-skin joke on a cosmic scale. Who but a God who had deigned to become incarnate could arrange things so? Encompassing in His love the suffering and the absurdity of His creation . . . Laughter, indeed, is God's therapy . . . in order that we might understand that at the heart of our mortal existence there lies a mystery, at once unutterably beautiful and hilariously funny.
>
> —Malcolm Muggeridge
> *Confessions of a*
> *Twentieth-Century Pilgrim*

We spent many of my childhood summers in Corfu. My two favorite summer dates were July 15—my birthday—and

August 15, the date when the whole of Greece paid homage to the Virgin Mary. I sat quietly in church among widows in black kerchiefs and younger women smelling of summer wool and candle smoke. I watched as deep faith and old memories moved them to tears of grief and hope. Heads bent in prayer, they had come to commune with Mary with a powerful woman's piety that in my own childish way I had shared ever since I can remember. I think I was three when, with no parental prompting, I knelt by my bed and prayed to the Virgin Mary.

Whenever I felt alone and afraid, I prayed to her. When schoolyard squabbles broke out, when my sister grew quiet and sick, when my father moved away and didn't come home at night, I prayed to her. Nor did I leave the Virgin Mary in Greece. She went with me to England and into adulthood. From the tumult of the debating chamber at Cambridge to the quiet of my first apartment in London, she was there. When I immigrated to a new homeland, took my husband's hand and made my vows, when I heard the truth I already knew about my unborn son, she was there. Beyond religion—beyond the icons that I took with me from Greece to England to America, and above the soaring melody of *Ave Maria* that I chose as a musical offering at my wedding—I have known Mary as a spiritual guide in my life. I met her early. We were introduced through the Fourth Instinct.

Religion is man's response to God; we come together, we bow our heads, we celebrate the spirit in song and prayer. But religion is also God's response to man, a channel for revelation and reconnection which is, after all, what religion means not only etymologically—from the Latin root *religio*—but essentially. When religion is alive and vital, it does just that: it helps us reconnect with God, with the spiritual reality in all things.

Spirituality, our sense of God and our search for Him, has been with us since the sixth day of creation, the day we were made in God's image. The Fourth Instinct longs for an active relationship with the divine. For thousands of years and millions of seekers, religion has served as the thread back to these spiritual essentials.

When I first started studying religion, I drew the conventional distinction between our Western view of God as remote, external, other, and the Eastern view of God as manifest in everything and everyone. But the more I delved into the esoteric depths of religious scripture, whether the Kabbalah, Lao-Tzu or the Gospel of Saint John the Beloved, the more inescapable became the conclusion that the truth is one and glorious in its simplicity: "The Kingdom of God is within."

Believing in an external God is only the first step on the way to experiencing Him. Then there is no question of "belief" and no wrestling with "doubt." Reconnecting with the divine is the first essential element of every religion. The second is manifesting that connection in our lives. The early Christian church ordained deacons to care for the poor, the widows and the orphans. To be a minister was primarily to minister, to be of service to those in need. Persecution drove the church into hiding, at the end of which a defining creed and an official hierarchy were both in place, and deacons who had gone into the caves as servants came out as bishops.

Christianity, embodied in the beliefs and rituals of the Roman Catholic Church, dominated the Middle Ages. Then the full force of Western thought bore down on the medieval church and individualism rose to challenge the clerics' claim to exclusive access to God. Luther's conviction regarding the priesthood of all believers was at the heart of the Reformation: God was accessible to everyone, always, everywhere.

The Enlightenment followed the Reformation and drained individualism of spirituality. It baptized the intellect, canonized empiricism and relegated religion to the safest of all possible places: somewhere else. The week belongs to man, but give God His due: an hour on the weekend. We lost our sense of mystery, of reverence and awe, and modern man, a man of reason, cannot stop shrugging his shoulders in disbelief. Yet awareness of the mystery of things has always been the only way for the human mind to look beyond its workaday world into the unknown, the world of the spirit, the only way to enlarge our capacity to experience wonder and reverence for the riddle of our creation.

When the eminent British philosopher Bertrand Russell was sent to jail for his anti-war protests in 1918, he was asked by his jailer some routine questions, including his religion. "Agnostic," Russell replied. "I guess it doesn't matter what you call it," came back the response, "as long as you believe in God." Agnosticism can either be a state of mind open to the pursuit of truth, or a state of pure skepticism fatal to its discovery. Obsessed, as William James put it, with "shunning error," the skeptics ignore our other major moral duty: believing truth.

The first person I knew to jump from agnosticism to unbelief was small for her age, and I'm not sure that she could even spell "agnosticism" or "unbelief." She was my best school friend in Athens. I remember standing in her bedroom, windows shut and shades drawn against the chatter and sunshine of a Sunday morning, begging her—again—to go with me to church. Her parents had christened her Theodora, "Gift of God," but with a skepticism far greater than her age, she spoke of God as a human invention and religion as a crutch for those too feeble to stand on their own. God and all his rituals, she informed me, were for dummies like me and my sister, not for smart little girls like her. She turned up her little nose at the conventionality of it all. And so each Sunday morning, after the rest of her family had gone to church, she would sit and silently sneer at Mass and the masses.

Years later, I discovered that while I had been missing her in church, she had been secretly missing God at home. In a room she had tried to scrub clean of God's memory, she felt an ancient longing she could deny but not extinguish. When she finally stopped denying it, she picked up the thread that led her out of that room, and through the labyrinth back to God. And the day came when we could light candles and pray together—and laugh at our earnest, all-knowing younger selves.

Theodora grew up and out of her arid skepticism. Not so our Western culture. Dominated by secularism, the twentieth century has been offering up its deluge of "isms": existentialism, communism, socialism, political salvationism. Like the one-year-old who "hides" by slapping his hands over his eyes, we have declared the divine missing, or dead, or generally irrelevant. And we have gone home to an aching emptiness.

We ache for spiritual truth, and at the same time we doubt both our longings and the experiences they lead us to. Many years ago, a friend and I shared powerful moments together at a religious retreat in London. I was, therefore, amazed and a little hurt when the next issue of *Private Eye*, a British satirical magazine, carried his sarcastic account of the experience. He had climbed to the safety of his critic's perch, from there to bring low his own spiritual insights and those of others. I have known well this temptation, and the fear from which it springs. It goes much beyond playful lampooning. Afraid of the power of our own spirit, and of the havoc it might wreak on our lives, we launch preemptive strikes to reduce its meaning. Our denigrating of spiritual experience is very different from a healthy, playful ability to laugh at all human attempts to describe adequately our experience of the divine. In the course of my research, and to satisfy my spiritual curiosity, I attended many retreats and seminars and I have to confess to having written several "Saturday Night Live" skits in my head, even as they were in progress, and sometimes even as I was learning, despite myself.

There is a part in us that is automatically suspicious of any dogma or ritual that threatens to become more sacred than the truth it seeks to evoke. At the roots of our secular age is the fatal error that has led us to regard organized religion and the spiritual truth man embodies as one and the same thing— and so to deny the reality of one because we have rejected the shortcomings of the other. But spiritual truth cannot be pinned down to one final dogmatic interpretation. The Book of Revelation is proof that, as Sir Laurens Van der Post has pointed out, the Bible itself ends "with the drawbridge of the Christian citadel let down and the road open once more for the spirit of man to travel to the end of experience and revelation." God is indeed one, but our Fourth Instinct insists on freedom as it leads us toward the truth.

Spiritual understanding is the process of anamnesis, the remembrance of forgotten wisdom lying latent within each individual. Our sacred texts can be the midwives to that spiritual rebirth, the thread that draws us to God, but not the fabric from which He is cut. As Karl Rahner, the German Jesuit theologian, put it, "the theological problem today is the art of drawing religion out of a man, not pumping it into him. The art is to help men become what they really are."

"We have all forgotten what we really are," wrote G. K. Chesterton. "All that we call common sense and rationality and practicality . . . only means that for certain dead levels of our life we forget that we have forgotten. All that we call spirit and art and ecstasy only means that for one awful instant we remember that we forget."

Radio commentator Gil Gross once reported on the young parents who brought home a new baby brother to his four-year-old sister. The little girl immediately wanted to be left alone with him, but the parents were fearful. They had heard of jealous children hitting new siblings and didn't want the baby hurt. "Why do you want to be alone with him?" they asked. "What are you going to do?" "Nothing," the little girl said, "I just want to be alone with him." But the parents weren't comfortable and so the little girl heard "no, no," and "not yet" day after day.

After one week of incessant entreaties, the parents finally gave in. There was an intercom in the baby's room. They would listen. If they heard crying, they could rush in and snatch up the baby. So the little girl went in, alone. She walked quietly to the crib where her baby brother slept. Then, after a minute, over the intercom the parents heard her plead, "Tell me about God. I'm forgetting."

Modern America and religion have had an uncomfortable marriage. And yet neither can afford a divorce. Because America itself is a deeply spiritual endeavor. Tocqueville summed it up in *Democracy in America:* "Religion in America takes no direct part in the government of society, but it must be regarded as the first of their political institutions. . . . How is it possible that society should escape destruction if the moral tie is not strengthened in proportion as the political tie is relaxed? And what can be done with a people who are their own masters if they are not submissive to the Deity?"

The famous painting of *Washington Praying at Valley Forge* is not a painting that sprang from a pious artist's imagination. It is rather an accurate account of actual events, as attested to by the diaries of Washington's soldiers. At St. Paul's Chapel in lower Manhattan, you'll still find, cordoned off to the right, the pew where Washington worshiped almost every Sunday of his presidency. The minutes of the Constitutional Convention record Benjamin Franklin, at one particularly contentious impasse, suggesting a group prayer. The day after the First Amendment was adopted, the Congress petitioned the President to issue a proclamation for national prayer and thanksgiving. The Declaration of Independence itself bears the signatures of several ordained ministers; and many citizens heard the Declaration read for the first time from the pulpits of their local churches.

The Founding Fathers lived and breathed the existence of God, His authority and influence, and yet were painfully aware of the great potential for the abuse of religious power. Their solution to this problem: government should stay out of religion and vice versa. Hence, all in one stunning breath, the rigid separation of church and state and guarantees of absolute freedom of religious expression. Brilliant concepts both, but what happened over the next two hundred years was the gradual erosion of belief in any moral authority in our political and personal behavior—a secular state and a secular society.

But today, in amazing numbers, Americans are rediscovering the truth inscribed above Woodrow Wilson's tomb in the National Cathedral: "The sum of the whole matter is this, that our civilization cannot survive materially unless it be redeemed spiritually." Many men of religious temperament, who in the past would have been led by the Fourth Instinct to seek this dimension of their lives in the churches, are now driven to seek it in a more personal search. At the same time, many who had spurned organized religion in favor of their own search are again filing back into church and temple.

The folksinger Arlo Guthrie turned a desanctified Episcopal church into a place where people can come and "express religious feelings or beliefs as service." "It's a Bring Your Own God church," he said. "When you think about it, every church is like that. Every synagogue and temple and mosque. Every hill with a view, every sunset, you're bringing yourself." Hank Donnelly, a journalist, is one of the seekers who returned to the church. "The story of my quest," he said, "is the story of always wanting to be hooked up to something greater than myself. I began to read about Zen Buddhism when I was sixteen. I kept walking around, thinking I'd catch *sartori* or something. When I started going to the Hare Krishna feasts after college, I got pretty wrapped up in meditating. . . . I went on to try lots of different things, then finally the unity of the various things became more important than their diversity. I asked myself: why not return to the dogma of your fathers?"

Whether we choose to infuse new life into the faith of our fathers or to find the connection between the transcendent and

137

our daily lives in our own way, God is unmistakably back and we are in search of Him. It is a process *Time* describes as "a quiet revolution" in which "increasing numbers of baby boomers who left the fold years ago are turning religious again . . . many are traveling from church to church or faith to faith, sampling creeds, shopping for a custom-made God."

Sometimes the shopping is very earnest, and in the sampling of the mind, we forget the wisdom of the heart. My first and favorite teacher, my mother, often had cause to remind her occasionally solemn daughter that "angels fly because they take themselves lightly." We heap weight on our souls, and between the expectations we place on ourselves and those imposed by others, life grows heavy. It is time we began to take ourselves a little more lightly and take God and service to others a little more seriously.

What we lack is a quiet center. Perspective. Balance. A sense of ourselves and of what really matters. A recognition of what is ultimately important, so that we are not overwhelmed by our daily distractions. There is nothing that we need more today than to have disproportion restored to proportion. The most prodigious variety of activities can coexist with harmony and a sense of order when there is an unambiguous center to our lives. The great altarpieces of the Flemish painters contain just such a prodigious variety of detail, and yet their central focus is unmistakable. There they all are, the shepherds and the angels, the kings and the philosophers, the fools and the burghers, the maidens and the clerics, with every feature, even the most insignificant, painstakingly executed—but in no way detracting from the central focus, the Lamb of God. It's when the variety of our lives lacks such a center that we get lost in trivialities and try to make fragments—our careers, our projects, our social status—stand for the whole.

We can't carry the weight of our lives without a spiritual center. It's impossible. And it was never meant to be possible. Man was not designed to pursue happiness without reference to the needs of his spirit. "A man who bows down to nothing," Dostoyevsky wrote in *The Possessed*, "can never bear the burden of himself." If we want to fly with the angels, we have to lighten the load.

There's a rhythm to practicing spirituality, like the rhythm of breathing in and out. I recognized the rhythm one afternoon when I was sixteen. I was sitting with others at the University of Shantaniketan outside Calcutta. We had come from all parts of the world to study the wisdom of the ages. We had taken in lectures and engaged in long conversations. But now the power of silence was making itself felt. Noise was all around me, from the quiet banter of friends to the fluttering leaves of the tree that shaded us; but I was being enveloped, as if in a bubble or cocoon of absolute silence. I felt reconnected. It was as if I knew, for the first time—only to forget and re-remember many times since—that God was both within me and all around me. When I left the university grounds to explore the world outside, the road was bright with mid-morning sunshine and the air was gorged with dust. I walked through sweet aromas and foul stenches, among snarling beggars and whispering holy men. I felt connected to it all.

The rhythm of that day—inward to the depths of soul, then outward to the noisy streets, seeking truth in the words of others, then listening to the wisdom of one's soul—is the pattern of spiritual practice that I feel most at home with. In the ordinary rhythm of our lives, it is this balance between soul and the world, between moving in and stepping out that so many religious practices strive for. We come to understand that we are not only made in God's image, but that we are made to image God—to reflect His freedom, joy, compassion and peace in our lives.

Yet, talk of soul and service—the quest for God and the search for meaning—must not become a new weight under which we collapse. "Angels fly because they take themselves lightly," I hear myself saying now to my own daughters as they pile onto our bed and nestle between Michael and me, sometimes for roughhousing and cuddles and at other times for a free-floating round of prayers in which each of us makes up a personal prayer. Christina sometimes sings her prayers, putting wings on her words. And then it's Mommy's turn and Daddy's turn and Isabella's turn, who normally just says "Amen" to everything. Those who think of prayer as something solemn and somber might have a much lighter step on their spiritual journeys if they listened to the prayers of children who find delight in talking to God.

· · ·

139

Mystery is at the heart of our religious quest. The completely rational man and the crime novelist both see mystery as something to be solved, not something to be entered into and explored. Embracing mystery means accepting that we see through a glass darkly, instead of assuming that if we were really clever, we would be able to eliminate it altogether from our lives. At the start of my own spiritual search, I went looking for God in books, in retreats and seminars, in trips to distant lands—all attempts to solve the mystery. And every time I returned home, I heard God calling from within myself. He had made every journey with me.

"Falsehood is never so false as when it is very nearly true," wrote Chesterton. When we take hold of true religion, we seize a thread of grace. But the agony of religion gone wrong—from children's blood flowing in a misbegotten crusade to the buzz of flies over Jim Jones's jungle morgue—shows the power of souls deceiving and deceived. Religion can be the fire that warms our spirits against the deadly cold of a secular world; but if perverted, it can become a holocaust sweeping over us and our sleeping children. It can be the cooling drink in the arid desert of our wanderings; or, adulterated by man, it can be turned into a deadly barrel of artificially sweetened death. In the name of God people can devote themselves to healing their community or stockpiling arms against it, awaiting Armageddon.

Nothing warns of this danger more surely than religious leaders who place themselves between God and the rest of humanity, arrogating to themselves the personal relationship with the divine. *Corruptio Optimi Pessima:* "The corruption of the best is the worst." No wonder Christ reserved his hottest fury for the false champions of religious authority and the scholars of dead orthodoxy: "Woe unto you . . . hypocrites! for ye are like unto whited sepulchres, which indeed appear beautiful outward, but are within full of dead men's bones, and of all uncleanness."

The Fourth Instinct continually urges us to move toward the divine, to immerse ourselves in soul and service. The more we listen to it, the more spiritually sensitive we become, and the more able we are to distinguish that thread of religion which leads to God from those false strands that take us into the wilderness. Religious traditions that have become calcified, dead orthodoxies, clannishness that turns a common crusade for spiritual renewal into petty squabbles over shared turf—these are all dead ends in our spiritual journey.

I have always laughed, and winced, when I remember the Yiddish story about the man stranded alone thirty years on an island. His rescuers noticed he had built two temples and asked why he needed two, since he was the only person there. "Simple," said the castaway. "One is the temple I go to, and one is the temple I don't."

When religion becomes reduced to an outward observation of rules and ceremonies and an intolerance toward the beliefs of others, we are mistaking the oyster for the pearl. The oyster is certainly valuable, but it is of infinitely greater value when it promotes the growth of the pearl. And like the sand that seeds the pearl, doubt can be a part of that process, the gentle prodding that will not let faith atrophy. As Tennyson put it in "In Memoriam," "There lives more faith in honest doubt, believe me, than in half the creeds."

> *He fought his doubts and gathered strength;*
> *He would not make his judgment blind;*
> *He faced the specters of the mind,*
> *And laid them: thus he came at length*
> *To find a stronger faith his own.*

There is a danger lurking in all threads through the labyrinth, the same danger lurking in the thread of religion. It is not that we might lose the thread. Indeed, most of us will more than likely lose the thread of our spiritual purpose more than once before we finally grasp it firmly and follow it home. The danger is something subtler and more insidious. It is what happens when we mistake the thread for where it is taking us, the map for the destination, the finger pointing to the moon for the moon itself, the means for the end.

"Those who make religion their god," wrote the theologian Thomas Erskine, "will not have God for their religion." And this happens when we stop using the thread as our guide, gather it up and wrap it around ourselves, wearing it as a badge of exclusive honor. Then the thread that pulls man most immediately to God becomes the one that holds him most ir-

141

revocably back. Religion "woven fine, clothing for the soul divine," becomes less a thread than a noose.

The thread of religion leads us to a relationship with God. But when the emphasis is on "our group" or "our faith," we are attempting to possess God rather than enter into a relationship with Him. And, as in other relationships, nothing shuts off communication with our own souls or those of others more surely than the impulse to possess.

But when we follow the thread of religion to its destination, we turn faith into the inner knowing that brings peace and purpose to our lives. We cannot reason our way back to the roots of religion. We cannot trap God in stale dogmas or narrow creeds. Our purpose is to make religion a continuous living experience, to lead us toward a resurrection not of the dead but of the living who are dead to their own truth. Then religion becomes a thread that can both link us to the past and guide us to our future.

8

To Be Knit Together: Community

> Our problem is not with the haters of
> the world who have nothing within.
> Our problem is with the lovers of the
> world who have something within and
> never let it come out.
> —Reverend Cecil L. Murray of
> First AME Church

We were gathered in the Junior Common Room, all gradu-
ating Girtonians—vintage 1969. Miss Duke, senior tutor, classical scholar, and resident perfectionist, was inspecting us to
make sure that we were each up to the vineyard's specifications
before being allowed to proceed to the Senate House, kneel in
front of the vice-chancellor, and be solemnly proclaimed a B.A.
Cantab. It looked as though we measured up: all of us in plain
black dresses with long sleeves ("of such a length that your
elbows are well covered when your arms are outstretched in
front of you"), white cuffs and collars, black shoes ("sandals
are not permitted"), and hired black gowns with furry white
hoods. I longed for a touch of loud, vulgar orange. I smiled.
Miss Duke half smiled.

"Your nails are painted red."

"Yes?"

"You cannot, of course, receive your degree with painted nails."

Of course? Of course.

"We must get hold of some nail varnish remover very quickly."

I wondered if Matron kept some in her special little cupboard in the sick bay. What, Matron a closet nail varnisher? No, not possible.

"Do you have your family with you?"

Did I have my family with me! While a member of my family was dispatched in search of polish remover, I thought that a Greek scholar and lover of modern Greece like Miss Duke should have known that it was only through extraordinary good luck that I didn't have my entire Greek village— Athens—with me.

Cambridge was a precious community for me. There was a sense of belonging that went beyond classes and tutorials that still lingers, sometimes even finding expression in the mock rivalry with "the other place"—Oxford. But the Greek community in which I was raised lingers in a way that is all-encompassing. It's in my cells, in my intuitive responses, in my deepest memories: the smells on Easter and summer holiday mornings, a delicious concoction of bread fresh from the oven and laundry fresh from the tubs scrubbed clean with home-made soap; sounds coming through our windows of children at play, shoppers in the street markets haggling over prices, women laughing over clotheslines. When I ventured onto the streets of our neighborhood, I was never far from home because I had learned from my earliest experiences that every home was open to me, and any woman on the block would mother me as surely as her own child—with a Band-Aid, a spinach pie, a scolding or a hug.

The call to community is a call to belonging, to being a part of something larger than ourselves, to making of our lives the latest chapter in the family's story. We want not only to know who we are, but of whom we are a part. These impulses, driven by our Fourth Instinct, weave the thread of community with which we connect with others and reconnect with ourselves.

. . .

Being raised in Athens, the City of the Gods, I was infused with that sense of community. Some of my earliest memories are of casual conversations with my father who drew lessons from Greek history as naturally as he drew breath, and spoke easily of our place in the legacy of the gods themselves. The Golden Age of Greece was taught to me not as ancient history, as my children will learn it in school, but as my personal roots and source of identity. Zeus and Athena, Plato and Socrates, the taste of stuffed grape leaves, the sound of my little sister being bathed in a tub on our terrace, the smell of incense and the Greek Orthodox chants—all merged together into a single story which offered a single identity. I knew myself as part of that timeless community. In the home of my childhood, there was no division between community and spirituality, history and current events, public concerns and private issues.

Philosophers and poets, wise men and dreamers—all have pursued the ideal of community. Plato came out of the caves with stories of blind kings who could see justice. Athens was built as a tribute to a goddess whose life was intertwined with the city's. Rome was proudest not of its remarkable feats of engineering, but of its laws that established justice and order. Israel traces its roots to the day God found a wandering clan and promised its childless patriarch children more numerous than the stars. Saint John had a vision of a New Jerusalem with gleaming alabaster and streets of gold, a vision the Pilgrims brought to New England, infusing American history with the sense of being a "chosen nation."

When I boarded a Pan American flight fourteen years ago from London to New York, perhaps I, too, was pursuing an ideal. England had given me an education, a career and a community of fellow journalists and authors. Still, there was a homesickness I couldn't quite express yet couldn't ignore. So I did something at once radical and traditional: I emigrated to America. I have always loved the fact that I was able to choose not just a new homeland but also a set of values, ideals, hopes and dreams that had drawn millions before me. Another writer who hailed from abroad captured the essence of this miracle. "America," wrote Luigi Barzini, "is alarmingly optimistic, compassionate, incredibly generous. It was a *spiri-*

tual wind that drove Americans irresistibly ahead from the beginning." And it is this spiritual wind that informs all true community.

The old image of America as a "melting pot" of cultures has fallen into disfavor recently. And while dismissing this ideal, many have also abandoned another dream: one nation, under God, made up of people whose primary sense of identity is not derived from the racial or ethnic traditions that distinguish us but from the transcendent spiritual values that unite us. Our diversity can make us a stronger, more vital, more enduring national community—as it can sometimes make a stronger family. My own family has certainly been strengthened by the merging of two very different traditions: my husband's which treasures solitude, and mine which includes the tribal chaos I have brought to our home in the form of live-in relatives and a deluge of friends who stay for weeks at a time.

In our calls for multiculturalism, however, instead of emphasizing the community strengths brought by diversity, we are promoting what divides us rather than what unites us. The legacy of "one nation under God" has been shattered into a secular set of competing claims. The "story" of America as a land of freedom and justice for all has been reduced to a tale of our divisions into classes and groups. To speak boldly of America as a proud nation, a strong moral force, a country of compassion and opportunity, is to invite outrage from those who cannot see in the ideals of our forefathers the only hope for our children. Speeches evoking such old-fashioned values are ridiculed for being as sentimental and unrealistic as a Norman Rockwell painting. Yet beyond the chaos and clamor, there is a call not to turn back the clock but to bring the rhythm of timeless values into our lives and our communities. It is the call of our Fourth Instinct.

Communities need absolutes, ideals of truth, transcendent sources of authority which are unchanged and unchangeable. In religious communities, the ideals are holy writings; in national communities, these truths are held to be "self-evident," captured first in declarations and eventually codified into law. Without the world of absolutes, we can neither create communities nor sustain them. When absolutes cease to exist, so do communities. As Ted Koppel put it in a commencement address: "What Moses brought down from Mount Sinai were not the Ten Suggestions."

The Founding Fathers grounded America in spiritual absolutes. The Declaration of Independence hinges upon the premise that "all men are created equal," which Lincoln called "the father of all moral principle." It is a truth self-evident only in terms of our spiritual heritage. Men are not self-evidently equal in talent, or intelligence, or physical appearance or by any other first-, second- or third-instinct criteria. They are equal by a standard perceived only by the Fourth, our instinctive grasp of the absolute. This does not mean that America was founded as a "religious nation." The Founding Fathers were not political men engaged in a spiritual enterprise. They were deeply spiritual men engaged in a political enterprise. They understood the connection between statecraft and soulcraft, and their purpose in separating church and state was not to rid society of religious influence, but to deny church and state alike the instruments of repression. Loyalty to the state, the Founding Fathers believed, can be nurtured only if the state is not the object of highest loyalty. In the language of the Fourth Instinct, the first three instincts can find their rightful place in society only if the Fourth is honored—in all its diversity.

The Founding Fathers, to put it more tangibly, would not see tyranny or religious coercion in a crèche or a menorah displayed in a public square. They would be more likely to see in these symbols a public reminder of our private devotion. No less a liberal hero than William O. Douglas, speaking in 1951 for a majority of the Supreme Court, affirmed this: "We are a religious people whose institutions presuppose a Supreme Being."

For our Founding Fathers, belief in a "Supreme Being" was the ordering principle of all human affairs, "indispensable . . . to private and public felicity," as Washington cautioned in his Farewell Address. And this belief, more than anything else, creates community. It is neither utilitarian nor utopian. It is prompted by the Fourth Instinct, not in its mystical but in its everyday manifestations: by giving, sharing, making "common" our blessings and burdens alike.

The call to community is not a hollow protestation of universal brotherhood. It is the call of our Fourth Instinct to make

147

another's pain our own, to expand into our true self through giving. If the second instinct ensures that we grow physically by what we take, the Fourth demands that we grow spiritually by what we give. This is not the cold, abstract giving to humanity in general and to no human being in particular. It is concrete, intimate, tangible. "To feel the intimacy of brothers," wrote Pablo Neruda, "is a marvelous thing in life. To feel the love of people whom we love is a fire that feeds our life. But to feel the affection that comes from those whom we do not know, from those unknown to us, who are watching over our sleep and solitude, over our dangers and our weaknesses—that is something still greater and more beautiful because it widens out the boundaries of our being, and unites all living things."

And those giving, even more than those receiving, tap into pools of connectedness fed by streams of grace—an experience that cannot be fathomed from the shore but only when we enter this cycle of giving and receiving. The nourishment, as it does in all sacraments, flows in both directions.

We know when we have entered the realm of the Fourth Instinct because its native language is that of paradox. In giving we receive, in serving we find our strength, in reaching out we are lifted up. We have stepped through the Fourth Instinct's looking glass into a place where the rules of survival are suspended so that we may truly live, and where experience contradicts the conventional wisdom of the first three instincts.

A few months ago I caught a glimpse of life through that looking glass when I watched a fellow volunteer at a shelter give a new pair of shoes to a homeless child. In her five or six years of life, the little girl had never even imagined a pair of *new* shoes. And in her forty years of privilege, the woman had never imagined anything less. They were each a little frightened of the other. Tentatively, the little girl took the shoes and slipped her feet into them, staring down in disbelief. When she looked up, all she could do was smile. The woman was equally quiet. She smiled—and she cried. And I, the unseen witness beyond the looking glass, wondered: Was the woman helping the child, or the child helping the woman?

Nicki Blackstone described herself and her husband David as "typical pioneer-stock farm people. We don't have a fancy lifestyle. We're not what you would call the beautiful people."

But because of her volunteer work through her church ministry, she said her life was "the happiest, most fulfilling, exciting that I ever dreamed of. . . . I am not on staff in a ministry. I am a farm wife . . . with three boys (ages eight, five, three) and a staggering workload. . . . We work eighteen hours every day, and we give and give and give and are happy, successful, and healthy. We live on a constant natural high. Our happiness and health are directly related to our giving and doing for others. Euphoria is a strong word," she added, "but it is an appropriate word." When she has helped someone, "a spiritual, emotional thing is taking place," she said.

This is the Fourth Instinct expressed in the everyday life and action of man—not remote, not mystic, not limited to the higher flights of religion or art. We discover soul in that which is intimate, close, familiar, engaged. In the political arena, names are attached to national efforts which bank on the Fourth Instinct's readiness to give: Kennedy's Peace Corps, Reagan's Volunteerism, Bush's Thousand Points of Light. No nation rivals America in terms of giving and volunteering— that very American urge to take matters small and large into our own hands, to get things done and meet needs unmet. We are enthralled by the Statue of Liberty and drawn to its ideal: "Give me your tired, your poor . . ."

New breath is being blown into this old ideal. Philanthropy has always been admired in this nation. But today we see that charity is more than a private means by which to solve public problems. By putting giving at the heart of our lives and service at the heart of our public policy, we reconnect ourselves with our forgotten instinct, with the spiritual and most neglected aspect of our nature that makes another's problems our own, that recognizes we cannot love God and ignore his children.

Tina Sipula, who works at a Catholic Worker hospitality home in Bloomington, Illinois, had no theories as to why the numbers of homeless were growing. But she had a solution. "If every church, synagogue or mosque in America had a house of hospitality, we could begin to eliminate welfare." Her belief emanates not from some partisan ideology or motive, but from a confidence born of daily experience that when the human spirit is awakened, there is no problem too intractable to solve. Catholic Worker's co-founder, Dorothy Day, has written of the way to light that inner fire: "To bring about a revolution of the heart, a revolution which has a start with each one of us. When we begin to take the lowest place, to wash the feet of others, to love our brothers and sisters with that burning love, that passion, which led to the cross, then we can truly say, 'Now I have begun.' "

Common endeavor leads to common identity: a shared narrative in which we each play a part, a common story weaving history, destiny and community. Shared religious beliefs have long provided a context for community identity. I have been at friends' houses during many a Passover meal and have always been drawn to the extraordinary community-building force of the Passover litanies. If you wish to understand what it means to be Jewish, to live as a modern child in an ancient community, listen to the Passover litany and see the child, his face lit by candlelight, asking his father the Passover questions. "Why on this night do we eat only unleavened bread?" asks the child. And the father responds: *"Avadim hayinu . . .* We were slaves in the land of Egypt." "Why on this night do we eat bitter herbs?" And again, *"Avadim hayinu . . .* We eat bitter herbs because the Egyptians made bitter the lives of our forefathers." Over and over the child asks the meaning of the litany, and with each answer, he both retraces and extends the long thread of community, as over and over the parent explains not just who our ancestors were but *who we are.* This is community in formation, a child learning an identity based on the reality of divine absolutes and his own participation in a continuing story, a spiritual drama with no bit players.

Community is less about what was brought down from a mountain chiseled in stone than what is captured in the heart of a living child who understands that his identity is found in a timeless community of which he is part. It is the nature of our Fourth Instinct to long for a timeless perspective. And community exists both within time and outside it, both within history and within myth.

In Third World nations, modern anthropologists have often discovered that what most defined a given tribe was not biological ties but participation in a common story. Once children of enemies captured in tribal battles were initiated into the unfolding story of the tribe—a narrative of gods and grandparents reminiscent of Athens itself—they were soon enough, and despite their biological differences, sons and daughters of the community. Wherever they find another who knows the story, they have found a brother or sister. Even in the modern, steaming cities of these Third World nations, bushmen who have come for work will find a spiritual home simply by repeating together the common story of their tribe.

We do not outgrow our need for a common story in our modern communities. Yet our search for the story that threads us all together is too often diverted by the daily barrage of journalistic detail—the "current events" of our public and private lives that may inform and entertain, but fail to satisfy our Fourth Instinct's longing for a spiritual context that brings meaning to our lives and frames our understanding. Our Fourth Instinct reminds us of a common history and a common destiny, of a unity which transcends our differences. It encourages us to seek authority rooted in a spiritual dimension.

The ideal of community was not conceived in the Magna Carta, the Declaration of Independence or the Bill of Rights; the ideal came from God and our covenant with Him. The latest documentations of this ideal merely echo the original source. The intent of our nation's founders—to prevent one religion from lording it over others, and to prohibit tyrannies of all kinds—was used by secularists to scrub the merest trace of belief from our communal life. When separation of church and state has been reduced to separation of all that is civil from all that is spiritual, civility and spirituality languish in the same grave.

If I speak of creating a community centered on God's love, I know I run the risk of being dismissed as quaint and culturally irrelevant. Why is religious devotion so trivialized in our culture? For years I blamed the heirs of the Enlightenment, who taught that only the intellect could be trusted. Ideas are sound, beliefs are dangerous; scientists speak truth, religious people talk nonsense. Like the cynic who knows the cost of everything and the value of nothing, modern man has been disconnected from all absolutes. But there's more to the story.

There is something about our modern culture that fears spirituality, and I suspect it is this: spirituality, like grace, is beyond our control. It is more subversive than any ideology or revolutionary cabal. It cannot be ruled by our will. To admit that there is God—not as some abstract principle but as a living personal Force—is to admit that our intellect is not the final source of authority. Deep down in every man, Arthur Koestler wrote, is a commissar yearning to be saluted. But even deeper than that is the part of us that is most attentive to the voice of the soul.

In the battle between spirit and the state for man's ultimate allegiance, the state has in the last few years clearly been winning. Indeed, even in our search for meaning, it is expected to lead the search party. Ohio State University President E. Gordon Gee did not exaggerate when he said, "We are in the midst of a third American Revolution. The first was waged to determine if we would become a nation. The second, the War Between the States, was fought to determine if we would remain one nation. And the third, our current revolution, must be fought to determine if we have the courage, the spirit, and the will to sustain our national character." And what did he believe was required if we were to succeed in this battle? "Nothing is more important to our future than building community."

The Fourth Instinct's call to community is not an invitation to utopia. We are not hounded to the shores of Walden Pond, needing to escape humanity in order to love it. Unlike the hippie havens of the 1960s, true community is not a withdrawal from the world for the sake of mountain-peak experiences. The Fourth Instinct urges us to engage the world directly and uncompromisingly, not to beat a retreat but to begin a reformation.

The woman who faithfully leaves her home each Tuesday to serve Meals on Wheels to those who cannot leave theirs, the eight-year-old who translates his passion for peanut butter into a school-wide drive to bring peanut butter to the homeless, the grieving widower who spends his mornings reading to children in an understaffed child care center—all are proof that the Fourth Instinct's call to community is being answered all around us.

When the need for true community is unfulfilled, pseudo-communities emerge, corrupt answers to an authentic call. The appeal of some destructive cults, like Jonestown, may be less the religion they offer than the community: the seduction of a place to belong, a sense of purpose and participation in a higher calling. The recent rise of fascism among European youths, with their British and American "skinhead" counterparts, offers another example of a warped response to our need for community. Rootless and alienated youth bond together in a common hatred, forging a new family ring. Like the Nazi creed they admire, they find their fellowship in bashing anyone who is "different" from them and unable to defend himself: a gay man, an African-American, a child of Haitian refugees whose only sin was birth.

Where the urge to find community, to belong, is unfulfilled, history teaches us that the emptiness that's left can be filled by enormous evil. Perverted responses to an aching longing for community have dominated our century. To be blond, blue-eyed and German was to be a member of a chosen community destined to rule the world. Communism could not quench the human craving for what Dostoyevsky called a community of worship and a universal unity. But it definitely appealed to it. Communism's promise of a perfect community through state action may be dead and Marx's promise that socialism could be the "functional equivalent of religion" may have grown as thin as Oliver's gruel, but we are still living in a spiritual orphanage where "the demon inherent in every political party," as C. S. Lewis put it, "is at all times ready enough to disguise himself as the Holy Ghost."

No government can legislate community. Government can no more save us from ourselves and mold us into a community of compassion than it can rescue our failing marriages or enforce affection within unhappy homes. At the core, we are dealing with a moral issue. Government can make good laws but it can't make men good, and without good men we cannot have a good society. When we follow the thread of community, we begin to respond to the cries of humanity with the same urgency that we bring to the cries of our newborn in the middle of the night. And it is out of our response to each other's suffering and each other's joy that we weave the delicate web of community.

When spiritual belief crumbles, community dissolves. Absolutes become suggestions. Authorities are viewed as hindrances. And the beliefs and ideas which once bound us together unravel in bloody confrontations of tribe against tribe, gang against gang. Race and gender, nationality and religion become the weapons we stockpile to wage war against each other. In the end, without faith, there is nothing and no one to whom appeal can be made. Without absolutes, even social protest becomes hollow. "If anyone doubts this," said Chesterton, "try to think blasphemous thoughts about Thor." We live in a nation under God, and a renaissance of community will require an acknowledgment of that fact. And it will be spearheaded not by government, but "by the better angels of our nature."

A child's identity and, ultimately, a citizen's self-concept are drawn from the story of which they are a part. If the story of my life begins with an immigrant grandfather who pulled himself up by his proverbial bootstraps, I am likely to see myself as the rightful heir in a community of opportunity. If the story of my life is littered with welfare checks and crack pipes, I am likely to see myself as the latest victim in a community of despair. And if there is no living national story, then there will be no national community.

In one of her last articles, Margaret Mead spoke urgently of the need for American children to hear the stories which would form their character. She remembered that a sense of community had been instilled in America "in small towns and neighborhoods" where teachers had "taught two generations of children and mellowed in the process, there to remind the children that their parents had once been young, played hookey, and passed forbidden notes in school." In neighborhoods where children had lost their parents, grandparents and neighbors told the stories that spun the web of community. She was describing my childhood in another country, the place and the people who gave me an experience of community that was full and tangible and from which I still draw strength.

9

Opening the Doors of Perception: Art

> This life, gentlemen, is much too short
> for our souls.
>
> —Goethe

I never suggested that Picasso should be drawn and quartered—although, if he weren't the star in the show, he might have enjoyed the sport of it. Here was a man who savored the sexual pleasure of regularly abusing one mistress, who beat another until she was senseless, who relished holding a lighted cigarette to the cheek of a third, and who left in his wake a series of breakdowns and suicides. A little blood-sport might have nicely sated his appetite for an afternoon.

What I suggested in my book on Picasso was that, although a great genius, he was not a great man. Based on the facts of his life, this seemed a reasonable conclusion. He undoubtedly was the greatest visual reporter of the twentieth century, a master at portraying in gritty detail modern man's degradation. From the pit of spiritual decay, awash in torture and death, he filed regular reports on canvas, showing in remnant body parts and faces distorted with pain all the darkness of our world. First-rate journalism, I said. But not—and here was where I gored the ox of his champions—the greatest of art.

One reviewer urged his readers not to see disintegration in Picasso's art. "The modern artist has no other world to draw on," he explained. A few others rushed forward to defend Picasso's character, but their task was large and their number small. The most virulent and steady attacks came from those who saw it as their duty to tell others what is art and what is not. By what conceivable right had I, an amateur in their exalted field, questioned their imperious judgment? The theme of the most scathing attacks was, basically, a wounded yelp: "How *dare* you?"

Within six months, more words had been written about my book than were in the book. Soon, the unabated hysteria of the indignant art experts became a story in itself. Paul Johnson did a column for *The Wall Street Journal* reviewing my reviewers. He surveyed the howling rage my book had inspired and observed that "a lot of powerful and highly vocal people have much to lose if their hero falls from grace." He asked by what standards they were employing "techniques of denigration and personal abuse alien to quality journalism" and then he answered his first question with another: "Can their rage be inspired by fear?"

The answer, plainly, was yes. But it was not just the fear that results from the investment of money, prestige and reputations in the propagation of a cultural idol. Worse was the fear that it is becoming increasingly hard to satisfy on a purely aesthetic diet the spiritual instinct in us that hungers for a larger meaning. With an almost pathetic desperation, our culture has overestimated the significance of everything "artistic," including Andy Warhol's cookie jars, with ever-diminishing
• emotional returns. Art was supposed to "redeem" us, and the artist was a stand-in for God the Redeemer. This time has passed. Aestheticism—the notion that all of existence can be sanctified as an aesthetic phenomenon—is exhausted, even though its champions still dominate the art world.

It will be another decade or so before Christina and Isabella may have any interest in the controversy their mother stirred sometime long ago. But even though that little skirmish will have faded, the battle itself never centered on a single book or a few homicidal reviews. The struggle continues against the belief that anything declared "art" is automatically insulated from moral judgment and spiritual perspective. This is dangerous stuff concocted in a culture that has forgotten that it is ultimately the connection between the aesthetic and the spiritual that gives art its dignity, its meaning and its power.

It is not a connection preached by the artist, but a connection experienced within ourselves when art pierces through the crusts of our everyday preoccupations and sparks the memory of who we are. The modern pilgrims lining up, sometimes for hours, outside museums, galleries and symphony halls are driven by more than the quest for an aesthetic experience. Consciously or unconsciously we seek the harmony that reconciles the inner with the outer man, the soul with the world. Art, whether carved into cave walls or cascading down the hallways of opera houses, is a bridge between the light we carry in us but may have never seen and the darkness we know all too well.

I was in San Diego in June 1993 to give a lecture on the occasion of the opening of William Paley's collection, which was on loan at the San Diego Museum of Art. I had arrived only moments before the festivities were scheduled to begin and I was being given a quick tour of the collection. Among the magnificent works on display, what caught my eye and held my attention was a small—almost tiny—oil of strawberries by Renoir. The curator, who wanted me to see the entire collection, was tugging me down the line and into the next room. But I was still looking back at that miniature miracle of creation. If art's true purpose is to open the doors of perception, then Renoir spoke to me "from soul to soul," revealing something transcendent even in the common strawberry.

Oils on canvas represent only one of art's voices. Music, sculpture, photography, cinema, architecture, literature, drama, poetry, dance—each can become a voice through which soul speaks to soul. Even an ancient art-form, rhetoric, becomes a thread of art through the labyrinth when it awakens the truth that slumbers within us. When Socrates in the *Apology* addressed his accusers for the last time—"Now it is time that we were going, I to die and you to live; but which of us

157

has the happier prospect is unknown to anyone but God"—
soul spoke to soul, and still does. When John F. Kennedy stood
within a rifle-shot of the Berlin Wall and declared, on behalf of
all who treasure freedom, *"Ich bin ein Berliner,"* soul spoke to
soul, and still does. When Martin Luther King, Jr., cried out,
"I have a dream," he crossed every barrier in a divided nation,
replacing angry profanities with soaring hopes as soul spoke
to soul, and still does.

Especially in America, where the arts have too often been
considered a luxury of the elite, we need to recognize art beyond the walls of museums and concert halls. I have been
transported by Beethoven's Fifth Symphony, and I have felt
my soul stir as I listened to a mournful gospel song. When first
I saw Nureyev leap from the ballet stage and, as if suspended
by God Himself, hang midway between heaven and earth, it
was art that took away my breath. I have sometimes wondered
if it was also art when Michael Jordan pirouetted toward the
basket in moves of strength and grace, or when Cecil Fielder
performs the miracle of hand-eye coordination required to produce a home run. There is something timeless in the beauty of
such sport, something awe-inspiring, that is also soul speaking
to soul. When we are absorbed not only in the score but in the
beauty of motion that was displayed in the first Olympics all
those centuries ago, our Fourth Instinct may have been tapped
by sport.

Widening the boundaries within which we recognize art
does not mean lowering the standards. While traveling the
lecture circuit, staying in hotels night after night, I usually find
myself complaining about art-as-decoration—"hotel-room
art"—by my third speech. "I have a collection of chiffon scarves
I carry with me," I once told an audience. "They add no
weight to the luggage, take up no space, and you can drape
them over the art in your hotel room before it depresses your
spirit."

At nearly the other extreme from hotel-room decoration is
work etched in the acid of rage. From the angry graffiti on
subway walls to the cries for freedom splashed on posters
borne through Tiananmen Square, unadorned expressions of
rage may be genuine, justified and powerful. But that does not
mean they are art. Paint-filled condoms thrown against bill-
boards may leave a "message" of some kind, but not every

message is art. George Halliday's tape of the Rodney King beating is not art even though it was dubbed "art" by the Whitney Biennial.

Rage, whether exploded on a canvas or a sheet of paper, in a rap chant or an underground film, is just rage even if it's called art. Some self-labeled artists are, in fact, suffering a prolonged adolescence, while the expressions of their rage have been elevated from an adolescent stage of rebellion to art that is encouraged and rewarded by our culture. At the moment, art that deals with rage, violence, disgust and brutality rises to the top. The message from the art world is clear: life is rotten, human beings are rotten, love is rotten, society is rotten. Instead of helping us recognize truth, art is reduced—and this at its most elegant—to a Beckettian monologue by a disembodied mouth. "I have nothing to say," explained Beckett, who once remarked that he would like to see *Waiting for Godot* play to empty houses, "but I can only say to what extent I have nothing to say."

There is plenty of darkness in Shakespeare's *Tempest* and Mozart's *Magic Flute*, but in the end it is overcome by love; there is chaos and ugliness but a new order of harmony and beauty evolves out of them; there is evil, but it is cast out by good. And there is plenty of darkness in the drawings of children trapped in the violence and the poverty of the inner city. I have a set of such drawings, and among them there is one that has become a thread of art for me. It is no less dark than any of the others; but through the darkness it is clear that this child has seen something beyond, and by seeing it, has given the rest of us access to that vision. In the same way, a collection of butterfly drawings, done by a child caged in a concentration camp, far from diminishing the horror, makes it starker and more horrible when set against the glimpse of another reality.

Art has, of course, long been accepted as a thread by which those who are emotionally distressed can find an inner peace. In the Old Testament we first meet David not in the story of his slingshot encounter with Goliath but in his role as music therapist. King Saul, suffering "an evil spirit" which goads him to fits of distemper, is counseled by his wise men that music could calm his soul. A servant remembers a shepherd boy with an uncanny gift for playing the harp, and when next the king falls into a rage, David is taken from his sheep and hurried, with his harp, to the palace.

Among those who have been disabled through injury or illness, many have found healing through art. Jack Hofsiss, who after winning a Tony award for *The Elephant Man* was left paralyzed from the chest down in a swimming pool accident, explained how life-restoring it was to get involved in the arts again: "When you work in the arts, the only handicap that counts is in your imagination and your dreams. We do what we can to help people with physical handicaps realize their dreams. . . . The arts have fed my soul in a very important way."

In studying the work of abused children, I've witnessed the power of art as spiritual therapy. A boy who had been repeatedly brutalized since infancy would paint only in dark blues and blacks, the colors of bruises that had covered his body and his life. After two years of love and safety, he began to reach for greens and yellows. A most moving moment, for me, was the Saturday morning this child gave me a finger painting of God. It was done in orange and red, "like the sunshine," he said.

I remember at Covent Garden in London a performance of *The Marriage of Figaro* under a guest conductor from Europe. I was sitting with a group of friends that included a brilliant English conductor when, very early into the performance, we realized that this would be a painful affair—especially for him. According to legend, the night *The Marriage of Figaro* was first performed, Count Zinzendorf went home to record in his diary, "The opera bored me." Zinzendorf would not have been bored this evening; he would have been, depending on his tolerance, irritated or incensed. When the string section was attentive to the guest conductor's unfamiliar rhythm, the brass was not. Soloists bolted off in their own directions, once taking a good share of the chorus—never, unfortunately, the whole lot—with them. Mercifully, it finally ended. And our conductor friend was the first on his feet, applauding loudly and long with what certainly appeared to be genuine appreciation.

As he applauded, a regular patron seated behind us leaned

forward and hollered, "What a terrible performance!" Over his shoulder, applauding even more enthusiastically, our friend shouted back, "What a great work!" When we are carried from one reality to another, it is a quantum jump. And we know we are in the presence of great art even when the conductor and the orchestra make mincemeat of the score.

It is a matter of recognition. The artist recognizes a timeless truth and, taking hold of it in his work, bears it over to the rest of us. There is a story in the Midrash that describes God, angry at Abraham, scolding him: "If it wasn't for Me, you wouldn't exist." "That's true, Lord," responded Abraham, "and do not think me ungrateful. But if it weren't for me, You wouldn't be known."

Artists are messengers between this world and the divine, which is why Goethe called art a sister of religion. We see the drama played out onstage as a smaller reflection of the divine drama. We read the plot of the novel as a shadow of the great battle of good and evil, fall and redemption. When the curtain is drawn between man and the divine, the true power of art is lost. "After the death of Henry James a disaster overtook the English novel," Graham Greene wrote, "for with the death of James the religious sense was lost to the English novel, and with the religious sense went the sense of the importance of the human act. . . ." Greene feared the demise not of religion but of art—because great art assumes the reality "of another world against which the actions of the characters are thrown into relief."

Through the Fourth Instinct the artist glimpses that world, a sound unheard, a sight unseen by others; on the strength of that glimpse, he writes, he paints, he composes, he choreographs. He is the conduit through which the divine is poured, the channel through which spirit flows. What we finally see from the audience, hear from the balcony, read from the page is the artist's most faithful rendering of his own vision. What is "borne over" to us faithfully becomes art—a penetration into the mystery of the world that transforms our everyday experience: "After all," wrote Walt Whitman, "the great lesson is that no special natural sight—not Alps, Niagara, Yosemite or anything else—is more grand or more beautiful than the ordinary sunrise and sunset, earth and sky, the common trees and grass." Art can awaken this certain vision in the soul

161

that removes the vagueness and dullness of habitual perceptions.

The primary requisite of art is that it move us. Different art
will move different people, but the greatest of art has spoken
through the centuries from soul to soul—a timeless and universal message. Art is a thread through the labyrinth because,
in the final analysis, it is, always, a connector. It links God with
man, spirit with spirit. It heals and makes whole by making
connections.

The creative artist who first sets down the vision, the per-
forming artist who takes up that vision and brings it to life,
and the members of the audience when they become active
participants—all are links in the chain of artistic creation. I
remember a performance of *Swan Lake* one winter's night in
New York, only a few years ago. As I left the theater, both I
and the city seemed transformed. The theater curtain had just
gone down, and mine had just been raised. I had never before
—and have never since—seen the city as it was that night:
streetlights twinkling, headlights glowing with warmth, side-
walks sparkling as if littered with the glitter of a dancer's dia-
dem.

I also remember the last time I was at Oberammergau in
Germany for the Passion Play. While the greatest story ever
told was being performed before us, hawkers were working
the aisles to move their merchandise. Wooden crosses were
going to Japanese salesmen who needed something to bring
home to the kids. In a moment of delicious irony, Christ was
onstage using a whip to drive a half-dozen money changers
out of the temple as two dozen vendors worked the audience,
making change for the latest tourist's buy. While Christ knelt
in the Garden of Gethsemane, begging his father to "let this
cup pass from me," Cokes were sold and consumed in almost
every row. And when the play was over, its power had been
undiminished for all the hubbub that had accompanied it.
When Christ cried, "It is finished," nothing of pure art had
been surrendered. Even amid the clamor and the commercial-
ism, I had felt the power of his inexplicable peace.

"But tell me," Herman Hesse's Narcissus asks Goldmund, a
seeker in life's labyrinth, "besides this desperate coming and

going between lust and horror, besides this seesaw between lust for life and sadness of death—have you tried no other road?"

"Oh, yes," comes the reply, "of course I have. I've tried art."

I have known a man who used to creep into his humidity- and temperature-controlled vault in the darkness of night to peer at his precious collection of paintings. He did not dare display his treasures for fear of theft. But he would visit his vault alone and kneel before his beautifully framed idols. I have seen other adoring worshipers venerate art in public. "From the museum orchestra down below," wrote Neville Cardus, a famous Wagnerite, from Bayreuth, "was wafted the incense, the enchanting fumes from the old magician's cauldron. Weak to the point of servitude, I succumbed, or rather relapsed, to faiths supposedly outmoded. . . . I am back in the thrall, actually glorying in the renewal of bondage."

I was at Bayreuth for the celebration of the centenary of Wagner's *Ring,* and I saw examples of that artistic bondage all around me. Unlike any other festival I have ever been to, this was a pilgrimage designed so that you breathed Wagner at every waking and walking moment—with Wagner records, Wagner pictures, Wagner plates and Wagner singers beaming at you from out of every shop window, from among the peaches, and among the face creams, and among the wigs and the sausages, and the baby food.

By three o'clock the magnificently laid-out park that leads up to the *Festspielhaus* was already dotted with dinner-jacketed figures and figurines in ball gowns (and I mean ball gowns), making their way up the hill in plenty of time for the four o'clock performance. The summons into the opera house itself came, of course, not with ordinary bells; as we were milling on the terrace of the theater, trumpeters appeared on the front balcony and played a theme from the first act. They repeated it once, twice, thrice. It was a curiously moving ceremony and by the end we were emotionally ready to enter the temple. I thought the grandiose austerity of the theater made every other opera house seem a mere entertainment pit, and its double proscenium arch, its invisible, sunken orchestra, its steeply raked amphitheater all seemed calculated (and in many ways they were) to transform us from an audience into communicants in a mystery.

There are many in the labyrinth who bow down to art rather than following it as a thread to God. They look for meaning *in* art rather than *through* it. They confuse the revelation of our soul—which, however momentary, overwhelms and glorifies everything it touches—with the circumstances of the revelation. If we have been moved by Wagner, nothing except Wagner will be true and divine for us; and if we felt the stirrings of our soul in front of Rembrandt's self-portraits, we will make a religion of painting and turn Rembrandt into our god. And our self-transcending emotions, unintegrated into life, will be nothing more than euphoric flickers of romantic enthusiasm, destined to atrophy and shrivel away. It is a trap into which millions have fallen.

The trap has by no means always been art. Indeed, it has much more often been a particular creed or dogma. And this is where idolatry and superstition begin. The trap is to take an intermediate stage for the end. And the danger is that, satisfied with the occasional life-giving artistic or religious ecstasy, we will forget that the end we seek is to allow these moments to penetrate our lives and transform them. Beethoven, Shakespeare and Shelley give us access to the highest truths, they raise the curtain of smoke and reveal a new world. But then it is up to us to integrate these insights into our life and make the new world manifest.

"Sacrifice," wrote Hesse, "is no longer a matter of doing specifically sacred things only on particular occasions, but of sacrificing (making sacred) all we do and all we are." Friends of mine who were decorating their New York apartment a few years ago had some bitter fights over art. She was hoping to introduce the sacred into their apartment through Old Masters and French Impressionists; he was hoping to stay within his budget for the project. There was one still life of fruit, done by a great master, that she was particularly intent on getting. Her husband balked and vetoed the purchase. Her response was a slammed door and a night in the guest bedroom. His response was to wake her up to the smell of morning coffee and fresh toast. Resting on a bed tray next to her was a three-dimensional still life: a bowl of fresh fruit. Exquisite still lifes, he was telling her, do not come only in gilded frames—when we learn to recognize the divine in the commonplace.

If an age is revealed most lucidly in its art, then the age that is dying was powerfully revealed in a symbolic moment in the fall of 1989. Thirty-seven Robert Mapplethorpe photographs were sold at auction for almost half a million dollars. Art dealers bid furiously against each other to take home photographs of leather-clad men in sadomasochistic poses. At the height of the controversy over Mapplethorpe's work, the Whitney Museum took a full-page ad in *The New York Times*. "ARE YOU GOING TO LET POLITICS KILL ART?" the ad asked in block type over a Mapplethorpe photograph of a tulip. I personally know of at least a dozen still life photographers, some much more talented than Mapplethorpe, who cannot get a showing in their neighborhood gallery, let alone the Whitney. The Whitney's trustees knew that Mapplethorpe's reputation was not built on tulips. It was his photographs of torture and degradation that had put him on the map, otherwise known as the "cutting edge" of art—what the art world decides is worth exhibiting, reviewing and talking about.

Those who call for censorship are missing the point. The real need is not to censor and suppress but to build a culture in which the art that is encouraged and rewarded is art that may show the darkness, but also gives us a glimpse of the light beyond—of another world of spirit, harmony and truth of which many fashionable artists in the contemporary world seem to know nothing.

George Orwell, forty-five years ago, wrote an essay on Salvador Dali. "Just pronounce the magic word 'art,' and everything is OK," he said. "So long as you can paint well enough to pass the test, all shall be forgiven you." Then he illustrated his point: "The first thing that we demand of a wall is that it shall stand up. If it stands up, it is a good wall, and the question of what purpose it serves is separable from that. And yet even the best wall in the world deserves to be pulled down if it surrounds a concentration camp." And photographs, films, novels or paintings extolling violence and degradation, no matter how brilliantly executed, cannot be made good by being called "art."

I said something to that effect on a Phil Donahue show dealing with the Mapplethorpe controversy, and another guest dismissed my concerns on the grounds that most of Mapplethorpe's violence involved consenting adults. When I asked if he thought the consent of his followers in Jonestown exonerated the Reverend Jim Jones, his response was clear and to the point: "Jim Jones was not an artist." The unstated assumption persists that there is one moral standard for ordinary mortals and another for artists.

The function of every thread through the labyrinth is the same: to lead us to a greater level of spiritual awareness and truth. We are taught to think of art as paint on canvas, notes on a score, words in print, scenes on the stage. But this is not the only stuff of art. Art is also made from dreams and visions —from what is still unspoken and unseen. Sometimes as I watch my children sleep I catch myself not wondering what they will be when they grow up but praying that, whatever they may be, they learn to turn dreams and visions as well as the everyday stuff of life into art.

Nearly every school teaches children something of art: tonal quality and phrasing, structural harmonies and literary analysis. We teach them to mold clay and splash colors, to recite the names of Renaissance painters and the poems of Americans long dead, to identify the composers of works that are perfect strangers to MTV. At this turning point in our culture, maybe we can also begin teaching our children to listen for the voice of God in art, to look for traces of the divine, to know that there is a greater reality from which art calls us and to which art points us, and at the same time to feel the wonder of our everyday existence. The musical delight of a two-year-old's first attempts at singing, the beauty of the window in the neighbor's vine-covered garage, the smoothness of a stone washed onto the beach, the sweet moisture of an icy watermelon on a steamy day, the distant church bells ringing down the evening's sun, the fragrance of a baby's skin, the sunlight dancing on a puddle left by last night's rain—this is the stuff of everyday life that, when our spirit is touched by our senses and our Fourth Instinct comes alive, we can turn into the thread of art.

When we nudge up against the end of our lives, with few days left to search the labyrinth for meaning, what will have made the difference is not how many times we saw Wagner's *Die Walküre* (Hitler claimed to have seen it over fifty times) or how often we have been transported by a painting or a sculpture, but how we have integrated into our lives intimations of another reality. Ultimately, the composition we create out of the stuff of our life, out of the darkness and out of the light, is the one work of art that really matters. If we can live our lives in that perspective, our aim becomes to make a living work of art out of the most everyday things and experiences, out of every action, every thought, every word, every relationship— and every work of art that moves us and awakens the memory of who we are.

10

Set Free to Wonder: Science

> There are only two ways to live your life. One is as though nothing is a miracle. The other is as though everything is a miracle.
>
> —Albert Einstein

It was one of those clear California evenings when the stars seem close enough to touch. Christina and Isabella were cradled in the crook of each of my arms as we lay on the grass watching the universe go by. And while Isabella was stretching out her little hands, trying to peel a star off the rind of heaven, Christina was, as usual, asking questions: "Mommy, what makes it go?"

It may be a little early to reserve Christina a place at MIT, but the questions she asks are as old as time itself. When men began to wonder about the hidden causes of things, they were on their way to the discovery of science. Our proud scientific age is rooted in wonder. "Men were first led to the study of natural philosophy," wrote Aristotle, "as indeed they are today, by wonder." Physicist James Clerk Maxwell's earliest memory was "lying on the grass, looking at the sun and wondering." And Einstein effectively defined wonder as a precondition for life when he wrote that whoever is devoid of the capacity to wonder, "whoever remains unmoved, whoever cannot contemplate or know the deep shudder of the soul in enchantment, might just as well be dead for he has already closed his eyes upon life." Throughout history, the greatest scientists have shared this sense of childlike wonder.

Now, as we leave the millennium that began in the Dark Ages to enter the millennium before us, the thread of science which was nearly buried when the Age of Reason dismissed its spiritual dimension can come to the forefront again. It's a thread which can take us directly into God's workshop where we can see His creative power and purpose—and discover our own.

I was living in London twenty years ago when I developed an adolescent crush on Albert Einstein. It wasn't his haunting look; it was his breakthrough equation, $E = mc^2$. I had never been a science buff, even in school. And I was in the process of writing a book challenging the Enlightenment's adoration of reason. So I started reading a book on Einstein without much expectation, until I realized that this little four-character formula had gripped me with an emotional force I did not usually associate with scientific equations. Here was the barest little formulation—$E = mc^2$—assuring me that nothing in the universe is unrelated to anything else, that energy is matter and matter energy, that nothing is static and dead, that everything is a living force or capable of being transformed into a living force. For the first time in my life, science had become a thread which pointed me—indeed, transported me—to a sense of meaning and understanding.

Man has always searched for reasons. Each generation looks up at the heavens and the search begins anew. Children move from the stage at which everything is "Me" to the stage at which everything is "Why?" "The cause is hidden, but the result is well known," wrote Ovid. When man begins to search for reasons about what is hidden—the unseen cause of what we *do* see—he is on the edge of becoming a scientist. Arthur Koestler described scientists as Peeping Toms at the keyhole of eternity. What becomes clear from the memoirs of many scientists is that the force of hard thought goes hand in hand with the almost sensual thrill of discovery—and reason blends with revelation. In fact, quantum physics, with its invisible parti- cles, whose existence is taken on "faith" because they can only be detected through their effects on matter, is closer to a sense of the miraculous than to our conventional view of "hard" science.

"The heavens declare the glory of God; and the firmament sheweth His handywork," the psalmist tells us, while Stephen Hawking's work is described as "reading God's mind." We trace the thread of science through both the outer reaches of space and the inner reaches of our own souls. But science is also churning up some queasiness. We are worried that our "know-how" has outpaced our "know-why." We have learned how to alter the genetic code of mice and sheep and are debat- ing the ethics of human engineering. We spent billions of dol- lars on a supercollider to smash atoms into the scientific equivalent of smithereens, an effort that its partisans hoped, until it was scuttled, would "reveal the source of the origin of the universe" deep in the heart of Texas. At the same time, as the English social anthropologist Dr. Edmund Leach observed, "Science offers us complete mastery over our environment and our own destiny, yet instead of rejoicing we feel deeply afraid. Why should this be?"

Hiroshima, Nagasaki, Three Mile Island and Chernobyl pro- vide at least part of the answer. The mushroom cloud drifting over humanity, more than any other symbol, challenged the Age of Reason's smug conviction that mankind would find salvation through science alone. Scientists themselves were once confident they would unmask all knowledge. One over- excited representative of this school of thought declared that physics was about six months from knowing all there was to know—this about one generation before Einstein revolution- ized physics with his theory of relativity. It was one thing for Einstein to make his famous declaration that God does not play "dice with the world." But when the searing heat of Hiroshima melted flesh from human bones, when the Cold War nearly erupted over Cuba into nuclear war, it was all too evident that it was man, not God, whose hand was rolling the dice. Science had given man new power, but no new wisdom to go with it. And so it is not the limits of science that worry us; it is the limits of man. What we know about the universe is already so awesome that if we really believed we had been left home alone in it, we would have every right to panic.

Not long after I had been captivated by Einstein's famous formula, I was taken by a friend to meet Arthur Koestler at his flat in London. He was fascinated at that time with the interplay between man's subconscious and his conscious mind, and was full of wondrous stories about great scientific discoveries that had been inspired by dreams. During his early years as a writer, Koestler had endured the worst of prosaic science. Those were the days when anyone who inquired about God at the house of science was sent packing for the nearest temple. But he remained convinced that scientific truth comes by intuition and revelation as surely as it comes by logical deduction and reason, and that great science and great faith always run in the same direction.

Why then, I wondered, do they more often seem to be running in opposite directions? No two threads through the labyrinth have been more tangled in misunderstandings and open enmity than science and religion. From those who in the nineteenth century attacked Darwin's theory of evolution to those who, based on a literal reading of Scripture, still believe that the earth is flat, people have used theology to defend ultimate truths that turned out, among other things, to be not true. Since Scripture speaks, for example, of "the four corners of the earth," to suggest that we inhabit a globe was seen—and still is by some—as a roaring heresy. In such moments, religion has been perverted from its purpose, and the damage done by this perversion has injured both religion and science.

But science, too, has been perverted from its purpose, particularly in the misbegotten notion that science had to declare its separation from God. Faith is excluded from the laboratory in the name of "scientific objectivity," ignoring the critical role our assumptions play in our conclusions. And God is asked, none too politely, to excuse Himself from creation so man can figure out what is going on in both the swirling solar system and in the tiniest particle of matter. Forgotten in this conflict between science and religion is that science is the study of God's handiwork. Its purpose is not only to seek technological solutions to life's problems, but also to illuminate the answers to questions about life's meaning by pointing to the order and harmony, to the delicate patterns and bold connections that pervade every inch of our universe—including the universe within.

Of course there have always been those who never subscribed to this false dichotomy between science and religion. Despite the grueling controversy that followed Darwin's *The Origin of Species*, days after receiving a copy of it, the Anglican clergyman Charles Kingsley wrote to him to say that his faith had been strengthened by reading Darwin's conclusions. Seeing God's hand moving through the stages of evolution is "just as noble a conception of Deity," he confided; perhaps, when contrasted to rigidly constructed creationism, it is even "the loftier thought." In our own day, physicist Edmund Whittaker echoed this same thought when he declared that the simplest explanation for the source of life is "to postulate creation ex nihilo—Divine Will constituting Nature from nothingness."

Science begins with doubt in its search for certainties, and it is this doubt that makes the religious mind uneasy. Yet if science goes about upsetting apple carts, it is in a mad search for the seeds of the apples. Religion may begin with our love of God, but true science ends there. In the very process of demystifying the world, we discover a new mystery, recognizing and celebrating God in everything. Those who want to use "the science of our fathers to combat the religion of our grandfathers" are fighting an unnecessary and outdated war.

With Einstein's proof that matter and energy are convertible, the dualities of science and religion—of a world of spirit and a world of matter—began to crumble. As the English jurist Frederick Pollock finally concluded, "There is not a world of thought opposed to or interfering with a world of things; we have everywhere the same reality under different aspects." And the greatest scientific search of all time for the Grand Unified Theory that will identify the single source of all reality echoes the wisdom of ancient philosophers and religions which placed the unifying *ether*, the all-animating *nous*, at the center of creation. "Everything is full of gods," said Thales, and for the Greeks this meant that everything is full of meaning and the living spirit. The Greeks did not believe in miracles because for them everything was a miracle. No part of life was complete without the Divine, and nothing was more natural than to be surrounded by gods and filled with them. Modern man leaves no room in his life for miracles, and when they happen anyway—as they do—he calls them coincidences.

Science is revealing that miracles are more than indulgent elaborations of a mystical mind. The descriptions of stigmata detailed in religious literature, for example, need no longer be dismissed as fiction, but should rather be read as if they were the long-lost lab notes of possibility. Reports of stigmata, a manifestation of marks on the body corresponding to Christ's wounds, are as old as Saint Francis of Assisi and as modern as a recent account from a Catholic church in suburban Virginia. Father Jim Bruse is a mild-mannered, middle-aged priest who has bled from Christ's wounds: "I think what's happening," he explained, "is Christ is saying, 'Hey, I'm here. This is real.'" In the case of Saint Francis, stigmata were accompanied by nails themselves formed out of his flesh and retaining the blackness of iron. Science that investigates such so-called "supernatural" phenomena is science that goes beyond delivering new technologies for our comfort and new trinkets for our delight; it is science as a thread to meaning and understanding.

"The scientist does not study nature because it is useful to do so," wrote scholar Henri Poincaré, "but because he takes pleasure in it . . . because it is beautiful. If nature were not beautiful, it would not be worth knowing and life would not be worth living." With our modern talk of beauty queens, beauty tips and beauty shops, we have diluted the timeless power of that term, but when scientists talk of beauty, they are describing images so aesthetically perfect that they inspire awe.

Koestler wrote about the two dominant emotions experienced by scientists in the early hours following truly great discoveries. The first was "the triumphant explosion of tension . . . so you jump out of your bath and run through the streets laughing and shouting Eureka!" But the second was "the slowly fading after-glow . . . a quiet, contemplative delight in the truth which the discovery revealed, closely related to the artist's experience of beauty."

Rhythm and harmony, order and symmetry, even color and flavor are terms regularly used by astonished scientists reporting on their scientific discoveries—they have even borrowed "quarks" from James Joyce. The universe is alive and dancing to an intricately choreographed script. What at first appears to be a chaotic explosion of stars moving in haphazard directions at unsteady speeds becomes, through the lens of science, a delicate pattern of heavenly bodies moving in precise patterns defined by absolute forces. The scientist searches out the harmony in randomness and the unity in fragmentation—which accounts for Einstein's remarkable observation that "without the belief in the inner harmony of the world there could be no science." And when life crashes around us in discord, we may take courage in the truth that harmony remains the dominating and abiding principle.

In science as in art, truth is often borne over to us by metaphor. In *The Double Helix*, James Watson told the story of how he and his fellow researchers had created a theoretical model of DNA's molecular makeup, and were struggling with it. "So we had lunch," he recalled, "telling each other that a structure this pretty just had to exist. . . . Almost everyone accepted . . . the fact that the structure was too pretty not to be there." Order and beauty permeate the structure of the universe itself —from the perfectly concentric circles of the black hole to the remarkable detail in a floating snowflake.

If our culture is going to reclaim science as a thread through the labyrinth, we need to recapture the sense of awe and wonder in the teaching of science. "Physics, as taught in the classroom," wrote Einstein, "was split into special fields each of which could engulf a short life's work without ever satisfying the hunger for deeper knowledge." Yet the trend toward greater, and still greater, fragmentation continues. So man, dissected, his world split up into a thousand specialties, lacks any meaning and central focus to hold him together.

When we face suffering or death, our tendency is to turn to science with demands to save us. Science may have nothing it can *do* for us at such a moment, no cure that will add years to our life or take away the pain. But, as a thread through the labyrinth which can turn us toward the source of peace and understanding, it has something to *say* to us, a timeless message to deliver: that there is a cosmic plan whose hallmark is an order and beauty that could never have come from chance, as broad as the universe and as delicate as an infant's tear. So when a summer outing turns to lasting grief, when the lump turns out to be malignant, when the phone rings in the middle of the night waking us out of a dream into a nightmare, we can have this one certainty: there is purpose beyond our pain.

Those who looked to science and technology for the salvation of mankind believed that by dissociating science from all that could not be subjected to test-tube experiments and mathematical analysis, they would be inoculating it against the twin errors of prejudice and faith. The consequence, of course, was quite the opposite. Steeped in the bias of secularism, those seeking truth exclusively by way of the prescribed scientific methods were often the least likely to find it and the more likely to excuse any evil perpetrated in the pursuit of knowledge or information—from the little bully who rips wings off butterflies to the Nazi doctors who performed hideous "experiments" on Jewish children in the name of science.

"I have a basically scientific world view," wrote science writer Robert Wright, "and it seems to basically work, but it isn't, by itself, very reassuring. Personally, I don't like the idea that we're mere specks in a universe indifferent to our fates." And we are all finding it increasingly difficult to silence the rumblings of our Fourth Instinct, even when they run counter to our culture's "scientific" worldview.

After we lost our son before birth, Michael was especially adamant about my being under strict medical observation during my next pregnancy. Although we planned a natural childbirth aided by a midwife, we had made arrangements for the delivery to occur at the UCLA hospital, a concession on my part to Michael's fears that some last-minute complication might arise. So, ten days before my due date, we moved into a hotel near UCLA. The idea was that I would go through as much of the labor as possible at the hotel and then we would scoot over to UCLA for the delivery. A fine plan, agreed to by all concerned.

Except the baby. We moved into the appointed hotel at the appointed hour, and waited the predicted ten days. Nothing. Fifteen days. Nothing. Twenty. Twenty-five. Not a thing. Meanwhile, the hotel had been sold to Japanese investors, creating a media flap over the price and the loss of another piece of prize California property.

On the thirtieth day of our sojourn at the hotel, there was, at last, some stirring of interest on the part of the baby. Within an hour, it was more than casual interest; I was unmistakably in labor. To manage the pain, the midwife and I started taking walks—I in labor, she monitoring my contractions—around the grounds, past the herb garden, across the grass and back toward the lobby. By now, of course, journalists and photographers from both Japan and America had descended on the hotel to cover the growing ownership fracas. So our strolls were punctuated by my occasional sharp intakes of breath, her quiet and confident words of support, and the stares of worried disbelief from tourists, Japanese cameramen and a couple of local television crews. When the midwife guessed I was under an hour to delivery, Michael piled us all—by then my mother and sister had joined us—in the car and we were off to the hospital. Thirty minutes later Christina was born.

The miracle of birth has, for all our scientific knowledge about it, never been diminished over the centuries. The staggering reality that we mortals have accomplished the act of human creation—matching in some sense God's creation on the sixth day of his labors—leaves us changed forever. It's a miracle that we celebrate with one another once a year until our death.

A few hours after Christina's birth, I had another experience which I have rarely wanted to discuss. But when on a few trusted occasions I have broken my silence, I have discovered that an amazing number of women have had similar experiences in connection with childbirth. Nor, as notes left in personal diaries from previous generations suggest, is this just a modern phenomenon.

Christina was with me for several hours after her birth. When I grew sleepy, we put her in a crib next to my bed. A few moments later, after everyone had left the room, I began trembling convulsively. I tried to calm myself with the same soothing words I had just offered to my baby: "It's all right . . . it's all right." I had turned down a ride in the wheelchair when I arrived because it symbolized a hospital's approach to childbirth as an illness; I didn't want to give in now. So I lay quietly, trembling.

And then my body was no longer shaking. I had left it. I was looking down at myself, at Christina, at the tuberoses on the nightstand, at the entire room. I had no fear at all, neither of the trembling nor of being away from it; I knew I would return. And I was being washed in a sense of enormous well-being and strength. It was as if a curtain had been pulled back to give me a glimpse of wholeness: birth, life and death—seeing them all at once, I could accept them all. For I don't know how long, I hovered in that state of almost tangible peace. I watched a nurse enter the room, and as she touched me, she jolted me back. I returned with a great sense of confidence and joy. The fear of taking Christina home to a pair of novice parents had disappeared. I somehow *knew* that our lives were in the right hands.

Which of these two experiences, the one of a body racked with the pain of childbirth or the other of a being draped in ethereal wonder, is the greater miracle? Which is most likely to be accepted as "natural" by someone who has never experienced either? Increasingly, as science opens to the importance of the Fourth Instinct, both experiences will be fitting objects for scientific review. Both will be explored by science, because for the first time, spiritual forces that have as yet hardly been considered will be seen as a legitimate scientific province. It is time to open the doors to mystery and let science loose to explore both *in*-and-*out*-of-body experiences, within and outside the bodies of knowledge that have confined it in the past few centuries.

The fatal mistake is to assume that the current limits of our understanding are also the limits of all there is to understand. And it's one of the more hopeful signs of the times that modern science, in the light of the laboratory or the darkness of the cosmos, becomes each day more aware of its limitations, less haughty in its account of "all there is" and so more profound in its grasp of what might be. The all-too-technological mind winces at the thought of fishes multiplied or virgin births, but what are such events if not variations on the miracle of creation itself? For if we accept that God speaks through nature, why can we not imagine that He sings?

It may yet be that $E = mc^2$, this simple expression of great truth, encapsulates in it the power of a science focused on spiritual forces. Imagine that extraordinary moment in which Einstein first realized not only that matter and energy are convertible, but that he could predict the conversion's pattern. Imagine the wonder of that first recognition that matter contains energy in such compact form that one bit of it encompasses energy equal to the speed of light (186,000 miles per second) multiplied by itself ("c^2")—34.6 billion "bits" of energy

177

for every one bit of matter. No wonder a nuclear power plant can light and drive an entire city on the energy released from just a few thin rods of radiation-enriched metal—and when the process is finished, still have nearly as much metal left as when the extraction began!

When in 1905 Einstein published his thesis, all the "evidence" thus far explored by the scientific method ran contrary to it. The tests and calculations other physicists subjected his theory to simply did not bear it out. But Einstein would not yield his theory to their "facts." His intuition for scientific truth had convinced him that such a harmonious pattern could not be wrong. It was his spirit, not barren logic, that inspired his world-shaking formula.

If Einstein were alive today, and if he granted me a one-minute interview, I would ask about the first letter of his formula. In the earliest versions of his formulation, it apparently did not read "$E = mc^2$." It read "$L = mc^2$." What the original L represented, and why it was changed, is not clear. But I am inclined to read it as did Pierre Boulle, whose short story "$E = mc^2$" revolved around his conviction that the formula itself "is the very symbol of love." Even if the L stood for Light rather than Love, if the formula is the symbol of ultimate union, where matter and energy are one, the difference between ultimate union and love is pretty slim.

As a young woman, distinctly uninterested in the thread of science, I was captivated by Einstein's equation. Now, twenty years later, I have discovered that my experience was not uncommon. The power of the equation transcends the physics that it represents. The gulf that would at first seem to exist between Einstein's revolutionary science, represented in $E = mc^2$, and John the Beloved's revolutionary theology represented in "God is love" may turn out to be no gulf at all.

We will need to trust both our reason and our intuition, in tribute to Einstein and to truth. If, in the millennium before us, we begin not only to scratch the surface of spiritual realities but to plumb their depths, my children will see a science that my parents—and even I—could never have imagined. Then, the most unexpected thread leading to a spiritual renewal in our journey through the labyrinth may be science—set free to wonder even about God.

11

The Unwelcome Thread:
Pain and Loss

> There is no coming to consciousness
> without pain.
>
> —Carl Jung

Night after night I had restless dreams. Our days were filled with the talk of all young—and in our case, not so young—couples expecting their first child. Michael was ecstatic. More than any other role in life, the one he had most looked forward to—and about which he had been disarmingly honest, even on our first date!—was that of father. We had been married for five months when I found out I was pregnant. Michael was in Brussels at an arms control conference, but I could not wait. I told him on the phone. I also told him that according to my famous intuition, our child was a son. He hurried back and, over dinner his first night home, we christened our unborn son Alexander Roy—Alexander because we had both always loved that name and Roy for Michael's father.

But in the days ahead, I did not want to tell Michael about my recurring dream. Night after night, I could see my son growing within me. But his eyes would not open. Nights became weeks, and weeks turned to months. Early one morning, barely awake myself, I asked out loud, "Why won't they open?" Michael turned and looked at me. "The baby won't open his eyes," I said. I knew then what was only later confirmed by the doctors. Alexander Roy's eyes were not meant to open; he died before he was born.

For Michael, the loss of his son, his first child, was grueling and bruising. But he never ran from the pain. He grieved openly, and in his grief I saw in him a courage from which I drew strength. He went into a period of total reflection and reassessment: spiritual and emotional, intellectual and even professional. In his search to understand the loss of a child he never knew, Michael came to a profound conviction about his own life's meaning, seeing it from that moment on more in terms of service than of success.

As for me, all I wanted to know was "Why?" And then I never wanted to know another thing for a million and one years. After five months of living in my womb, my baby had been born dead. "Why?" I asked of the nurses, of anyone, of no one, of God. For five months my heart had swelled with love as my belly had swelled with new life. How was I to know that I had cradled my child in his grave?

Women know that we do not carry our unborn babies only in our wombs. We carry them in our minds and in our souls and in our every cell. And now everything felt broken inside. As I lay awake that night, and the many still and sleepless nights to come, I began to sift through the shards and splinters, hoping to find reasons. I looked for answers, perhaps too hard at first. Gradually, I began to realize that the answers would come in God's time, not mine.

Through this field of hard questions and partial answers, I began to make my way toward healing. Dreams of my baby gradually faded, but for a time it seemed as if the grief itself would never lift. My mother had once given me a quotation from Aeschylus that spoke directly to these hours: "And even in our sleep pain which cannot forget falls drop by drop upon the heart, and in our own despair, against our will, comes wisdom to us by the awful grace of God." At some point, I accepted the pain falling drop by drop, and prayed for the wisdom to come.

I had known pain before. Relationships had broken, illness had come, death had visited people I loved. But I had never known a pain like this one. Drop by drop the pain splashed against my heart until, despite my questions, the first light of understanding began to appear. I began to accept that the meaning of life, even the purpose of the pain that accompanies it, would be found not in the questions I asked of life, but in the questions life asked of me.

We had been married less than a year when Alexander Roy came and went too soon. More than the many good things our marriage has brought to us, the pain wrapped around the loss of our first child has strengthened each of us as individuals and has, especially, strengthened our relationship. A sense of wisdom—clearer priorities, a more definite understanding of what matters and what does not, a deeper joy in each other and our daughters—did, in fact, come through our loss. I would never seek such pain, nor wish to learn these lessons in such an agonizing classroom; but looking back, I do see grace flowing into our lives during these months. And I see the changes that resulted.

As we were growing up, my mother used to remind us that this world held defeats and disappointments for everyone. Some, she said, are ruined by their defeats, others are corrupted by their victories. She tried to teach us to master both defeat and victory. The triumph over defeat was not a pep talk about "looking on the bright side of life," but rather the meaning we find in our brokenness. What good, after all, is having our hearts broken if we cannot let God in through the cracks?

Yet the great and false assumption persists: that life's purpose is found in accumulating victories, wonderful things and wonderful experiences. In fact, many people are turned by success into failures, because the goal of life is not to see what we can make of it, but what it can make of us. We are here to be whittled and shaken down and sandpapered until what's left is who we truly are. And this is not a painless process.

In the grim days following his wife's death, C. S. Lewis said that the conclusion he dreaded was not "so there is no God after all," but rather "so this is what God is really like. Deceive yourself no longer." Pain is *not* what God is really like. But pain is a condition of human life. "In sorrow thou shall bring forth children," God said to Eve, and since giving up the innocence of Eden, we have made pain our companion. No one can escape it. Indeed, we are no more exempt from heartaches than from heartbeats. When we enter life's labyrinth, pain enters with us. Therefore, the question isn't whether we can avoid pain in life—we can't—but what we can do with it. How do we bear up when we are broken down? Where do we turn when it feels as if we have nowhere left to go? What do we grab for, what do we hold on to, when we are set adrift? And above all, how do we find meaning in our pain?

Dennis Potter, a television writer whose hands and body have been cruelly bent by a twenty-seven-year battle with a combination of psoriasis and arthritis, found the answer in the paradox of embracing pain as an ally: "It could also be said that my illness, although my enemy, is also my ally, my ally in that it removes me from the hustle and bustle and makes me redefine myself. I've had to face questions about God and pain and humiliation that normal people postpone asking. But when they come crashing in like the tide, there's no time not to answer them."

When, in our pain, we turn our attention to life's purpose, we take up pain as a thread through the labyrinth. Unlike the other threads, this one we do not choose; it is thrust upon us. But if we cannot choose whether or not to pick up this thread, we can choose what to do with it when it's handed to us. We can run from pain, denying its reality, or we can choose to evolve through it.

When our hearts break or our lives seem useless, some of us deny the pain, deaden it with drugs, sedate it with alcohol, or lose ourselves in busywork or shallow relationships. We look for a way to build a wall between our day-to-day lives and the night-by-night agony which consumes us. But when we deny pain, we are denying life itself. When we flee from pain that we cannot escape, we are fleeing from an opportunity to grow.

"The way we respond to pain," wrote Stephen Levine, who has done a lot of work with the dying, "is the way we respond to life. When things aren't the way we want them to be, what do we do? Do we close down, or do we open up to get more of a sense of what's needed in the moment? Our conditioning is to close down—aversion, rejection, denial. Nothing heals. . . . Most of what we call pain is the resistance that clenches down on the unpleasant. The word *surrender* is so funny, because most people, particularly in the case of illness, equate surrender with defeat. But surrender is letting go of resistance. . . .

Well, the hardening has become involuntary. As for the softening, it takes remembering priorities, that this is the only moment there is, and this is the moment to open."

Holding on to the thread of pain, although it may drag us to our knees, is an act of courage—and of trust. We have all heard the clichés about what life is *not*—a bed of roses, a bowl of cherries, a barrel of laughs. Parents die. Marriages crumble. Children get sick. In these moments false idols topple. But in the empty places where they once stood we may, if we will look, find the grace of God. In these empty places there are no distractions, no excuses—indeed, there is nowhere left to hide.

The power that courses through this unwanted thread is what Terry Anderson, a hostage for five years, found in the silence of his cell: "We come closest to God at our lowest moments. It's easiest to hear God when you are stripped of pride and arrogance, when you have nothing to rely on except God. It's pretty painful to get to that point, but when you do, God's there." It was what Quincy Jones found when he was struck down first with aneurysms that required two brain operations and then with the collapse of his marriage: "I went through changes like you never saw in your life. I just stayed with the books (the Bible, *The Essene Gospel of Peace*, *The Rays of Dawn* and *The Road Less Traveled*) and went inside myself. I wanted to build a spiritual base that would be strong enough for the rest of my life. That means turning negative energy into positive energy and living by the Golden Rule. You must love the joy of giving. You can care for people you love and some you don't love too. And you don't worry about what you get in return. It may sound corny, but it feels great."

Lee Atwater, the pugnacious chairman of the Republican National Committee, followed that same thread when he was suddenly confronted with cancer and, as it turned out, death: "Long before I was struck with cancer, I felt something stirring in American society. It was a sense among the people of this country . . . that something was missing from their lives, something crucial. . . . My illness helped me to see that what was missing in society is what was missing in me: a little heart, a lot of brotherhood." Norman Cousins picked up the thread when, at the age of nine, he contracted tuberculosis and was confined to a public sanatorium: "My life became entirely different, because I had been sheltered up to that point. . . . I learned a lot about survival during that time and it has affected my entire life. It helped me to come to full possession of my powers."

The image of forced, accelerated growth appears again and again in the stories of those who have courageously grappled with suffering. Neither turning their faces nor shielding their eyes, nor stoically resigning themselves to the pain, they use their agony to break through to the next level of their evolution —to bring perspective to their lives and find meaning in them.

Not long ago, a friend, devastated by her husband's sudden death, took to her bed and lay unblinking, not talking, not reading, not bothering to throw out the flower arrangements which friends had sent and which had died days ago. The only child of doting parents, she had married quite young a much older man who had doted on her all the more. I visited her soon after his death. I talked to her and read to her and held her hand. And, more than once, I wondered if she had even heard me. Then one day she stunned me—by showing up at my front door carrying a bouquet of fresh-cut flowers for me. She had emerged from her chrysalis of grief with a clear conclusion: "I've spent a lifetime looking for the child within. There's got to be more to life than Me!" she exclaimed. The end of her husband's life signaled another end: the end of one life centered around pampering herself, and the beginning of another, devoted to caring for others.

It is often the depth of our love that is reflected back in the breadth of our pain. We may minimize our risks, of course, by taking care not to love, so that we will feel no pain. We can gird ourselves against the possibility of loss, but only if we shroud ourselves from the possibilities of life. "Anxiety is painful," Judith Viorst wrote in *Necessary Losses*. "Depression is painful. Perhaps it is safer not to experience loss. And while we indeed may be powerless to prevent a death or divorce . . . we can develop strategies that defend us against the pain of separation. *Emotional detachment is one such defense.* We cannot lose someone we care for if we don't care. . . . We learn at an early age not to let our survival depend on the help or love of anyone. We dress the helpless child in the brittle armor of the self-reliant adult."

When we fail to be vulnerable to pain and loss, we have failed to answer the call of our Fourth Instinct—to be open to life *and* to death. I have a friend in New York who finally gave in to her husband's insistence that they have no flowers in their apartment. "Flowers are messy," said the husband, "their petals fall off, the water spills—and aside from that, they die!" And so they lived without any fallen petals or spilled water, and with not one flower, fragrant or wilting, to mar the sterile beauty of their apartment.

We may try to protect ourselves against loss with plastic flowers and lukewarm attachments, but there are some losses we cannot ignore—and these, ultimately, are our own: the loss of health, the loss of strength, the loss of youth, and the loss of control. In a culture that is embarrassed by death, illness with its intimations of mortality has become one of the most painful ways through which the Fourth Instinct brings us the recognition that the greatest loss in life is not death but what dies inside us while we are still alive. "Man," wrote the French critic Leon Bloy, "has places in his heart which do not yet exist, and into them enters suffering, in order that they may have existence."

It's hard to look at illness as an awakener, bringing dormant parts of ourselves to life, but this is what it has been for thousands of people. Life is pared down. The things that seemed urgent yesterday become increasingly irrelevant—and so do all our false idols and dead ends. We are thrown back on our own inner realities. And yet while illness denies all our little lies, it also has the power to awaken us to some of life's greatest truths. We may have preferred to sleep, but to wake is to know. Pain breaks our protective shell. With nerves exposed and eyes unpeeled, we see the world as we never have before, and we are led beyond the last horizon of our known self toward a wiser, more loving, more luminous state of being. Close friends of mine who lost a child to cancer endured the cautious hopes and terrible, crashing defeats during the progression of the disease. They now live on with a wisdom which I am in awe of and pray that I never earn this way.

There are no pearls without grains of sand. Mary Fisher, a mother and an accomplished artist, is HIV-positive, traveling at an uncertain pace toward AIDS. She must be tired and, sometimes, afraid—especially when she tucks her two small sons into bed. And yet she goes on, speaking through the pain, smiling through the fear, sharing the wisdom she has found.

Speaking to a church congregation in Van Nuys, California, she said, "Most of us would gladly take a pass on grief; but we cannot. Unavoidably, inevitably, the moments come when we are drenched in grief. . . . But grief is only one pole. Grace is the other, and it is the one that surprises us most. We leave the mortuary feeling empty and wasted; a week or two later, we notice the gentle curve of a rainbow and feel a strange peace. A friend we admire at school tells us we are her hero. We feel the delicious joy of a child's morning hug after we spent a sleepless night. We hear the quiet whisper of 'I love you,' coming out of the darkness from someone we thought was sleeping. We are surprised by grace." Mary Fisher has been there, on the "far side of despair"; she has wrestled with pain's demons. Life asked and she answered: "Having discovered, however painfully, that I cannot save my own life, I have decided to contribute it."

Illness, disability, disfigurement, death—these are blows that can make of life a living hell. If hell is truth seen too late, then illness, although it tries us with the fires of purgatory, also grants us a glimpse of heaven's light. It often begins with the revelation of deceit, the discovery of heartbreaking betrayal by our closest ally, our very self. "Lying to ourselves," wrote Dostoyevsky, "is more deeply ingrained than lying to others." These are not the little fibs we fob off on our friends. These are the lies that lives are built on. And when we begin to question their unspoken premises, we may shake our lives to their foundations. In its most intensified form, this phenomenon of coming to consciousness through pain often accompanies not only physical illness, but mental illness as well. And whether we are bringing forth art, new life or ourselves, there are labor pains involved. It was, after all, Van Gogh, a man in great pain, who painted *Starry Night*.

My mother is an artist whose only canvas is life itself. It is one she has painted, not just with the pastel palette of her days of peace and harmony, but with the raging reds, acid yellows and deep blues of her pain and passion. The British writer Bernard Levin was asked once by *New York* magazine what my mother was like, and he replied: "Like the atomic bomb—only nice." To this day, she refuses to let any of us refer to the enormous pain she suffered after her divorce in any way that would seem to either pity her or belittle her experience. "It was not a breakdown," she declares with her mischievous smile and thick accent. "It was not a breakdown—it was a *breakthrough!*"

Suffering may be the circumstance of revelation or of degradation, but it remains a circumstance, nothing more or less. As such, it slows us down a step, takes us back a pace, stops us and asks us for the passwords to grace. In the answers we give, we reflect whether our pain has served as a thread or a noose—whether we have, through it, inched forward, or whether we feel trapped, disempowered, unable to move in any direction.

I once read of a young man who moved through life on just one leg. The other had been amputated at the hip after doctors determined it was riddled with bone cancer. For many, many months after the operation and the addition of an artificial limb, he carried a great bitterness, a seething anger at the world and all the two-legged people walking about in it. But Rachel Remen, who was one of his doctors, detected a difference emerging after more than a year. "He began 'coming out of himself,' " she said. "He began visiting other people in the hospital who had suffered severe physical losses and he would tell me the most wonderful stories about these visits."

One day he visited a young woman near his own age. As Dr. Remen told the story, it was a hot day and he entered her hospital room wearing running shorts, his artificial leg clearly visible. But she didn't see it—indeed, she wouldn't look. She had just lost both breasts to cancer and had sunk into a bottomless depression. Someone had left the radio playing, perhaps to cheer her up. The young man decided there was only one way to get her attention and help her out of the dark place from which he had not long ago emerged. He unstrapped his artificial leg and began to hop around the room on his remaining one, snapping his fingers to the beat of the music. She looked at him, transported by the absurdity of it all, and finally burst out laughing. "Man," she said, "if you can dance, I can sing."

The young man's transformation is a journey chronicled in the drawings he made. Among his earliest sketches was a self-portrait in the shape of a vase with a deep, black crack running through it. Consumed with rage at the time, he had drawn the crack over and over, crushing the black crayon. When he saw the same picture two years later he said, "Oh, this one isn't finished." Taking a yellow crayon from the box, he drew rays of light streaming through the crack, spraying sunshine on the rest of the vase and the entire page.

To suggest that pain might have a purpose in our lives is in no way to romanticize it. "He jests at scars that never felt a wound," Shakespeare warns us. Pain is a howling, screaming demon. It is bones broken, skin flayed, insides eaten away. It is an incubus, feeding on what is good, corrupting what was once unadulterated flesh. Anyone who has seen a loved one wasting away on the white sheets of a hospital bed has had to shed any illusions about a painless transcending of pain. The Filipino worshipers who annually have themselves nailed to a cross, the Eastern gurus who sleep on a bed of nails—these devotions, however sincere, trivialize pain and make a maudlin mockery of the suffering we cannot evade.

"All losses are so painful," the playwright Neil Simon once remarked. "After a while you forget what the loss is even about —it's just a loss." Indeed, it is this very trap that misfortune challenges us to hurdle. When, instead of releasing the power of our Fourth Instinct, we rely solely on our first instinct to survive and on our second to control, we may briefly find victory, but we will never find peace. I remember one friend who, before she turned to her powerful spirit, tried to defeat her breast cancer with a furious declaration of war. She was angry and she wanted that lump to know it. One morning she launched into a tirade against her cancer that went on and on, building in intensity until she shouted, "I'm going to beat this thing even if it kills me!" And, at that, we looked at each other, struck by the strangeness of her words. She hadn't known what she was saying—and, as her outburst made clear, she didn't know what she was doing. If we wrestle our pain to the ground, if we try to pinion it down, we will have to remain there with it.

The test of whether pain has served as a thread is whether it has helped move us forward or whether it has simply ensnared us. It is the difference between spiritual unfolding and spiritual refolding, between evolving and revolving. Driving through Washington not long ago, I spotted a glaring graffiti message on the side of an abandoned building. "I RECYCLE PAIN," it informed the world. Some anonymous urban artist had given expression to the anxiety-addiction plaguing many of us—a vicious cycle of pain, which leads to blame, which leads to guilt. For some, feeling the pain of the victim has become a form of empowerment—through the pity of others. For others, the guilty ones, suffering is the corner we always thought we deserved, and so we are eager to occupy it. Still others stay within the confines of a nightmare because, to them, it is at least familiar territory. This is the darkness not of accepting pain, but of clinging to it.

The line between masochism and heroism was drawn by Viktor Frankl: "It goes without saying that suffering would not have a meaning unless it were absolutely necessary; e.g., a cancer which can be cured by surgery must not be shouldered by the patient as though it were his cross." Even Christ himself, in the long night of Gethsemane, bowed to the enormous authority of pain: "Father, let this cup pass from me," he asked, adding the supreme surrender: "Not as I will, but as Thou will."

It is, ultimately, this understanding which allows us to use pain as a thread. "Why?" is the question we try to answer by following the other threads through the labyrinth—the question pain will simply not let us avoid.

Inevitably and irrevocably, life sends suffering our way. How we bear up—whether we are left redeemed or resentful—brings meaning to our suffering and reveals the mettle of our souls. To be open to the grace of pain is not to underestimate the gravity of what is thrust upon us. But just as a kite may rise higher against a strong wind, so may we be lifted higher—as though when we are buffeted by the turbulence of life, God is reeling us back to Himself.

There are, of course, many who become embittered, not ennobled, by pain. Suffering becomes the misunderstanding which is never resolved, the slight which is never forgiven. Like star-crossed lovers, man and God remain separated by suffering, pain becoming the great divide. But it is man, not God, who made the whips, the guns and the gas chambers. Human suffering does not refute God but rather, as C. S. Lewis pointed out, calls out for him: "God whispers to us in our pleasures, speaks in our conscience, but shouts in our pains: it is His megaphone to rouse a deaf world."

To embrace our own suffering as a thread thrust into our hands, the wounds through which we are healed, is the greatest challenge. But what, we demand to know, are we to make of random violence, raped innocence, babies thrown behind barbed wire? "If the suffering of children," Ivan cries out in Dostoyevsky's *Brothers Karamazov*, "serves to complete the sum of suffering necessary for the acquisition of truth, I affirm from now onward that truth is not worth such a price. I would persist in my indignation even if I were wrong."

It is life's great paradox: the indignation at the suffering of the innocent and even the determination to try to put a stop to it, coupled with a deep trust that it is neither a cruel joke nor proof of an indifferent universe. I'm always suspicious of easy explanations when confronted with evil and suffering, especially when they are offered by those who have not experienced them firsthand. Reticence, even ineloquence, is a more appropriate response. So is listening, with awe, to the testimony of those who have experienced evil and were blessed with the grace of acceptance and understanding. "It was granted me," wrote Solzhenitsyn, who lived through the inhumanity of the Gulag Archipelago, "to carry away from my prison years on my bent back, which nearly broke beneath its load, the essential experience: *how* a human being becomes *evil* and how *good*. In the intoxication of my youthful successes I had felt myself to be infallible, and I was therefore cruel. In the surfeit of power I was a murderer, and an oppressor. In my most evil moments I was convinced that I was doing good, and I was well supplied with systematic arguments. And it was only in the Gulag Archipelago, on rotting prison straw that I sensed within myself the first stirrings of good. Gradually it was disclosed to me that the line separating good and evil passes, not through states, nor between classes, nor between political parties either—but right through every human heart and through all human hearts. . . . And that is why I turn back to the years of my imprisonment and say, sometimes to the astonishment of those about me: 'Bless you, prison!' "

"Quo vadis?"—"Where are you going?" This is the question that Peter, fleeing Rome to escape martyrdom, supposedly asked Christ whom he met on his way. "To Rome to be crucified again" was Christ's reply, which turned Peter around, back inside himself and back to Rome to meet his fate. Whether

in the clutches of mortal suffering or with our fists clenched in mortal fear, at the heart of our response to suffering is our attitude toward death. That it is life's inevitable destination we all know. But is death a new beginning or a final end? Is it a door to another reality or a solid brick wall?

Dr. William Grossman, a New England cardiologist who has witnessed many deaths, found that the ease with which we leave our bodies has less to do with science and more to do with soul—with whether we see death as our existential end, or as a transition to another state. "You can tell by the hands," he said. "I know it sounds strange, but it's true. In the difficult deaths dying patients grasp onto your hand—as if by sheer grip they could hold on to life. I try to tell them whatever I can, to comfort them and say it will be all right. But in the easy deaths it's the other way around—the dying man or woman will reach out and take *your* hand. They are trying to comfort *you.*"

The sense of light, of illumination, is at the heart of many near-death experiences—and the sense that there is nothing to defend, that when you are falling back, you are going to be held, that there is safety in surrender. I remember all the preparations during my pregnancies: the Lamaze classes, the breathing exercises, the endless hours of yoga. How strange, I thought to myself one day, to spend hour upon hour learning how to *bring* life, but hardly a minute learning how to *leave* it. Where are the mortality classes? What are the preparations for leaving life with gratitude and grace? These are the uncomfortable questions that modern man would rather not try to answer, or even ask. In a secular culture that shivers at the implications of death, we require quiet in our waiting rooms, a stillness laden with anxiety and fear.

A friend who has a high-powered executive position lost her husband recently after thirty years of marriage. He died suddenly of a heart attack while on a trip to London. When my friend returned to Washington after dealing with the shock, the funeral arrangements and the grief of her four children, she was informed by the personnel department of her company that "we give five days for death." During these five days, our culture expects those left behind to deal both with the logistics of death and the logistics of loss—so that they can again become a fully functioning unit of the company and of society. When we allow grief to spill its tears over more than a mere five days, we accord it the respect it deserves, and the pain becomes a thread to answers not only about death but about life.

"In working with people who are dying," wrote Dr. Remen, "and in reading a lot about near-death experiences, people seem to arrive at a sense of what life's purpose is. The purpose of life is to grow in wisdom and to learn to love better. If life serves these purposes, then health serves these purposes and illness serves them as well, because illness is a part of life." And in illness, in pain, in death we can find purpose.

The thirty-eight notes of the trumpet call in *Fidelio* which announce that when all is lost, all is saved—that when Florestan is about to die, he is about to live—announce Christ's message of renunciation, redemption and resurrection more powerfully than any collection of dry theology. It is the assertion that there is nothing final about our final hour, the truth expressed by Whitman:

> All goes onward and outward, nothing collapses,
> And to die is different from what anyone supposed, and
> luckier. . . .

Traveling around the German countryside a few years ago, I came upon a small village cemetery. I have always had the habit of visiting graveyards—not only as a memento mori but to absorb the past, the spirit and even the pain of the place. In this particular graveyard, there were many small markers. One little headstone read "Hans Werner 1911–1914." Another, "Marta Fuchs 1914–1915." Row upon row of tiny graves, grouped around the same set of years, bore silent testimony to the grim harvest of war. I bowed my head, not only in prayer, but under the weight of what I had seen. When I looked up, right in front of me there was another small gravestone which read simply: *"Auf Wiedersehen!"*—"Until I see you again!" What it communicated to me was not wishful thinking but the truth.

In death, pain ends; in life, it has its way with us. In fact, it sometimes takes more courage to face life than to confront death. Pain is not a pleasant teacher and suffering is not a thread we would ever willingly choose. Yet life thrusts the thread of pain into our hands, and even though our hands and our hearts may still ache, when we look back we may see how far this thread has brought us and how much we have learned along the way.

When we have supper together as a family—something which doesn't happen nearly as often as we would like—we hold hands and say a blessing. We take turns, and the blessing varies, but there is one that since we lost our first child has particularly touched my heart: "Thank you, O Lord, for all you have given us. Thank you for what you have taken away. And thank you, Lord, for all that you would have remain."

It is not the pain for which we offer thanks. It is the wisdom, and the grace, and the God who brings us both.

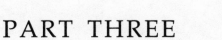

PART THREE

---

*Life under the Reign of
the Fourth Instinct*

12
Choosing to Evolve

It did not last. Before the year was out,
The Count was once again a slave to women,
The Countess had a child by Cherubino,
Suzanna was untrue to Figaro,
Young gallants went to bed with Barbarina.
But for a moment, till the music faded,
They all were ravished by a glimpse of heaven,
Where everything is known and yet forgiven,
And all that is not music is pure silence.

—John Press
(On the end of Mozart's
The Marriage of Figaro)

I had always thought of evolution as something that had already happened. It was history, biology—a series of minute, and grindingly slow, changes taking place over eons of time. An eternity, it seemed, divided into massive epochs in which environmental and biological shifts irrevocably altered life on this planet. As history, it might have explained, in part, how we got here. But did it have anything to say about what we *do* here? An explanation about the past and the present, it was an idea to be taught, not a choice to be made. Like gravity, it happened—and, probably, still happens—whether we choose it or not.

Over a dozen years ago, while I was talking with Jonas Salk on the terrace of his California home, we wandered into a conversation about evolution. "If we look at evolution as an error-making and an error-correcting process," he said, "and if we are ever so much slightly better at error-correcting than at error-making, we'll make it." It was no surprise that the man who had patiently corrected volumes of errors to produce a single life-saving vaccine believed mankind could do the same. Salk the scientist was sure we would "make it."

But then he began speaking of evolution in different terms. Spiritual terms. "The evolutionary instinct compels us to bring out the best in ourselves and in others, to recognize our inter-connectedness with everyone else," he said. He was referring not to the first instinct, survival, but to the Fourth. Jonas Salk believed that man needed to make a choice: he needed to choose "to bring out the best."

Man, created in God's image, has free will. We have exercised it to pick our mates and plague our enemies, to forge our steel and launch our rockets. We determine, we decide, we choose. And we can apply this same will to our evolution. We may evolve whether we choose to or not, but suppose we were determined to choose the direction and purpose of our evolution, suppose we decided to seek every opportunity to "bring out the best" and to "recognize our interconnectedness." What then?

The lofty idealism soaring from Salk's oceanside terrace landed, with a thud, in the everyday reality of my study. My two-year-old daughter, all red curls and outstretched arms, walked—or rather hopped—into the room. She wanted Mama. Mama, after two decades of carrying this book in her heart and mind, creating files and producing drafts, had two weeks to finish putting it down on paper. I had heard from my editor, now I heard from my child. Neither will wait. Irresistible baby meets immovable deadline. I must choose.

These are the choices that are all too often grounded in the survival behavior of our first instinct. I felt the rising frustration of competing demands, the anxiety about whom I was going to disappoint. Life calls our bluff every time we declare ourselves in control—of our time or our existence. The baby I love more than anything in the world together with her older sister wanted me. The mother in me wanted nothing more than to respond; the writer engaged not only in the fulfillment of a deadline but in the passionate pursuit of ideas wanted to abdicate from the rest of life—at least for two weeks.

I give an evening speech on peace and centeredness, but in the morning I'm uncertain about which of four ringing telephones I should answer first. All the metaphysical rhetoric about peace evaporates and what I am left with is reaction—survival behavior, expressing itself in anxiety and tension. The charge of our Fourth Instinct is to move us from the tyranny of the fight-or-flight mechanism of our first instinct to the liberation of a practical spirituality that affects our everyday lives. Time and time again, whenever I got too intense or grandiose in my spiritual search, my mother would remind me of one of her favorite sayings: "You are scrambling about in the sands, looking for bits of mica to piece together a mirror. Do you not realize that the sand *itself* is capable of becoming the purest glass?" Our life's pattern is not built on a few grand metaphysical themes but on the day-to-day, real-life decisions that we make—and that is also where our life's meaning will be found.

We scramble around looking for bits of meaning in our lives. We dash from museums to churches, from the analyst's couch to dream workshops, but we often forget that it is the way we choose to lead our everyday lives that gives them purpose and meaning. The Fourth Instinct urges us to treasure peace and compassion and oneness so deeply that we don't just wish for them, or wish others would search for them; in our everyday actions and routine decisions, we consciously choose them for ourselves.

I have heard speakers who describe the search for meaning in ways that leave me exhausted. They advocate a kind of ferociousness in the search that would be terrifying at the breakfast table, as if we must launch each day by tightening our fists, gritting our teeth, tensing our muscles and telling ourselves through clenched jaws, "Now *search!*" Such an approach seems less like a spiritual exploration and more like an existential aerobics workout. My hope—based on my own experience—is for a more natural seeking, perhaps at times intense and painful, but always prodded by the voice of our Fourth Instinct which encourages us to choose, at every moment, our own path to meaning.

Truth may break into our lives in electric moments of high drama, but such moments are rare. We are more likely to hear truth whispered in a quiet voice than in a thunderclap from heaven. With a bit of practice, we discover that listening and yielding do not require a forced intensity. This is a difficult proposition for many high-powered, high-performance, high-octane Americans to accept. Yet when it comes to increasing our inner awareness, we cannot push that door down; the moment comes when we realize that the door is opening toward us.

When Darwin first published *The Origin of Species*, clergymen gasped and fought. A century and a half later we know that God was done no more damage by the theory of evolution than by the discovery that He made the earth round. Since Darwin, evolutionary scientists have used evidence of structure to draw conclusions about purpose. They find incisor teeth in the remains of a mastodon; the structure of a jaw with such teeth has a purpose: to eat meat. They uncover the skeleton of a reptile which bears a perfect set of delicate wing bones; the structure of this skeleton speaks to a purpose: flying. We have proceeded, in the study of evolution, from the question "How does it work?" to answer the more important question "What is it for?" Evidence of man's spirit abounds throughout human history, and instead of endlessly probing the nature of our feelings, we begin to ask, what are our feelings for? So feelings become clues to our destiny, emotional signposts pointing us toward our lives' ultimate purpose.

What was true in the past will be true in the future. Man is going to evolve. It is our destiny. As in any evolution, parts of us will die in order for other parts to be born. Choosing at each moment the feelings, attitudes and values—acceptance, cooperation, caring, loving, forgiving—that will be the building blocks of the emerging reality is what it means to choose to evolve. At each moment we can choose to behave as natives of this new reality and co-creators in our evolution.

And the way we live our lives, the choices we make, the thoughts we gravitate toward—all these very personal, every-day and every-night aspects of our lives are at the same time the means by which we influence something as grand and monumental as the next stage in our evolution. The brontosaurus had no way of influencing its evolution and, therefore, no responsibility for its extinction. Unlike any other species, through our Fourth Instinct, we are called to be the cause of our next evolutionary breakthrough—to claim our inheritance and become what we were intended to be, to master life's secret, not by understanding it but by living it.

When I was younger, I thought a day would come when our lives would trace the flight path of an arrow, as if fired by a master archer straight at the mark. I was wrong. But those who see life as a random path are equally mistaken. There is purpose and direction; there is progress and evolution, even when it may sometimes seem that we are moving in circles.

"First I took a degree in one field, then I shifted to another and, finally, to a third." My friend was describing her life in the labyrinth: "First a marriage and a family; then a breakup and divorce. Another marriage, with new hopes and challenges. First I was in education, then broadcasting, then government service, then business. Zigs and zags, sometimes by the hour. Now, looking back, it seems different. Each degree and every turn had somehow shaped who I was and what I did. Each relationship, each glory, each failure and defeat—all stand in an ascending line from there to here. Coming forward, it was life in a corkscrew; looking backward, it's a spiral leading me right up to this moment."

It was very empowering for me to see life not as a series of ups and downs, but as a spiral in which even as you are moving *down* you are still moving forward. Ira Progoff, the psychologist who invented journal therapy, found that "a good many other journals were just diaries: without a project to be done, people's diaries just went around in circles." Then he discovered a project for his patients that fit everybody, no matter what they did. The project was life.

When we recognize our everyday lives as the raw material of our evolution, we move beyond our instinct for survival and self-assertion, beyond even the timeless ecstasy of physical union, and begin to listen to our Fourth Instinct. When hurt, we learn to forgive; when angry, to seek peace. As Laurens van der Post said in an interview, "One of the great problems for mankind has always been how to combat evil without becoming another kind of evil." If years of oppression by South African whites evokes years of retribution by blacks, then South Africa will be "merely repeating a discredited pattern of history . . . an endless despairing cycle of action and reaction." Van der Post's view of South Africa is true of every nation and every person. To set behind us this discredited pattern of history, this despairing cycle of revenge, we must choose action, not reaction. We must choose—not wait—to evolve.

At first, our choices may seem strange. We may be as awkward at our new decision making as two-year-olds at ballet. We may leap only to fall, turn and spin only to get dizzy. But discouragement, giving in to the inevitable disappointments, is the only real enemy; endurance, the ultimate ally. Evolution, after all, is about getting up one more time than you fall down, juggling the balls in the air one more time than you let them drop. And even the most expert juggler will still occasionally drop the ball. The more uncomfortable we are with dropping balls, the more judgmental of ourselves every time we make a mistake, the harder the journey will be. There may be electrifying breakthroughs, but it is in the quiet, daily persistence of practicing that we will master the art of choosing to evolve.

Mere understanding of the concept is about as useful as understanding a book on piano playing. However clearly we may understand about chords and keys, we will only be able to play the piano after hours and hours of practice. And whether learning to play an instrument or learning to live life, we need to give up any idea of doing it perfectly. Life is not a dress rehearsal in preparation for a flawless opening night. Every night is opening night, but we are practicing and improvising as we go along. In survival thinking, the dominant illusion is that once we vanquish the next enemy, overcome the next obstacle, get over the next hill, life will be secure, free of problems, perfect. In real life, on the other hand, I have yet to meet a person who has said, for any length of time, "I'm done!" Humans have desires, dreams and goals beyond their current reality, no matter how magnificent that reality might be. It is never done, and it is never perfect. And then, even if it momentarily seems to be, there is always the Fourth Instinct knocking on our door, nudging us on beyond our present state of consciousness.

When we choose to evolve, we choose to communicate—with ourselves, with each other, with God. And when we communicate, we share not just information, but ourselves. In times of tension and hurt, our survival instinct urges us to withdraw and withhold, waiting on cue to fight or flee. The

Fourth Instinct insists that we remain vulnerable and take the risk of expressing what is true even when we fear disapproval, ridicule or rejection. A woman I know was committed to being "nice." That was her most precious self-image. As a result, she would hold back any communication that might provoke dissension or bring up uncomfortable issues. If her boss took advantage of her, she accommodated him uncomplainingly. If her husband never lifted a hand to help with the household chores, she said nothing. It was a pattern that permeated almost every aspect of her life. And while she thought she was amiably "letting things go," she was secretly letting things build, slowly but surely isolating herself from those with whom she could not be honest. Finally, she found herself in a failed job, a failed marriage and failing relationships. And all the hurt, anger, pain and frustration that she had not dared express even to herself were making her sick.

At last she started to talk, at times stumbling over words, at other times terrified about admitting certain feelings that "nice" women were not supposed to have. And she began to discover that the feelings and thoughts she had been most ashamed of were not unique to her—and neither were they who she really was. By acknowledging them, she could, most easily, move both beyond them and beyond her plastic niceness, and connect with her true strength and wisdom. At the same time she acquired a much needed sense of perspective. "I realized," she told me, "that this life is like the twinkle of an eye in eternity, so it began to seem really absurd to get upset about every little thing—whether it was my husband squeezing the toothpaste in the middle, the plane being three hours late, or a colleague at the office being rude to me." When we choose to evolve, that same sense of perspective will permeate our lives, not only in the way we deal with our hurts, but even in the way we approach our successes.

"It seems to me as I write this hardly important to have been emperor." It is the great Roman emperor Hadrian delivering one of my favorite lines in literature as he contemplates his death in Marguerite Yourcenar's novel. His life and times had been spent at the height of temporal power. Now, with death approaching, he looks back to see that power and glory had been "hardly important." In our own day, we have amputated the dimension of death from life and so have lost the perspective that only the awareness of death can bring us. It was for reasons of right living, not morbid fascination, that *Memento Mori*—"Remember Death"—was carved all over Rome. Western civilization has taken a different tack. We adore youth, deny age, and live as though death will never catch up with us. We are embarrassed by it, as if we know that it's important but we don't know what to do with it.

A friend once told me why he had decided not to marry the woman to whom he was engaged. His brother had suddenly died, and he said: "I was devastated, in a grief I hadn't imagined possible, and the woman I was about to marry sent me a box of chocolates and a Hallmark card." Someone so uncomfortable with death that she can get no closer than mailing chocolates and condolences seems a bit extreme. But I have been to many a funeral or memorial service where more than sadness thickens the air. There is a sense of strained discomfort, an anxiety that doesn't know where to put its hands or rest its eyes. We cross our arms. We steal a glance at the grieving family. "I hope the service will be quick," a friend sitting next to me in the pew whispered in my ear once, "and without too much morbid talk."

When we choose to evolve, we recognize that there is a purpose to life beyond physical existence, beyond being born, growing up and dying. We are not prisoners of the time by which we measure our lives or of the fear of death which punctuates our life story. Life lived under the eye of eternity changes our relationship to time. Without that dimension, it remains that of a slave to a master. A friend, for whom an appropriate epitaph would be "She lived in the fast lane," complained recently that every time she looked at her watch, it was later than she thought. "If life is a race with time, well, I'm losing it," she said. "The simplest task takes longer than I think it should take. Even sleep takes longer."

The timeless world has disappeared from the horizon of our everyday lives; clock and compass are used to calculate the span of our every action, desire and thought. All that can be, and all that should not be, is being measured, and time is being treated as an absolute reality, with death as its unspoken end.

Our first two instincts nail us to the cross of time. Through our sexual instinct, at least until the ardor is spent and the ecstasy subsides, we enter a world of timelessness. But only through our Fourth Instinct can we muffle the sounds of the clock and touch that place in our souls where linear time—that was then and this is now and tomorrow has not yet come—is suspended. We plunge into this timeless peace for moments that may equal seconds by the tick of a clock, or half a revolution of the stars, and we reenter our temporal world restored, liberated—even if only for a short while—from the tyranny of the urgent.

We have been sacrificing the important on the altar of the urgent for so long that our lives have lost their balance and we have lost our center. And we have massively redefined the urgent. It's no longer just dealing with a blazing fire; it's rather worrying about the probability of a fire starting and especially about the possibility of missing some fireworks. Some of my most beloved friends feel alive only when they are living life on the brink, dealing with half a dozen crises, wallowing in the drama of it all, and having to drug themselves before they can go back to sleep when they wake up in the middle of the night.

To move the important to the center of our existence and tend to our souls, we need to bring timelessness into our lives —by some form of spiritual practice, and also by rediscovering the sacred in the most mundane and often most resented ritual of our day: sleep. Sleep, or how little of it we need, has become a symbol of our prowess. We pride ourselves on how little of our precious busy time we sacrifice to an activity as useless as sleep. Maybe insomnia is merely the stubborn refusal of our hyperactive minds to surrender to a temporary nonexistence and yield control for a few hours to the mystery of sleep.

In my years as a mother—between nursing a newborn, comforting a crying baby or holding a feverish toddler—sleep has become a survival tactic. Time disappears into the night. On one such night my mind wandered to the "sleeping chambers" in the Egyptian temples I had visited some years ago, chambers in which initiates would retire after they had prepared, through prayer and meditation, to receive in sleep divine guidance and inspiration. In stark contrast to the modern habit of drugging ourselves senseless, hoping to "crash" for a few hours before having to face another frantic day, they went to sleep expectantly. Following this ancient tradition has helped

205

me make of sleep—of whatever length—a time not only of rest but of regeneration. I have even noticed that when I prepare spiritually for sleep, I'm more likely to bring back remnants of my dreams and notes from my night travels.

Not all dreaming takes place when the sun goes down and the lights are turned off. All of us daydream to a certain extent, but when we are consciously choosing to evolve we can focus on the quiet moment of reverie we call "daydreaming" and shuttle back and forth between our ordinary and our heightened consciousness. Dreaming, daydreaming, meditation, prayer—all are gates through which we pass between the world seen through the eye and the universe glimpsed through our Fourth Instinct. One world is governed by our appetites: the next promotion, the next conquest, the next hot meal. The other is a land of miracles and wonder, the land where fishes and loaves can multiply and we can love our neighbor as ourselves.

The world of dreams, far from shutting us off from what we consider "the real world," opens us to another world, another reality where there is no past and no future. It's all now—which explains why people have reported seeing disasters in their dreams before they actually occurred. Graham Greene wrote late in life of such a dream he had when he was five: "On the April night of the 'Titanic' disaster, I dreamt of a shipwreck. One image of the dream has remained with me more than sixty years: a man in oilskins bent double beside a companionway under the blow of a giant wave." London businessman J. Connon Middleton had more reason than Greene to worry about such dreams. He had already booked passage on the *Titanic* when, after a richly detailed dream of the catastrophe, he canceled his trip. When we accept the fact that dreams can be messengers "bearing" information from outside time itself, we will be able to accept a message about the future as easily as a memory from the past.

Hardheaded "realists," who think of dreams as floating bits of nonsense, and want their worlds served up in tangible chunks of testable material, are holding a concept of reality which isn't real and isn't holding. Jungian analyst Harry Wilmer listened to the dreams and the most grisly nightmares of more than a hundred Vietnam veterans. And he tracked the dreams of an AIDS patient, John Ficht, whose dream images were dominated by a spiritual journey accompanied by light, peace and beauty. "Within each individual," Wilmer concluded, "there exists a healing force that manifests itself in dreams. . . . No matter how awful things [get] physically, the dreams reflect the growth of this spirit." Dreams can be messengers of healing from within ourselves, if only we learn to listen to them.

Sometimes, during question-and-answer sessions after a speech, I'm asked how one should first start writing. Rather than recommending courses on composition or weekend seminars with famous writers, I have always given this advice: Begin by writing down what you see and hear in your dreams. Resolve not to show it to others, so you have no need to censor what your dreams have told you, or how you report their messages. Several people have later contacted me to talk about their experiences with this technique—including a few whose works, not dreams, were eventually published.

An image that I brought back from a dream a few years ago has become a sustaining metaphor for me. I am on a train going home to God. It's a long journey and everything that happens in my life is scenery along the way. Some of it is beautiful; I want to linger over it awhile, perhaps hold on to it or even try to take it with me. Other parts of the journey are spent grinding through barren, ugly countryside. Either way the train moves on. And pain comes whenever I cling to the scenery, beautiful or ugly, rather than accept that life is never static, but always in movement toward our spiritual destiny.

My family is, of course, on board with me. Beyond our families, we choose who is on our life's train, with whom we will share the journey. The people we invite on the train are those with whom we are prepared to be vulnerable and real, with whom there is no room for masks and games—and they are, therefore, the ones with whom we are least protected. If they are fellow seekers, looking in the same direction, they can strengthen us when we falter, remind us of the journey's purpose when we become distracted by the scenery. And we do the same for them. These are the friendships of the soul, and even if this is all that brings us together—not common interests or common causes, not intellectual fascinations or sexual pleasures—it is a powerful bond.

"Desireless desire" is a state taught by many spiritual masters. It is a desire with no attachment—a state not many of us are familiar with. It does not mean we love our children, our parents, our work any less—just that there is a destination to our lives that is not about our relationships and our projects. It is a state personified in Greek mythology by the god Hermes. He embodies the longing in us to move beyond fantasy and beyond experience in our ever-expanding reality, always en route, never trapped by the magic, the glamour of any stage in the journey, yet fully enjoying the scenery along the way. He is involved but never caught, which is why he is the winged messenger, always in movement, a bridge between ourselves and what we dimly perceive and yet feel called upon to become.

When we reach this next stage in our evolution and look back, we will be astounded at how little time we have given to this other world and how little we have cared for our soul. "Ask your soul!" pleads Herman Hesse in *My Belief*.

Ask her who means freedom, whose name is love! Do not inquire of your intellect, do not search backwards through world history! Your soul will not blame you for having cared too little about politics, for having exerted yourself too little, hated your enemies too little, or too little fortified your frontiers. But she will perhaps blame you for so often having feared and fled from her demands, for never having had time to give her, your youngest and fairest child, no time to play with her, no time to listen to her song, for often having sold her for money, betrayed her for advancement. . . . You will be neurotic and a foe to life—so says your soul—if you neglect me, and you will be destroyed if you do not turn to me with a wholly new love and concern.

Learning to listen to our soul until it becomes the guiding force in our life is the essence of choosing to evolve. The people who are doing this are my heroes: the men and women who have taken the base metals of their lives and turned them into the gold of godliness and service. When I met Mother Teresa a decade ago, as she toured the Bronx, she told me that people in the West should stop trying to portray her as flawless. "Spiritual people," she said, "are not perfect people. They are only imperfect people who have put the Lord first." I wondered then if she knew how heroically her life has communicated to our modern age the ancient call: "Seek ye first the kingdom of God."

When we put spirit first, interesting things begin to happen. Some habitual patterns of thought and response—vindictiveness, keeping score, getting even—are squeezed out. Of all the precious needlepoint pillows I have seen in well-appointed living rooms, my least favorite over the years was the one that read: "Living Well Is the Best Revenge." Even in jest, the attitude captured on that pillow is obsolete. Revenge is outdated—and irrelevant. The more courageous alternative, forgiveness, will permeate a world dominated by our choice to evolve. Forgiving, which starts with self-forgiving, shedding past resentments and moving on, will become a constant process, a way of living. It's not easy, and we will by no means be perfect at it, but any other approach to living ignores the reality of our Fourth Instinct.

I have observed such powerful moments of forgiving and self-forgiving in many of the spiritual retreats I have attended. I have heard people speak of painful secrets that had haunted them for a lifetime, and I understood, then, why the confessional was the first place built in a cathedral. The power of confession is the power of acceptance and of forgiveness—of our own trespasses, and of those who have trespassed against us. I have seen the grace that comes from confession and repentance and the liberation from guilt. I have seen people able to accept the spiritual side of themselves only after they had put aside their grievances and their sense of unworthiness that had become walls, separating them from others and from God.

Nothing impedes our evolution more surely than our inability to forgive. By its very nature, forgiveness implies a forgetting, a letting go, a moving on. When we "hold a grudge" against someone, we remain—just as the words imply—there with them, holding on to the very thing we hate. A friend of mine was once mugged on his way to work. Although he was not seriously injured, he was knocked over, robbed of all his money, his briefcase, even his wedding band. When we talked about the experience afterward he was visibly and understandably shaken. A few months later I ran into him in the street. His experience had deepened into a resentment he seemed unable to shake. His eyes narrowed as he surveyed his surroundings, his fists clenched tightly when a homeless man asked for spare change. A deep mistrust of his environment and of other people had become a dead weight around him. His anger had moved from outrage over the past to a belief about the future—expecting a mugger to emerge from behind every tree—and a determination never to forgive or forget.

The Tibetan Buddhist monks embody the opposite attitude. Their expressions of forgiveness toward their Chinese Communist oppressors are sometimes difficult for outsiders to understand. On numerous occasions, during lectures and in answers to pointed questions, I have heard the Dalai Lama reaffirm his conviction that feelings of revenge only bind you more firmly to those you hate. In the midst of oppression, forgiveness allows the monks to experience freedom.

There is nothing mushy, vague or softheaded about loving and forgiving. In fact, a life led with love and forgiveness takes on the intensity of an adventure that can transform our world. At first it may seem forbidding, but it is worth remembering other challenges that seemed forbidding and indeed "impossible": heavier-than-air flight, electricity, television, space travel.

Evolution has always proceeded in increments—sometimes imperceptible ones. So if we can be courageous one more time than we are fearful, trusting one more time than we are anxious, cooperative one more time than we are competitive, forgiving one more time than we are vindictive, loving one more time than we are hateful, we will have taken the next step in the evolution of our species—and we will have found a new peace and meaning to our lives.

My unerring barometer of where I am on my spiritual journey is the way I respond to what people say about me—whether it's negative hearsay or negative press. Not the way I respond in public, but the way I respond inside myself. When my first book was published I was twenty-three years old. A nasty article would send me under the covers for a day of brooding about an unjust world. Two decades and a lot of writing later, I no longer dive for the covers. And it's not because, as the saying goes, one grows a "thicker skin." I prefer to keep a thin skin that lets the hurt in, and right out again, that lets the spirit flow through and wipe the emotional slate clean every day. The problem with growing a thicker skin is that if criticism and pain can no longer reach us, neither can love and caring. "Let the dead bury the dead" and "The evil of today is enough" are powerful expressions of the need for forgiveness. When we overprotect ourselves out of fear that life's blows will undo us, we barricade ourselves not only against our detractors, but against life and the spirit.

During the controversy surrounding the publication of *Picasso*, there was one headline about me in *The New York Times* that Michael taped to our refrigerator door as if it were my report card: "Serene at Center of Furor." My attitude was certainly not a lack of passion for my cause, but rather evidence of a still center in the lives of all of us that is not susceptible to the erratic buffetings of success and failure, criticism and praise. Kipling called it keeping your head while those all around you are losing theirs. It is one of the signs that our journey can transform our lives. It does not mean that we will stop losing our heads, but it does mean that we will know how to find our way back to that still center, and learn to build a secure structure of inner support.

When we choose to evolve, all our negative emotions—pain, fears, attachments, shame, guilt—present opportunities to achieve the greater inner freedom and strength that are necessary for us to evolve from complacency into completeness. When I'm going through my day and suddenly something in the present—perhaps reactivating something unresolved from the past—triggers a painful emotion, I consider that, once again, "school is in session." If our life's purpose is not merely to achieve our goals but to achieve greater spiritual awareness, we welcome such sessions as opportunities to separate more dross from the gold at the center of who we are.

When we choose to bring God's light into every part of our lives, we must include the dark and shameful corners. Saint John of the Cross's "That which I am, I offer to you" is at the heart of our choice to evolve. Wherever we find ourselves, right here and right now, with our last promotion behind us, or a pink slip in our hands, on our honeymoon or heading for divorce, holding a sick child or our third Oscar, we can make the choice to evolve rather than merely survive.

However great may be our achievements, they are inferior to ourselves—the self unfolding in us. "Greater is he that is in you," the Bible reminds us, "than he that is in the world." But we don't have to retreat from the world. We don't have to go east or west, to India or Walden Pond. Such false dualities are another obstacle over which to stumble when setting out on our journey.

Living in New York for four years, I had the feeling at first of having gained the heights and lost the depths. But the more I cultivated the spirit inside me, the more I harvested it around me—in the mystery of an alleyway, in the smile of a stranger, in the energy of a rush hour sidewalk. Nostalgia for a simpler way of life may lure us but, as psychologist James Hillman put it, "it places city and soul in opposing camps, resulting in soulless cities and citiless souls." Souls can still be nourished in the shadow of city towers when we connect with the inner depths that serve to balance the heights around us. When we tap into these depths, we redeem from them the spirit, the imagination and the intuitive abilities that have been crushed under the pressures of modern life and the worship of material values.

Intuition reconnects us with our natural knowing; it acknowledges something in us before we know, sees before we see, and sends its vision to the surface in the form of a faith which although at first inexplicable, is neither illusionary nor elusive. Rabindranath Tagore, who founded Shantaniketan University which I attended in India, called faith "the bird that feels the light when the dawn is still dark." The book of Hebrews calls it "the substance of things hoped for, the evidence of things not seen." The Fourth Instinct goads us to turn faith into understanding and experience. When we choose to evolve, our intuition that may have remained dormant for years is activated and becomes our guide, seeing what is not seen through the eyes and hearing what the noise of life drowns out.

"Knowing without knowing *how* you know" is the way Laurie Nadel described intuition in her book, *The Sixth Sense*. It is another channel bringing us information we can't pick up through our first five senses. "Woman's intuition" is a familiar description of this sixth sense that points to a certain reality, but also perpetuates the duality between the intuitive and the rational, the feminine and the masculine. Many men are just as intuitive, although they are generally more comfortable calling intuitive messages "hunches." Accounts of intuition—among both men and women—are, in fact, legion: from the newsman who moved his film crew just before disaster struck, to the father who rushed home to save his children from a fire not yet reported, to all the thousands of women who "just knew" when they had conceived.

Sometimes the stories are not of the whispered voice followed, but of the whispered voice ignored or denied at our peril. To develop our intuition, to bypass our intellect and emotions and learn to reach our inner wisdom, there is no substitute for time alone—not with a good book, not contemplating a Rembrandt or a sunset or listening to Mozart—but alone. Alone, with God. Or, until God speaks, simply alone—waiting for revelation but accepting God's timing. "Everywhere, wherever you may find yourself," says *The Way of a Pilgrim*, "you can set up an altar to God in your mind by means of prayer."

What modern man calls "intuition" the ancients often understood as spiritual guidance from another realm. Divine tidings, prophetic warnings—these have traditionally been borne to men by angels. The word "angel" is a derivation of the Greek *angelos*—a messenger or "one who is sent." In the Koran, angels preceded humans in the order of creation and serve as emissaries and witnesses: "Ye who believe! Celebrate the praises of God, and glorify Him morning and night. He it is Who sends Blessings on you, as do His angels, that He may bring you . . . into Light." In the Catholic tradition, angels are our guardians and guides: "For to His angels He has given command about you, that they guard you in all your ways." I have always particularly loved the prayer I have taught to my own children: "Angel of God, my guardian dear, To whom God's love commits me here; Ever this day be at my side, To light and guard, to rule and guide."

The presence of guardian angels is very real in many people's lives. Joan Anderson, author of *Where Angels Walk*, reported the story of a woman who was walking alone down a dark city street late at night, when a man suddenly appears in front of her. Afraid, she prays for help, and as she passes the man looks away. The next morning she learns that another woman was attacked the night before in the same spot, almost the same time, by a man resembling the one she saw. When he's arrested, she goes down to the police station, IDs him, and has an officer ask the man why he hadn't attacked her: "She was walking down the street with two big guys, one on either side of her."

Survivors of near-death experiences often describe meeting

213

angels—"bright beings of light"—along the way. Whether in the form of angels or intuition, God speaks to us in many voices. And when we choose to evolve, the challenge is to welcome these voices into our life, not only as we leave it, but as we live it more fully. We are called to let them guide us, whether they whisper to us through that intuitive part of ourselves, visit us through the door of faith or speak to us in our dreams. Our relationship with angels moves from receptivity to responsibility when we follow the "better angels" of our nature. As Cicero said so many centuries ago: "In nothing do men approach so nearly to the gods as doing good to men." Goodwill becomes God's will. Or, as the Hasidim say: "Every time one man helps another, an angel is born."

Every spiritual tradition, East and West, insists, in different language, that to reach a higher level of being requires devotion, service and some form of spiritual practice. Beyond our spiritual practices and answering the call to service, choosing to evolve means bringing a new attitude to everything we do, starting with the major areas in our lives—family and work. If loving each other is not only looking into each other's eyes but traveling together in the same direction, nowhere is this more important than within a family. The large aims of our journey —loving, forgiveness, cooperation—are, within the family, brought into focus every minute of every hour. And our choices inevitably serve as models for our children. Our involvements with our community, our service to those in need, become central to our lives and theirs. As well as taking our four-year-old to the zoo, we can take her to serve soup at the local homeless shelter. Christina is at least as engaged when she puts cans of food on the shelves of the Unity Shoppe, which provides food for those who would otherwise go hungry, as she is when she is painting a picture for her daddy for Father's Day. She may not quite understand what she is doing, but in some sense we are preparing her, doing what we can now, so that she will make the right choices later.

Watching my daughters grow, I again recognize the wisdom of the ancient truth: while we grow physically by what we take, we grow spiritually by what we give. On one of our long flights from Los Angeles to Washington, Christina told me she had noticed that many of the other children on the airplane didn't have crayons, and she wanted to distribute hers along with some of her drawing paper. I followed her as she went up one aisle and down the other giving her crayons away. Her eyes were glowing and she looked as happy as I had ever seen her.

Children are already so connected with God, it is our responsibility to keep that connection alive, to focus on their spiritual development, until it is not merely confined to Sunday school or temple, but becomes part of their everyday life. We learn to pray with them as we play with them, to share moments of silence so that we might better learn to communicate with each other through words.

When I watch my children work—whether it is helping Mommy wash the vegetables, or folding the towels, or bringing Daddy a snack, or tidying up their rooms—I am struck by how, in the integrity of childhood, work and play, duty and joy are merged. But today, when there is barely any cultural memory left of a family both living and working together, the prevalent attitude about work is "It's only a job." Most of us leave our lives to go to work rather than continuing to live them there. We bring no meaning to work and we certainly don't find it there. Knowing that what we do makes a difference to an organization or a community brings meaning. But what will transform work *and* life is the recognition of the infinite significance of everything we do.

When we recognize the sacred in the mundane, we allow gratitude to enter our lives. Gratitude has always been for me one of the most powerful and least practiced emotions. Living in a state of gratitude is living in a state of grace. Gratitude is a central theme in most major religious traditions. According to my Greek Orthodox tradition, the role of humankind is to reflect the glory of creation back to the Creator. The Russian Orthodox priest Saint John of Kronstadt said, "If I do not feel a sense of joy in God's creation, if I forget to offer the world back to God with thankfulness, I have advanced very little upon the Way. I have not yet learned to be truly human. For it is only through thanksgiving that I can become myself."

Gratitude can be the gateway to grace, animating our life with meaning. "What a wonderful life I've had!" the French writer Colette said. "I only wish I'd realized it sooner." Choosing to evolve is about realizing it sooner—and about manifesting that realization in every aspect of our lives.

13

A Future Waiting to Unfold

> A map of the world that does not include Utopia is not worth even glancing at, for it leaves out the one country at which Humanity is always landing. And when Humanity lands there, it looks out, and seeing a better country, sets sail. Progress is the realization of Utopias.
>
> —Oscar Wilde
> *The Soul of Man under Secularism*

It was a steamy August afternoon, the kind of day when I couldn't wait to get out of the city. I was driving along the expressway, hurrying to meet friends on Long Island. Although I had made this trip countless times, I had never before noticed whatever it was that now caught my attention, looming like a strange vision in what appeared to be a park. There, on my left, stood what looked like relics of another civilization, as if Atlantis had risen from the sea overnight—strange and mysterious like the Athenian ruins I remembered from childhood. There was some sort of abandoned amphitheater, and nearby, a huge ribbed hemisphere, which looked as if an indifferent Atlas had dropped his globe in this corner of the cosmic yard.

A Future Waiting to Unfold

When I regaled my friends with my vision of these vestiges of otherworldly proportions, they were amused. They were, they told me in a chorus, the remains of the New York's World's Fairs of 1939 and 1964, left to age with fading dignity for the past several decades. Built to signal America's emergence from the Depression and to trumpet the industrialized world's vision of a triumphant future, the 1939 fair opened only months before the first shots were fired in a war that would forever change the world.

Curious to discover what kind of future had been predicted for a world that was only moments away from war, a few days later in the New York Public Library I looked up a copy of *The New York Times* World's Fair section, dated March 5, 1939. The supplement, entitled "The World of Tomorrow," carried a series of articles designed to give readers a preview of the fair that would give visitors a preview of the future. The articles had big, bold titles like "Building a Better Society," "New Health for a New Age," and "The City of Tomorrow." They had been written by titans of industry and pillars of society, including Henry Ford and Charles Kettering. As I read them and looked at the illustrations, I thought how extraordinary it must have been in 1939 to pass through the gates of the World's Fair and, in a single step, walk into the future.

If there was one theme running through the supplement it was "The Glory of the Machine Age." The fair was a three-dimensional prospectus of the tools and technologies with which the world of tomorrow would be built. Looking back to those who were looking forward in 1939, I realized that the reason it's so hard for our age to imagine our future is that we are still infatuated with, and trapped by, the same technological model praised in those prewar years. We are still looking through the outdated lens of machines, the "wheels, keels, and wings" described in the yellowing pages of the *Times* supplement. We still imagine that technology is what will both evoke and enrich the future.

But what if we opened some toolbox of tomorrow and discovered not more "machines as ministers to man"—to quote Henry Ford's hope—but the makings of a new world-view based on *inner* tools? What if, instead of an updated technological prospectus, we stepped into an ancient spiritual perspective?

217

The World's Fair of 1939 consisted of buildings and exhibits all demonstrating life in the world of the future. That future, the one anticipated in 1939, is now. Our future, shaped by the Fourth Instinct, will be different. The landmarks of our lives—birth, marriage, children, death—may be the same. But a revolution of understanding will alter how we live our lives because our inner focus will be redirected, and the attitudes and perspectives we bring to all we do and think will be transformed. As a man thinks in his heart, so he becomes, the Bible tells us. And in the new world waiting to be born, the truth of the spiritual teachings from which Western civilization has derived its vital force, will finally be demonstrated both in our lives as individual men and women and in our communities and culture.

Since the time of the 1939 fair, men have taken to discussing fundamental revisions of human understanding in terms of "paradigm shifts"—advances through a progression of steps in which, at each stage, we exchange one model for another, trading in one set of assumptions for another, an old premise for a new one. The shift in understanding that would come from looking at life through the Fourth Instinct is more radical than a paradigm shift in any one aspect of reality. It is a paradigm shift in the *whole*—not only in the way we understand the world, but in the way we live in it, in the way we choose to evolve rather than merely survive. The paradigm shift from the Old Testament to the New was from law to grace. Life under the reign of the Fourth Instinct will witness the fulfillment of the spiritual truth of our being, not merely by reading about it, or talking about it, but by actually manifesting it in our lives.

Syndicated journalists who write regularly on the importance of caring for those in need will not feel that they have finished their task until they begin to live the message of their columns. Churchgoers will leave Sunday Mass not just absolved, but energized, ready to breathe a little more life into the word of God through good works. Activists of all stripes will spend less time scoring rhetorical points on their opponents or lobbying their congressmen and more time getting involved—whether it is caring for the sick, planting trees or setting up neighborhood-watch groups. Under the reign of the

Fourth Instinct we will move from theory to practice, from argument to proof—from wholesale to retail.

The World's Fair, a half-century ago, displayed in spectacular ways the applications of a peacetime technology that would soon be harnessed for war. Europe had already heard the first tremors of Hitler's goose-stepping march across the continent as the fair's spokesmen were confidently predicting a juggernaut of material progress and the dawn of a new civilization. "Steadily, in the near Tomorrow," wrote H. G. Wells at the time, "a collective human intelligence will be appearing and organizing itself in a collective human will." This faith in a collective human will based on man's intellect, rather than man's spirit, was about to be brutally shattered. The war showed in all its horror the animal grimace behind the mask of civilization. All the cruelty and violence that we secretly harbor could recoil on us again, unless we address the root of evil in the heart of man. Under the reign of the Fourth Instinct, when we recognize our spiritual power, we will begin to transform the dark forces within us—the forces which, in every century of human history, have risen up and overwhelmed us.

In retrospect, the World's Fair of 1939 was a celebration more of toys than of spirit. Despite tremendous technological achievements, we have, as Newton put it, been "playing on the seashore . . . while the great ocean of truth lay all undiscovered before us." It is the spirit of man, not his technological achievements, that will lead us to discover that ocean of truth. This is the dimension missing from our culture and from ourselves. As a result, most of us make use of only a very small portion of our spiritual resources, much like a man who, out of his whole body, has got into the habit of using only his little finger. Or, in the words of the inimitable Charles Schulz: "Life is like a ten-speed bike. Most of us have gears we never use." The future envisioned at the World's Fair of 1939 was based on visible realities and the presumed superiority of the first three instincts that drive us to conquer the world. My glimpse into our future in the new millennium is based on the power of the Fourth Instinct, the invisible realities of the spirit within.

. . .

Perhaps, inevitably, the prophets of the World's Fair of 1939 saw science as the salvation of mankind. According to the *Times* supplement:

> A graphic picture of this rise of techniques to the crescendo in which we are living will be presented at the New York World's Fair. Here the prominent place of science as the foundation of our organized life will be made clear. One will see how the growth of technology has changed our social life and customs, and has supplied the tools with which we can shape our world to fit our needs.

The role of science under the reign of the Fourth Instinct will be diametrically different from the vision celebrated at the 1939 World's Fair. The technological changes that are still emerging in the nineties—however great they may be and however great the social, psychological and political upheavals they may cause—will be trivial when compared to changes brought about by men and women tapping into the wisdom that flows like a river through the deepest caverns of the human psyche.

There is indeed nothing new under the sun. The quest for knowledge may be pursued at higher speeds with smarter tools today, but wisdom is found no more readily than it was three thousand years ago in the court of King Solomon. In fact, ours is a generation bloated with information and starved for wisdom.

The most profound forces acting upon us and influencing our world—love, hate, faith, fear, courage—remain as much a mystery to the technocrats of our civilization as they were to the cavemen of Lascaux. We still cannot account for love, explain the character of hatred, prove the origins of faith, make sense of irrational fears or reproduce human courage. Even the most advanced recording equipment, able to amplify with the utmost verisimilitude vibrations inaudible even to the ears of bats, is a mystery not one-thousandth part as great as the mystery of the C-major piano concerto of Mozart that pours from its speakers. A more homely enunciation of that same principle was offered by Thoreau: "We are in great haste," he said, "to construct a magnetic telegraph from Maine to Texas; but Maine and Texas, it may be, have nothing important to communicate."

Under the reign of the Fourth Instinct, science will cease to be the province of technocrats. Not only will the greatest scientific discoveries of the future be made in the realm of the human spirit, but they will be part of everyone's life. Today, our fascination with the occult often finds expression in magic tricks and trivialized prophecies—spoon bending, Ouija boards, newspaper astrology and year-end tabloids carrying next year's predictions. Having defined much of reality out of existence, when something occurs in our "normal" lives that transcends our known realities, we simply call it "paranormal." This will change. When the paranormal—such things as near-death experiences and the prophecies of dreams—is understood as the normal that has been neglected by the modern rationalist mind, our eyes will be finally opened to the deep mystery of the whole of our lives, and we will no longer be as driven to dabble in the silly side of transcendentalism.

Twenty or so years ago, Arthur C. Clarke, often called "the father of science fiction," gave a radio talk in which he made a series of informed guesses at what the future might hold in the way of technological advances. He prefaced his predictions with the remark that had we been told half a century ago about television—the talk was given, incidentally, before men had relayed to earth live pictures of themselves landing on the moon—we would have rejected the truth as too inherently improbable to be worth considering; yet here that truth is, all around us.

When we talk about scientific advances along spiritual lines —such as telepathic communication, cell memory, the unified field effects on human behavior—they also now seem too inherently improbable to be worth considering. But once our Fourth Instinct is activated, once it transforms first our vision of ourselves and, gradually, our lives and our world, these inner breakthroughs will occur all around us. We will have finally reached, as Joseph Campbell predicted, "the inner reaches of outer space."

What sounds like a paradox to the untrained ear actually contains the outlines of science's emerging truth. Science under the reign of the Fourth Instinct will uncover the unity of all things, a dawning discovery that will render divisions like "inner" and "outer" obsolete. When the quantum mechanical revolution was launched, we began to explore a view of the universe in which everything was an interrelated part of an overarching whole. Our habit of segregating ourselves and our surroundings into separate entities was really nothing more than an optical illusion of our limited consciousness. When, during an illness, Einstein was asked whether he feared death, he replied, "I feel such a sense of solidarity with all living things that it does not matter to me where the individual begins and ends."

Although Einstein instinctively grasped the grand unity of the universe, the actual theory eluded him. As Stephen Hawking put it, a grand-unification theory would merit not just a Nobel Prize, but perhaps the last one ever given: "There would still be lots to do [in physics], but it would be like mountaineering after Everest."

Will this mark the end of science, or perhaps a new sort of beginning? When Einstein was asked what was the most meaningful question a human being has to answer, he replied, "Is the universe a friendly place or not?" Science under the reign of the Fourth Instinct will reveal that it is.

At the time of the World's Fair of 1939, the *Times* supplement lamented the decline of the human spirit in the art it foresaw in our mechanistic future:

> The danger of modern art, which is so closely allied with technic and machinery, is that it may lose too much of the personal touch, of the imprint of the hand and mind of the master which makes art what it is.

There would come a day, in fact, when pictorial and musical compositions created by computers would try to pass themselves off as art. But just as dehumanizing would be the predominance of "art for art's sake," separate from meaning and divorced from the inner realities of our lives. Under that banner, the aesthetic experience is idealized irrespective of its spiritual dimension (or, more likely, lack thereof). Light, if thought of at all, is considered solely in terms of chiaroscuro, not as composer Robert Schumann used the word when he described the duty of the artist: "to send light into the darkness of men's hearts."

Under the reign of the Fourth Instinct, once we wake to the possibilities of ultimate reality within us, we will see signs of this same reality everywhere around us. It is as if the world fully reveals itself only after we, too, have laid bare our souls. And then it becomes, as Baudelaire described it, "a spiritual house. . . . Man walks there through forests of physical things that are also spiritual things, that watch him with affectionate looks."

As we become more sensitive, less blinkered and more vulnerable, our aesthetic sensibility will at last be integrated with the rest of our lives. Viktor Frankl observed this transformation even in the cold gray of a Nazi death camp: "As the inner life of the prisoner tended to become more intense, he also experienced the beauty of art and nature as never before."

Under the reign of the Fourth Instinct, art will be restored to its original function as a thread through the labyrinth, a sister of religion, helping reconnect man to his divine source. When these threads are increasingly interwoven, creating new tapestries of meaning, the spiritual yield will be enormous. In *The Shell Seekers*, Rosamunde Pilcher predicted this future: "One day, they will come. As we came. Young men with bright visions and deep perceptions and tremendous talent. They will come, not to paint the bay and the sea and the boats and the moors, but the warmth of the sun and the color of the wind. A whole new concept."

The modern trends of deconstruction and disintegration will have run their course. Our goal will be to do much more than merely "contain" the culture of disintegration. We will roll it back: intellectually, artistically and commercially.

Culturally, Americans have been living on a deprivation diet. The emerging art will help provide spiritual sustenance. In the meantime, to hasten its arrival, we must do more than just snipe at television sitcoms or rap lyrics. We must give voice to a new vision for our culture rather than merely a distaste for the one we see about us.

Kandinsky, always fascinated by the spiritual in art, was prophetic about what he called "the great epoch of the Spiritual which is already beginning . . . and will provide the soil in which a kind of monumental work of art must come to fruition." The monumental work of art is man himself, and when we choose to evolve we will bring this work of art into glorious being.

. . .

Paradoxically, religion occupied a prominent place in the temporal setting of the World's Fair of 1939. The *Times* supplement insisted on its importance:

> It is, therefore, no small matter that at the center of the World's Fair the Temple of Religion will stand in quiet, noncontroversial testimony, not an outward form only but an inward reality.

This aspiration for religion in a central place—not only in our public squares but in our hearts—remains sadly unrealized. Indeed, we have wandered further away from this hope than was imagined possible at the 1939 World's Fair. But the embarrassed consensus of silence that built over decades and has surrounded spiritual realities in our culture is already being broken. And questions about life's meaning and God's purpose are again being asked with increasing urgency. In life under the reign of the Fourth Instinct, we will welcome God back into our hearts, our homes—and, yes, our World's Fairs, our classrooms, and town squares.

In the third century A.D., Ptolemy laid down the premise that the sun revolved around the earth. This one premise constrained the progress of astronomy for over a thousand years. It wasn't until Copernicus took the heavenly sciences back to the drawing board, and proposed the revolutionary premise that it was indeed the earth that revolved around the sun, that astronomy was able to move forward. If we wish to move forward again, our culture must acknowledge the existence of a higher power not as an opinion but as a fact—a truth as fundamental and far-reaching as the truth that the earth revolves around the sun.

There are still flat-earth societies and people who join them, persuaded that the earth is flat and the sun revolves around it. In life under the reign of the Fourth Instinct, people will be free to believe this as individuals, just as they should be free to believe that there is no God and that we are all alone in an indifferent universe. But the culture as a whole can no longer afford to remain agnostic. To continue to do so would be much more destructive in terms of human casualties than if we were to build our principles of navigation on the basis that the jury is still out on Copernicus.

"Despotism may be able to do without faith," wrote Tocqueville, "but freedom cannot." At a time when our social fabric is frayed by competing claims of fairness and vociferous arguments of blame and victimization, spirituality provides the only fixed point from which we can experience our interconnectedness regardless of race, creed, gender or circumstance. Throughout our nation's history, at times of tension and grave social discontent such as ours, men of vision have always appealed to transcendent truth and helped usher in a new era. Jefferson trembled for his country when he contemplated its compact with slavery, reflecting "that God is just; that his justice cannot sleep forever." Lincoln later argued that slavery was incompatible with the beliefs enshrined in the Declaration of Independence: "these principles cannot stand together. They are as opposite as God and mammon." And Martin Luther King advanced the cause of freedom by appealing to "individuals who are willing to be co-workers with God." Underlying each of these appeals is the understanding that, ultimately, justice exists, and that its origin is divine. "The sacred rights of mankind," as Hamilton put it, "are not to be rummaged for among old parchments or musty records. They are written, as with a sunbeam, in the whole volume of human nature, by the hand of Divinity itself; and can never be erased or obscured by mortal power." Jefferson agreed: "Can the liberties of a nation be thought secure when we have removed their only firm basis, a conviction in the minds of the people that these liberties are the gift of God?"

Those who would rant on about some imagined unholy alliance between church and state forget the fact that the principle of the separation of church and state was intended to protect spiritual freedom, not to eliminate any sign of God or spirit from our schools, our ceremonies and our communal lives. The concept has become so perverted that anything resembling prayer at school—a moment of silence, a general blessing—is branded as sectarian and banned as unconstitutional. What can we say about a society that is not willing to allow its children one minute of even *silent* prayer each day—that, in fact, considers such a moment of silence as a coercion?

In "Faith for Groping Man," the pastor of the Riverside Church in New York celebrated the representation of religion at the 1939 fair "under the united sponsorship of Roman Catholics, Jews and Protestants, with the emphasis on the common and universal elements rather than on the particular and sectarian." Under the reign of the Fourth Instinct, religion will once again be a force for unity rather than division, reconnecting us with God and with each other. It will not be a skylight opening on the next world, nor a theological structure of creeds and dogmas, but a new window opening on this world—our world—changing our perspective and our priorities.

Under the reign of the Fourth Instinct, religion will fulfill its destiny, becoming, as Tennyson described it, "the perpetual ministry of one soul to another." The original vision of ministry —a vision that will again animate our lives under the reign of the Fourth Instinct—is one of service. *Minister*, after all, is the Latin word for "servant," which has at its heart a sense of self-giving and submission. It is the sense evident in Christ's reply to apostles James and John when he was asked if, as his ministers, they might someday sit in glory at his left and right hand. He answers that this gift is not his to give, adding: "But whosoever will be great among you, let him be your minister; and whosoever of you will be chief among you, let him be your servant; even the Son of man came not to be ministered unto, but to minister, and to give his life in a ransom for many."

The early church struggled with the tension between this call to humble service and the need for authority—between ministering and administration, Christianity and Christendom. The original vision of the church, Paul Johnson wrote in *A History of Christianity*, was "a community where the spirit worked through individuals, rather than an organized hierarchy where authority was exercised by office." In this very important sense, the Fourth Instinct makes "ministers" of us all, incorporating us, through religion, into the priesthood of all believers. God, addressing Moses in Exodus, called Israel a "kingdom of priests." The "kingdom of priests" became, with Christ's descent on earth, every man's unconditional birthright. The Book of Revelation speaks of the God "who loves us and freed us from our sins by his own blood, who has made us a royal nation of priests in the service of his God and Father. . . ." The idea of an informal, lay priesthood revolving around self-giving will be at the heart of religion under the reign of the Fourth Instinct.

The priesthood of all believers will minister not just heavenly truths, but earthly comfort and care. An expression of the reli-

gious spirit that will prevail under the reign of the Fourth Instinct appears in the preamble to the Constitution of Mother
Teresa's Mission: "The International Association of Co-Workers . . . consists of men, women, young people and children
of all religions and denominations throughout the world, who
seek to love God in their fellow men, through wholehearted
free service to the poorest of the poor of all castes and creeds."

The ministering spirit will manifest itself more and more as
we move toward the millennium. The Fourth Instinct encourages us to minister, as fathers, mothers, employers, employ-
ees, wherever we find ourselves—in our work, in our families,
in our communities, ordering our little patch of the world according to God's plan. The ministry of all believers is not about
distributing authority but about diffusing responsibility. It is
what Solzhenitsyn meant when he said that "the salvation of
mankind lies only in making everything the concern of all."

At the center of life under the reign of the Fourth Instinct
will be an inward, spiritual renewal that precedes all other
renewals—social, political and aesthetic. In 1939 we were told
that the Temple of Religion at the World's Fair represented "an
endless quest of the human spirit, not simply for the means by
which to live but for the ends for which to live." The Fourth
Instinct gives us an understanding of life's purpose, a longing
to live our lives according to it, and a recognition that when we
actually choose to evolve, every aspect of our lives will become
a tool for our inner transformation—and the transformation of
the world around us.

The *Times* supplement of 1939 accurately predicted fragmentation in our families and our relationships:

Maybe people's lives will fall into phases. . . . Home will be a
family nest—and it will come to an end when the last chick has
flown.

Relationships under the reign of the Fourth Instinct will be
less about phases and empty nests and more about evoking
the Fourth Instinct in all our interactions. The people we share
relationships with—whether family, friends or the checkout
girl at the local grocery store—will present us with opportuni-

ties both for recognition of our flaws and reconciliation of our differences and for celebration of our common divine potential. In fact, mirroring and evoking in others their potential for godliness is one of the greatest ministries we can provide in relationships. "A rock pile," wrote Saint-Exupéry, "ceases to be a rock pile the moment a single man contemplates it, bearing within him the image of a cathedral." In the same way, a man ceases to be a mere mortal, a pile of ailments and grievances, when we see him through the eyes of the Fourth Instinct. He becomes instead what he has always been, a child of God ready to claim his rightful spiritual inheritance.

When we recognize man's unexplored possibilities, we motivate him with a vision of becoming; encouraged, he sets off on his journey. But relationships are not only about seeing and evoking each other's spiritual potential. They also challenge us by exposing our fears, attachments and insecurities—and the more intimate the relationship, the more likely are these challenges. When we enter relationships our "school is in session." By bringing our soul into our relationships, we will turn everyday pains and frustrations into grist for the mill of our awakening.

Looking into the future of health, the soothsayers of the World's Fair pointed to a destination that would be determined by man's technological achievements, not by the resources of his spirit. The *Times* supplement predicted:

> In the battle for health—the resources of modern medicine are pitted against disease. . . . In the future hospitals will no longer be regarded as places where people go to die but where people go to have better health for the enjoyment of life and better performance of their normal pursuits.

Healing under the reign of the Fourth Instinct will be about keeping people *out* of sickbeds and hospitals, as well as redefining what we mean by "the enjoyment of life" and what we consider "normal pursuits." In 1939 it would have seemed impossible that a third of Americans would today consult alternative healers—among them chiropractors, acupuncturists and a variety of homeopaths—spending nearly $14 billion a year for their services. We are going back, unearthing the wisdom of the ancients to help modern medicine meet the challenges of the future. It was Hippocrates who equated health to a harmonious balance of mind, body and the environment and declared nature as the healer of disease. Modern medicine is not being supplanted; it is being supplemented. And in the process, it is embracing once again the conviction that we have within our human nature massive, untapped and unrivaled potential to heal ourselves.

As the daughter of a woman who was absolutely assured by three eminent physicians that her virulent tuberculosis would leave her barren for life, I was recently delighted to read Sir William Osler's observation: "The care of tuberculosis depends more on what the patient has in his head than on what he has in his chest." And my mother's mind had been made up: She *was* going to have children.

Skepticism about holistic medicine still dominates some corners of the medical profession. When I was dating Michael—then a firm believer in the supremacy of conventional medicine—he was getting ready to run the Houston Marathon. He had been training hard for months, so he was extremely disappointed when he ripped a tendon running up and down bleachers at UCLA. After seeing three well-known osteopaths, he gave in to their conclusion. He simply had to forgo running the marathon; there was no way the tendon could be healed in time. I wondered: Do I dare show my holistic stripes so early in our courtship? Would he dismiss my advice—and maybe me!—and question my judgment? I took the risk and, on the grounds that he had nothing to lose, he agreed to see my chiropractor. Seven days later his mother and I cheered roadside as he crossed the twenty-mile mark and kept going. Seven years later he has seen in his own life, and in the life of our family, the benefits of chiropractic, homeopathy and relaxation techniques—even in the middle of a grueling eighteen-hour-a-day campaign.

The study of the interaction between the brain, our immune system and our health is now at the cutting edge of the healing arts. It's called "psychoimmunology," and behind its imposing name hide laughter, optimism, imagination and a caring spirit. The writer Max Lerner—after he was hit on three fronts with lymphoma, prostate cancer and a heart condition—learned to marshal inner resources to combat these unseen enemies. Spending weeks in the hospital, he began to feel powerless: "You are expected to surrender your selfhood to the doctors and their apparatus." And, even as he craved the authority of his doctors and the stability of their environment, he saw the need to define his own involvement in his recovery.

He came, as he described it, to a new understanding of health as an equilibrium of the various functions of our being. Illness disturbs this balance and throws the system out of whack. Adopting what is called "will therapy," Lerner rebelled against the essentially passive role of the patient (the Latin root of the word "patient," *pati,* meaning, after all, "to suffer"). "In my most troubled illness years," he wrote, "I would jot down a phrase in my journal, *I must live,* and when that resolve turned to possibility, *I can live.* It was not so long before *I can live* moved to a final stage, *I will live.*" These words were uttered at age eighty-eight—ten full years after he first contracted cancer. His "will" had found a way, not through the assertion of the second instinct, but through the optimism and faith of the Fourth.

What we will see emerging is more than just a new technology of healing; it is a new philosophy of health. Under the reign of the Fourth Instinct, healing will involve cross-pollination between different healing techniques. Even more important, the patient, instead of being merely plugged into a machine, will become replugged into himself and assume responsibility and a role in his own healing process.

Responsibility in this context does not mean blaming ourselves for our illness, or seeing sickness as what we "deserve." It is rather the ability to respond to our illness or trauma with imagination, forgiveness and optimism. Under the reign of the Fourth Instinct, we will become partners not just in our own personal healing, but in the healing of our communities—however variously defined. Healing moves us beyond being victims or even survivors of our experiences of abuse or illness. Instead of staying within the confines of our own private hell, we become the shepherds who guide others out of theirs.

How, finally, did the spokesmen for the 1939 fair envision the society of the future? Predictably, perhaps, community was conceived in economic rather than spiritual terms. And the *Times* supplement issued a call to action:

A chance to share in the economic life of the nation under just and safe conditions is, perhaps, one of the most important of all the things we must provide for the children of the oncoming generation.

Here it was, the clear-cut and unarguable objective of 1939: a just and safe society. And we were told that these were commodities "we must provide." But who were "we"? In the years that followed the war, "we" came to be seen not as the individuals, parents, families and communities of which society is comprised, but as the collective "we" of government, whether democratic or despotic. And insofar as that "we" had faces, they were the faces of the politicians, government bureaucrats and social engineers of a technological age. It was they who came to bear the chief responsibility for righting society's wrongs. So began the gradual takeover of our lives by government as the sole agent of social and economic change, the sole guarantor of a just society.

Under the reign of the Fourth Instinct, we will see ourselves, not government, as the most effective agent of social change. We will both recognize the need for a sense of community that transcends our collective economic life and choose to begin working together as individuals, with commitment and compassion, to build such communities. This choice—actually a pattern of choices—will replace the compulsory compassion and nationalized generosity that have dominated our lives since the World's Fair while insulating us from the experience of giving and the spiritual growth that it yields.

By a large majority Americans today would like less government, not more. They would like a government which lives within its sphere and within its means. In 1992, all three candidates for the presidency promised to reduce government, because whether they *believed* it or not, all three knew it was what the voters wanted. To quote George Will, most Americans today regard government as "an overbearing and overreaching underachiever that is suspect regarding both its competence and motives."

Yet we continue to put our trust in princes and to ignore

231

Madison's warning that "if men were angels, no government would be necessary." Most of us can see through the promises of the Ku Klux Klan and the neo-Nazis, but we continue to be seduced by the promise that government can create a just society. We are more vulnerable by far to articulate men in three-piece suits who preach political salvation on C-Span and CNN. We are lured not so much by political extremes but by the extreme blandishments of politicians. We expect government to save us, to rescue us from our spiritual rootlessness and provide us not only with economic security and social justice, but also with community.

In the middle seventies I wrote in *After Reason* about the rise of political salvationism in America. "The state," I wrote, "has no salvationist function whatsoever. . . . It is a military, political and economic force, and no amount of fictions, catchwords and state philosophies will turn it into an ethical entity." Since then the most extreme manifestations of political salvationism have collapsed, but we continue to be lured by a government that has for decades promised more than it can *ever* deliver.

It's an explosive mixture when we introduce a government which wants to save the people to a nation of people who want to be saved. When we are standing on our tiptoes to see hope for our cities and promise for our children, it's tempting to accept the government's offer to lift us higher through special funding and legislation. When we see the bloody aftermath of racial tensions which lacerate our communities and destroy our sense of unity, it's appealing to believe that the cure will be found in more social spending. When we see the child's eyes dazed from years of abuse, or the homeless schizophrenic shadowboxing on the street corner, we are tempted to turn our eyes toward government and lobby for redemption. We want community, and we want government to give it to us. And when government is in the hands of marketers and pollsters, that's just what it promises to deliver.

The fundamental role of government—the role in which it is failing miserably—is to secure the safety of its citizens. It's much harder to foster community in America when we are leading the industrial world in violent crime, when every stranger on the street is viewed as a potential assailant and seven-year-olds are kidnapped off front lawns and murdered in back alleys. It is time not just to "reinvent" government, but to reorder its—and our—priorities.

The realization is growing that deep cultural change cannot be imposed from distant quarters even by sincere politicians and earnest reformers. In life under the reign of the Fourth Instinct, we will finally expand the national debate beyond what government can do *for* you, beyond what government can do *to* you, beyond even what you can do for government. All of these views are based on the false premise that government is at the center of all problems and solutions. Samuel Johnson's wisdom still rings true today: "How small of all that human hearts endure, That part which laws or kings can cause or cure."

Society will not be changed unless individuals change themselves. The greatest tragedy of the modern welfare state is that we have allowed it to deprive us of a fundamental opportunity to practice virtue, responsibility, generosity and compassion. The welfare state has usurped these practices to itself, and since giving and caring for others add meaning to life, it has deprived us of meaning as well.

For generations, we have vociferously exercised our rights as individuals, and ignored our responsibilities as members of a community. If something challenged our narrowly defined self-interest, it was an unwelcome intruder. Under the reign of the Fourth Instinct, we will discover that we cannot create and sustain community without transcending selfishness, and we cannot keep taking, caged away from our fellow men and from our own souls, without giving back.

In the new millennium, giving will expand well beyond our own preconceptions of community as modern technology and the global information network radically alter our understanding of time and space. Under the Fourth Instinct's reign our generosity will take full advantage of modem, fax and fiber optic. We may reach out to that wider world with the latest technological gadgets, but our compassion will be motivated by age-old values.

I read recently one story that illustrates that neighborliness is now "on-line," expressed through the magic of modem. "Call it a barn-raising—on the electronic frontier" was how *The Washington Post* described it. A man named Mike Goodwin had just arrived at his new home in Washington, D.C., when he learned that the moving truck carrying all his belongings had exploded in flames somewhere in Delaware. "He did the profoundly human thing. He turned to his community and wailed in anguish." This, however, was no ordinary neighborhood. It was an electronic information network that serves as sort of a common computer green where people sign on, meet, send messages and merge into community.

"I'm devastated. It is almost impossible to grasp how much is gone," Goodwin typed into his information network. Soon responses were gushing back: "Good God, Mike, unimaginable." "A real sick-to-the stomach feeling—who among us is ready for that kind of ugly surprise?" And then came help: irreplaceable books, personal mementos, sound advice, offers to lend money. As Andrew Alden, another computer crusader put it, "This is how life should be. Modern American life is the aberration, where people who return dropped wallets are lauded in editorials and sent marriage proposals. . . . So, if this is a frontier, it's one on the edge of the old true ways, not a new one."

Margaret Mead predicted on her deathbed that the survival of civilization will depend not on governments and bureaucracies but on "citizen volunteer associations, gathering together, deepening and growing together, and going out and taking social action." When we discover not only new ways of giving but new ways of *living*, we will pit the truth of spiritual renewal against the lies both of political salvationism and of narrow individualism that see men connected with others by little more than utilitarian self-interest. As Frankl described it, many of us "have enough to live by but nothing to live for; we have the means, but no meaning."

The instinct to serve is potentially at least as pronounced as the first and second instincts to survive and to assert oneself. Over 80 million Americans volunteer nearly one billion hours to philanthropic activities. William F. Buckley describes in his book *Gratitude*, a "huge body . . . of unmet needs, finding its way to a huge appetite to meet their needs." It is a new way of matching supply and demand through the Fourth Instinct.

The time is ripe and, by many standards, the harvest of giving is richer than ever before. In 1992, a year of troubled times and tightened belts, we broke all records for charitable giving. Americans poured more than $124 billion into the coffers of charity—a 6.4 percent increase from 1991. Yet statistics cannot capture the silent revolution of social responsibility sweeping the country. Night after night television news parades endless images of suffering and wanton violence. But these pictures paint only part of the story and not even half of the truth. Millions are seeing the challenges and rising to them —whether the cause is a hurricane, homelessness or hunger.

This expanding ethic of altruism comes at a time when the failures of the welfare state have grown too glaring to ignore. It has become a modern monster—grotesque in its proportions, insatiable in its appetites, detrimental to the very people it claims to serve. It was Einstein who predicted that "the significant problems we face cannot be solved at the same level of thinking we were at when we created them." We need to come to a new level of understanding. Decades after "The Great Society" first dawned, many who once handed government the wheel have now grown frustrated and angry with the direction we have taken. Yet their solutions tend simply to grease government's axles and give it more fuel. Equally frustrated are those who accepted the premise that the government would be responsible for others while we cared only for ourselves.

Both these perspectives—that the government is responsible for us, and that we are responsible only for ourselves—are dehumanizing. To be fully human, we can neither give up responsibility for ourselves nor refuse responsibility for others. Indeed, we need to redefine individual responsibility to include social responsibility. We need to obey both of Saint Paul's admonitions: "Bear one another's burdens" and then a few verses later, "Every man shall bear his own burden." Responsibility for ourselves, a value which matures within the first three instincts, becomes responsibility for others when visited by the Fourth.

Americans have a truly historic opportunity to create community and effect a merger between the two greatest strengths our country has to offer: our intrinsic generosity and our entrepreneurial creativity. In his 1991 encyclical on capitalism, Pope John Paul II wrote that man was blessed with an "ability to perceive the needs of others and to satisfy them." If Americans can harness this "creative spirit"—or rather, set it free—it can

235

achieve for community what self-interest achieved for Adam Smith's capitalism. It is time to lift the *other* invisible hand.

The modern carnage of urban neighborhoods, wracked by poverty and inhabited by grim survivors, cannot be redeemed by bigger and better programs conceived in a distant bureaucracy. It will take a much greater infusion of spirit than is found in the experiments of social engineering. It will demand of us not just our taxes but our compassion, which is to say, the resources of our hearts. The answer to the accumulating casualties of the welfare state's "war" on poverty is the home-grown, grass-roots, all-volunteer army of ordinary people armed with food, books, skills and a determination to make a difference. The entrepreneurial creativity that catapulted this nation to a position of global leadership can now be harnessed to do for community what it did for productivity. When we provide imaginative, entrepreneurial alternatives to the welfare state, we won't need to confront it. It will simply wither away. And the rewards of this work are a bounty of spiritual renewal: an abundance of love, meaning and connectedness. From the blue-collar worker to the pampered socialite, from the big-time donor to the small-town doer, from the urban executive suite to the rural farmhouse, life takes on meaning when we answer the call of our Fourth Instinct, and live it responsibly on behalf of all those within our reach. And each of us will decide how wide our reach will be.

What we need is nothing short of a crusade. We need, first, to defeat the belief that any actions requiring more than individual efforts—any collective engagement, any organized response to social problems—should default to anonymous government. When the worker scans the list of required deductions from his weekly paycheck, he doesn't feel generous or compassionate; he feels gouged and angry. The poor do not become the brothers of those more fortunate; they become the objects of resentment and prejudice, responding, in turn, not with gratitude, but with the righteous entitlement that the welfare state promotes. And even beyond these tragedies, there is a great national loss, a missed opportunity for all of us to become deeply—emotionally and spiritually—engaged in the intimate cycle of giving and receiving. We have forfeited our own answer to the question posed by philosopher Erich Fromm "of how to overcome separateness, how to achieve union, how to transcend one's own individual life and find atonement."

This spirit is an essential part of our American identity. Indeed, John Winthrop, the first governor of Massachusetts, wrote in 1630 what amounts to a spiritual charter for American community: "We must be knit together in this work as one man; we must entertain each other in brotherly affection; we must uphold a familiar commerce together in all meekness, gentleness, patience and liberality. We must delight in each other, make others' conditions our own, rejoice together, mourn together, labor and suffer together; always having before our eyes our commission and community as members of the same body."

It is one thing to march and argue and debate about the homeless, the battered, the abused. It is quite another to actually go out and feed, clothe and care for them, to move from being good-time social spectators and part-time social lobbyists into the arena of hard-times social action. Mother Teresa is right: "If you can't feed a hundred people, then feed just one." We have too many people filming the hungry and not enough preparing food; too many in advertising and not enough in production.

The line between doing good and do-goodism is thin. We know we have crossed it when we grow fondest of those acts of charity which fetch us headlines in the Style sections of the local papers. There is a world of difference between social *activism* and social *action*. One demands change from others, chiefly in America through the intercession of the government; the other delivers the goods. One is dominated by high-sounding words; the other by heartfelt actions.

From those who have been given much, much will be demanded. If we have wealth or influence, if we have developed special gifts, our Fourth Instinct teaches us that they are not our own private possessions to be squandered on self-amusement. They are given to us in trust. Talents—from making music to making friendships, from healing the sick to comforting the grieving—will become sources of meaning when they are turned to the good of others.

Time and time again, working with other volunteers, I have observed what a two-way street the experience of giving is. I have seen people who have never given the needy the time of day—much less a hot meal—who, in a moment I cannot describe as anything less than an epiphany, suddenly make that one connection that changes them forever. I was at the Council of Christmas Cheer—a bazaar of giving, organized like a shop, where needy families are given Monopoly money to pick up clothes, food, toys for their children. A man came in, a prominent citizen and patron of the arts, prepared to put in his hour and a half of good works. But then something happened to him. Something changed about him, something (after having witnessed several) I have come to call a compassionate conversion. In one magical moment, all the dead statistics, all the cold numbers and anonymous faces were recast for him in the form of living beings—neighbors, brothers, friends. In the instant when he saw their humanity, he experienced his own. It was an awakening during which this man of privilege had recognized his interconnectedness with everyone else, however different their circumstances, and in the process discovered new depths in himself.

Giving is essential to our evolution—both as individuals and as a society. As new research is showing, it may also be essential to our health. A study in Tecumseh, Michigan, showed that doing regular volunteer work dramatically increased life expectancy: "Men who did not engage in volunteer work were two and a half times more likely to die from various causes than their peers who did volunteer work." The study also showed that doing good for others enhanced the immune system, lowered cholesterol levels, strengthened the heart, decreased chest pains and generally reduced stress. "Helping others helps you, too," said Dr. Chris Kiefer of the University of California. "A survey of well-known altruists showed that they are unusually healthy and emotionally secure." Many involved in volunteer activities have remarked that the resulting feeling of well-being relieves headaches, alleviates depression and heightens self-esteem. In the words of the ancient Chinese proverb: A little bit of fragrance always clings to the hand that gives the rose.

It is the truth so many volunteers discover: When you help lift someone else's burden, it makes it easier to bear your own. Valerie, a forty-five-year-old recovering alcoholic, helped cure her own sickness by caring for others in need. Eleven years ago she looked at life through the dark glasses of the scotch she drank morning, noon and night. She lived with the curtains drawn, not bathing or seeing anyone for days. "At the time," she told me, "it made no sense to me how helping others would help me."

Today, Valerie has exchanged alcohol for what she calls "the juice I get out of helping other people." She has volunteered at a neonatal clinic. She organizes "Safe Rides" so kids won't drive drunk. And she helps bring others into the sunshine of sobriety. "I feel like I have a purpose other than myself," she said. "It's amazing how it works. I get back tenfold what I give."

Erich Fromm expressed the same feeling: "In the very act of giving, I experience my strength, my wealth, my power." This will be the everyday experience under the reign of the Fourth Instinct. When we decide to lend a hand, we will discover what strong arms we have. When we choose to give to others, we will appreciate how much we have—no matter how little it may actually be. And when we start to love our neighbors, we will end up also loving ourselves.

14

Critical Mass

> If mankind is not to perish after all the dreadful things it has done and gone through, then a new spirit must emerge. And this new spirit is coming not with a roar but with a quiet birth, not with grand measures and words but with an imperceptible change in the atmosphere—a change in which each of us is participating and which each of us regards as a quiet boon.
>
> —Albert Schweitzer

In 1953 monkeys living on the Japanese island of Koshima began to wash sweet potatoes in a stream or in the ocean before they ate them. The potato-washing habit spread gradually until 1958, and then—so goes the story—something remarkable happened. "In the autumn of that year," wrote anthropologist Lyall Watson, "an unspecified number of monkeys on Koshima were washing sweet potatoes in the sea. . . . Let us say, for argument's sake, that the number was ninety-nine and that at eleven o'clock on a Tuesday morning, one further convert was added to the fold in the usual way. But the addition of the hundredth monkey apparently carried the number across some sort of threshold, pushing it through a kind of critical mass, because by that evening almost everyone in the colony was doing it."

It's a great story, but it's a myth. The facts do not support it. There was no hundredth-monkey phenomenon that occurred on the island of Koshima in 1958. There was no hundredth monkey that, by learning to wash sweet potatoes clean of sand and grit, carried this wisdom across some critical threshold until the practice appeared spontaneously not only all over the monkey colony of Koshima, but in monkey colonies on surrounding islands and on the mainland of Japan.

The story of the hundredth monkey is a myth. But a myth is not a lie. And the truth—in this case, that when a change establishes itself in a critical mass of a few, it mysteriously and automatically spreads to the many—is often best captured in a myth. Whether in religion or in fairy tales, myths point to realities hard to communicate in fact alone. They correspond to spiritual realities within ourselves that teach us their truth long before we are able to analyze and understand them. Myths may not correspond to historical facts, yet they may teach more history—and psychology and religion and truth—than any list of facts ever could. They spring from the invisible, primordial times in man's soul, delivering ancient wisdom to modern cultures.

"Myth is the foundation of life," wrote Thomas Mann. "It is the timeless pattern, the religious formula to which life shapes itself. . . . There is no doubt about it, the moment when the storyteller acquires the mythical way of looking at things, that moment marks a beginning in his life." Facts are important, but they do not have a monopoly on truth. The ancient claim that God's spirit goes to the four corners of the earth may fail the test of fact, since the world is a globe, but it is eminently truthful. And within a culture, embracing a more mythological way of looking at life is a sign of longing for what is truthful not just what is merely factual.

The hundredth monkey story may lie in the realm of myth rather than science, but the critical mass phenomenon is no less real for that. For a physicist, critical mass is the amount of radioactive material that must be present for a nuclear reaction to become self-sustaining. In chemistry, it's illustrated by the process of titration: Drop by drop, one solution is added to another, but nothing happens until that critical drop is absorbed and the solution is suddenly changed from blue to red. In biology, critical mass occurs on a cellular level. A mutation appears to happen overnight, but it's actually the end result of a genetic process that may stretch back for generations.

The critical mass phenomenon also manifests itself in the realm of cultural and social change, and it is based on this observation: Any new principle of existence first establishes itself in the few and then in the many who most readily resonate with it until, finally, it is realized in all. Social scientists have found in the critical mass phenomenon a useful theoretical concept, not just a loose, metaphorical way of speaking about breaking through some threshold of participation. Pamela Oliver and Gerald Marwell from the University of Wisconsin have argued that "collective action usually entails the development of a critical mass—a small segment of the population that chooses to make big contributions to the collective action . . . that will tend to explode, to draw in the other less interested or less resourceful members of the population and to carry the event toward its maximum potential."

The broad, cultural event toward which a critical mass is now building is the next breakthrough in our evolution. It is the widespread acceptance of the imperatives of the Fourth Instinct to seek the truth and to follow the call to service in our lives. As yet, the contributions of those pressing forward, working toward the explosion of spiritual interest and community involvement that signals the achievement of critical mass, may not yet be fully measurable by social scientists. The force of such phenomena is rarely seen until the explosion actually occurs. The achievements of those men and women who will raise mankind to new possibilities will at first be achievements of the spirit, and will, therefore, most likely go unheralded for a time. But by conquering the challenges of expanding to a higher consciousness, they will have raised the rest of us to the possibility of a similar transformation. When the critical mass has been reached, and what has brought us to the new consciousness becomes clear, those once regarded as eccentrics may well be enshrined as pioneers.

After centuries of believing that social change can only be brought about by centralized government action, we are now recognizing the truth taught by the greatest spiritual teachers and documented by the greatest modern scientists: The moment *we* begin to change, the world starts changing with us—because we are all a vital part of the world itself. The moment our Fourth Instinct is activated and we take our first steps back to God, every other consciousness—however imperceptibly at first—is affected. Once the seed takes root and the shoot breaks through the ground, it is forever growing, covering and changing the landscape all around it.

Since people inherit not only genes but habits of being, when change establishes itself among a critical mass of pioneers, it is not only behavior that is altered, but the memory of who we are. The memory implanted in our cells and our souls, Jung's concept of the collective unconscious as the inherited memory of mankind, will trigger the quantum leaps in consciousness in the nonlinear manner in which change spreads through a culture.

From the pre-Platonic philosophers to the Pythagoreans, from the Pythagoreans to Einstein's unified field theory, and from Einstein's to Hawking's efforts to substantiate the existence of this universal field, the dominant impulse has been to discover the principle by which the world is knit together. The existence of this universal, unified field that underlies everything makes it easier to understand how people can resonate to changes in a different part of the field without experiencing them firsthand.

Science provides an illustration in the crystallization of various chemicals, an event which sometimes takes months to achieve even under conditions of supersaturation. But when it finally does occur, it becomes easier for it to recur, and the chemical reaction becomes more common all over the world. So whenever a critical mass, whether of chemicals or creatures, is reached, change accelerates, becoming self-sustaining and far-reaching.

Another example of this process can be found in the properties of the laser beam. When scientists use stimulated emissions to produce photons (light particles) that are "coherent" —in step with each other in phase and frequency—they have found that these particles can bring others into coherence, almost as if incoherent photons begin to mimic more coherent ones. A beam of light past the threshold of coherence becomes so powerful that it can shoot all the way to the moon, while the ordinary light bulb, however bright it may be, is actually extremely incoherent, with photons canceling each other out, instead of building a powerful beam of light.

A parallel process is already under way in the realm of spiritual awareness and cultural change. People are choosing to pick up the threads of grace that lead us through the labyrinth, coalescing to follow the light that will illuminate the darkness. Few in number at first, they will blaze the trail to the next stage of our evolution. "A normal lizard," wrote Hermann Hesse, "never hit upon the idea of trying to fly. A normal ape never thought of abandoning his tree and walking upright on the ground. The one who first did that, who first tried it, who had first dreamed about it, was a visionary and eccentric among apes, a poet, an innovator, and no normal ape. The normal ones, as I saw it, were there to maintain and defend an established way of life, to strengthen a race and species so that there might be support and vital provision for it. The visionaries were there in order to venture their leaps, to dream of the undreamed of, so that perhaps sometime a land animal might emerge from the fish and an ape man from the ape."

Venturing leaps—this time spiritual—is also at the heart of the descent of God to earth. This is the view of Christ not as an isolated prodigy but as one who manifested the new reality for the rest of us. So powerful was this image that the New Testament letter to the Hebrews, to comfort the martyrs who were being slain for their beliefs, urges them to follow their Christ, "the author and finisher of our faith."

"The world," wrote Teilhard de Chardin, "seems to me to 'tumble' forward and upward upon the spiritual. . . . Entropy has been replaced for me by the highest consciousness as the essential physical function of the universe." In this view of cosmogony, the spiritual progress—the upward tumble—of the world depends unequivocally on our choosing to follow our Fourth Instinct, not in order to produce a sprinkling of self-realized experimental men, but so that the universal truth of our spiritual destiny, so far manifested only in a few visionaries and pioneers, can, in fact, be realized by all.

Critical mass phenomena are happening around us all the time, not only in the laboratories and the outer reaches of the cosmos but in the mundane, trivial moments of our everyday lives: the way a new style catches fire, a new joke becomes the rage, new jargon sweeps the airwaves, rumors magnify as if in an echo chamber. In the realm of ideas, yesterday's heresies flick around from influential mind to influential mind until they become the conventional wisdom of the day. When I was majoring in economics at Cambridge, Milton Friedman was introduced in our lectures as a professor from Chicago who didn't understand Keynesian economics—an eccentric, if you will, among the apes. Two decades later Friedman had won a Nobel Prize, and Keynesian economics—the standard by which he had been judged the fool—was discussed only in embarrassed whispers.

On Capitol Hill the critical mass game is played by both the political stalwarts and the political rebels. Elected officials speak, for example, of creating a "critical mass" of opposition to a tax on energy, or a "critical mass" of support for tougher crime legislation. In politics, majority rules, and once a critical mass is reached, it is easy to transform it into a majority— whether of votes or of adherents to an idea or belief.

Lewis Thomas describes the human brain as "the most public organ on the face of the earth, open to everything, sending out messages to everything. To be sure, it is hidden in bone and conducts internal affairs in secrecy, but virtually all the business is the direct result of thinking that has already occurred in other minds." Because most of our thoughts are borrowed, the state of our culture—from which we borrow every day—is of paramount importance in determining what we believe and, in consequence, how we live. Some psychologists, observing this phenomenon, have gone too far and argued that we are blank slates on which society imprints our entire identity. Far from it. Each of us is unique, but we are all incomplete, and therefore most susceptible to filling ourselves with the nostrums we inhale from our culture. This very incompleteness, this longing for meaning and direction, can either be exploited by evil, as it was when the people made Adolf Hitler the ruler of Germany, or it can lead to our liberation. We witnessed the latter when a critical mass was achieved in the struggle against communism. The walls came tumbling down in what appeared on the surface to be the *sudden* collapse of totalitarianism, but which was, in fact, an eruption of forces that had been gathering imperceptibly underground for years until a critical mass was reached.

Social scientists have proven that people's behavior often depends on how many others are behaving in a particular way. Parents have long been aware of this truth. "But, Mom, *nobody's* wearing that anymore!" is the wail that announces the newest teenage clothing fad. It's the same pattern of behavior that is put to positive use in any social activity. Whether it's a political campaign or a fundraising drive for the local homeless shelter, it can become self-sustaining and even accelerate once it passes a certain threshold, a certain critical mass of energy and involvement. At that moment, a back-breaking effort that felt like Sisyphus forever pushing a rock uphill becomes an endeavor that seems unrestrained by the normal laws of gravity, tumbling forward and upward.

At its best, once critical mass has been reached, neighbor helping neighbor starts a chain reaction of compassion that spreads throughout the community and beyond. At its worst, a corner crime spree erupts into nights of rioting and violence across an entire city. One tragic critical mass hypothesis, documented by research, involves suicide rates in thirty-three industrial nations: Once the number of suicides reached a critical level, in every instance there was a sudden jump in the absolute number of suicides.

Society as an organism is a metaphor that has been applied to many different cultures throughout history. The metaphor has been carried over in our language in phrases such as the "head of state," the "body politic," or the "long arm of the law." In religion, the Christian church is often described metaphorically as the "mystical body of Christ" while Christ compared himself to the "vine" and the faithful to the vine's "branches." Connections do resonate within our society as if it were a living organism. But unlike colonies of butterflies and schools of fish, we don't carry imprinted in us unambiguous instructions about where to go and how to get there. We make choices all the time, and some of these choices are little more than wild guesses. We take strolls that lead to dead ends; we pick up false threads that fall apart in our hands. The subjects of the animal kingdom are governed by the first three instincts, but we have access to the Fourth. The distinctive feature of being human is our capacity to make moral choices. And with our choices we can rain down on ourselves untold disasters or open up unimagined possibilities. We can choose to self-destruct, or we can choose to evolve. Given our free will, the critical mass phenomenon is another way God's grace extends to us. Everyone does not have to choose to evolve for everyone to end up evolving. Once critical mass is reached, it's as if God's grace will reach out and lift humanity closer to its spiritual destiny.

"People become infected with good will and compassion," Jonas Salk told me once. "It's a state of being as real as any physiological condition—and it spreads to others just like a virus." Under the influence of the Fourth Instinct, habits of selfishness and cynicism can be transformed into new habits of empathy and hope. "If a man have not order within him/He cannot spread order about him," says Ezra Pound's Confucius. "The principle of good is enunciated by Confucius," Pound explains. "It consists in establishing order within oneself. This order or harmony spreads by a sort of contagion without specific effort."

In the same way that the human soul encounters thresholds that it must cross, so does society. As human history amply demonstrates, progress is not automatic. In fact, to assume progress is to deny what is at the heart of the human adventure: free will. A critical mass is significant because it dramatically increases the *probability* of social, cultural or spiritual breakthroughs, but it does not make them inevitable.

We were not made to be members of a mindless herd, but to affect the course of our lives and of history. As in the poetic dialogue recounted by Wallace Stevens in *Man with a Blue Guitar*, we influence all that we touch:

> *They said, "You have a blue guitar,*
> *You do not play things as they are."*
>
> *This man replied, "Things as they are*
> *are changed upon the blue guitar."*

Things as they are are changed when we demonstrate a new reality. A very small change in perception can result in a change in behavior and, cumulatively, in a very large change in cultural patterns. Our purpose and destiny are encoded within us. But they do not automatically propel us to the next act in our day, let alone the next stage in our evolution. Our

Fourth Instinct allows us to see that next stage, and our free will enables us to act on it so that it can become a reality. "Every transformation of man," wrote Lewis Mumford, "has rested on . . . a new picture of the cosmos and the nature of man."

America began with a clear vision of the future, *Novus Ordo Seclorum*—"a new order of the ages"—as it is printed on the back of the dollar bill. Now, after all the glorious achievements and tragic dead ends of the last two centuries, we have reached the point where we can make this vision a reality. We need only a critical mass of pioneers who will choose to follow the voice of our Fourth Instinct—to answer the call to meaning and manifest spiritual truth in our lives, and to answer the call to service and put giving and caring for our communities at the center of each day. Then values like responsibility, forgiveness, gratitude and compassion will be practiced with the same frequency that they are preached. It is a big dream, but a dream based on the inner reality of our Fourth Instinct—a reality whose time has come.

Acknowledgments

This list of acknowledgments is an expression of deep gratitude to all those who helped make this book a reality—a dedication to all those who have dedicated themselves, for a few months or for many years, to *The Fourth Instinct:*

To Michael, Christina, and Isabella for being an unending source of energy, enthusiasm, and anecdotes.

To my editor, Fred Hills, for believing in this book from the beginning, believing I would return to it after two babies and one campaign, and providing—for our third book together—masterly editorial direction in the long months between the time the first draft was delivered and the time the final draft went to press.

To Burton Beals for his incisive and relentless green-pencil editing, paragraph by paragraph and chapter by chapter, with marathon bargaining sessions on the telephone in between.

To Jennifer Grossman for working with me on the book through every draft from the massive four-hundred-page outline to the final line editing and for "choosing to evolve" with me through successive deadlines, sometimes as an all-night editor and sometimes as a "Camp Cutie" counselor to my children when no one but Mommy or "Jayfer" would do.

To Jim Heynen for encouraging me to find a new voice for this book and for helping me refine it.

To Matthew Scully for all his help with research, ranging from the founding fathers to "the ministry of all believers."

Acknowledgments

To Louisa Oliver for all her research into the first three instincts, the threads through the labyrinth, and especially the thread of science.

To Darian Strain-Valdez, Andrea Latham and Kelley Goodsell for offering creative alternatives to all the sentences that did not work as they were updating new drafts on the computer—Kelley staying until four o'clock one morning to get revisions faxed to Fred on time.

To Maryann Stevens, without whom it would have taken me months to settle in my new office in Washington. To Randy Fetting, who helped computerize our world and always responded late into the night to our urgent beeper calls for help. To the Federal Express couriers who visited us nearly every evening and would occasionally give us those few extra minutes we needed to send successive drafts on their way to New York.

To Robert George, Maren Lee, Louisa Barker, Christine Serrano and Kate Flaherty for all their help in checking the facts, statistics, and quotations accumulated over twenty years.

To Mark Kelly at Pacifica Institute, Larry Arnn, Father Constantine Zozos, Coleman Barks, Ann Driscoll, and Dr. William Grossman for their help with books, quotations and articles.

To Jonas Salk for all our discussions through the years that helped crystallize my own thinking about spiritual evolution; to Leda Cosmides for her painstaking commentary on my chapter on instincts and for all the help I received from her own pioneering work on evolutionary psychology; to Professors Jerome Spanier at Claremont Graduate School and Alex Pines at UC Berkeley for their scientific vetting of the "Critical Mass" chapter; and to Jane Bedford for her invaluable transatlantic edits—for my fourth book running—and for ensuring that all Americanisms got converted to universal English.

To Gail Gross and Jodi Evans for being at the heart of the Healing chapter, and to all the people who appear namelessly in so many stories throughout the book but who are to me anything but nameless.

To my mother, Elli, and my sister, Agapi, who have been an endless source of encouragement and wisdom. And to Bernard Levin, my writing mentor from the beginning, who not only read and greatly improved what I thought was the final draft, but who also had an inscription made for my desk, which read:

Acknowledgments

"You can break any and every grammatical and syntactical rule consciously when and only when you have rendered yourself incapable of breaking them unconsciously."

To my agent, Gloria Loomis, who helped me stay focused on the book even through the years that I immersed myself in motherhood.

Finally, to Frank Metz and Jackie Seow for the creativity and loving care they brought to the jacket design; to Victoria Meyer, Seale Ballenger, Lynn Goldberg, Camille McDuffie and Sandy Bodner for making sure that the book, once written, would also be read; to Laureen Connelly Rowland for steering the manuscript into production even through her wedding preparations; and to Leslie Ellen, Eve Metz and everyone at Simon and Schuster for helping me turn an idea into a book.

when I was sixteen. I was sitting with others at the University of Shantaniketan outside Calcutta. We had come from all parts of the world to study the wisdom of the ages. We had taken in lectures and engaged in long conversations. But now the power of silence was making itself felt. Noise was all around me, from the quiet banter of friends to the fluttering leaves of the tree that shaded us; but I was being enveloped, as if in a bubble or cocoon of absolute silence. I felt reconnected. It was as if I knew, for the first time—only to forget and re-remember many times since—that God was both within me and all around me. When I left the university grounds to explore the world outside, the road was bright with mid-morning sunshine and the air was gorged with dust. I walked through sweet aromas and foul stenches, among snarling beggars and whispering holy men. I felt connected to it all.

The rhythm of that day—inward to the depths of soul, then outward to the noisy streets, seeking truth in the words of others, then listening to the wisdom of one's soul—is the pattern of spiritual practice that I feel most at home with. In the ordinary rhythm of our lives, it is this balance between soul and the world, between moving in and stepping out that so many religious practices strive for. We come to understand that we are not only made in God's image, but that we are made to image God—to reflect His freedom, joy, compassion and peace in our lives.

Yet, talk of soul and service—the quest for God and the search for meaning—must not become a new weight under which we collapse. "Angels fly because they take themselves lightly," I hear myself saying now to my own daughters as they pile onto our bed and nestle between Michael and me, sometimes for roughhousing and cuddles and at other times for a free-floating round of prayers in which each of us makes up a personal prayer. Christina sometimes sings her prayers, putting wings on her words. And then it's Mommy's turn and Daddy's turn and Isabella's turn, who normally just says "Amen" to everything. Those who think of prayer as something solemn and somber might have a much lighter step on their spiritual journeys if they listened to the prayers of children who find delight in talking to God.

.   .   .

Mystery is at the heart of our religious quest. The completely rational man and the crime novelist both see mystery as something to be solved, not something to be entered into and explored. Embracing mystery means accepting that we see through a glass darkly, instead of assuming that if we were really clever, we would be able to eliminate it altogether from our lives. At the start of my own spiritual search, I went looking for God in books, in retreats and seminars, in trips to distant lands—all attempts to solve the mystery. And every time I returned home, I heard God calling from within myself. He had made every journey with me.

"Falsehood is never so false as when it is very nearly true," wrote Chesterton. When we take hold of true religion, we seize a thread of grace. But the agony of religion gone wrong—from children's blood flowing in a misbegotten crusade to the buzz of flies over Jim Jones's jungle morgue—shows the power of souls deceiving and deceived. Religion can be the fire that warms our spirits against the deadly cold of a secular world; but if perverted, it can become a holocaust sweeping over us and our sleeping children. It can be the cooling drink in the arid desert of our wanderings; or, adulterated by man, it can be turned into a deadly barrel of artificially sweetened death. In the name of God people can devote themselves to healing their community or stockpiling arms against it, awaiting Armageddon.

Nothing warns of this danger more surely than religious leaders who place themselves between God and the rest of humanity, arrogating to themselves the personal relationship with the divine. *Corruptio Optimi Pessima:* "The corruption of the best is the worst." No wonder Christ reserved his hottest fury for the false champions of religious authority and the scholars of dead orthodoxy: "Woe unto you . . . hypocrites! for ye are like unto whited sepulchres, which indeed appear beautiful outward, but are within full of dead men's bones, and of all uncleanness."

The Fourth Instinct continually urges us to move toward the divine, to immerse ourselves in soul and service. The more we listen to it, the more spiritually sensitive we become, and the more able we are to distinguish that thread of religion which leads to God from those false strands that take us into the wilderness. Religious traditions that have become calcified,